JSM

John Stuart Mill at about thirty-four years of age

John Stuart Mill

A MIND AT LARGE

❋ *EUGENE AUGUST* ❋

CHARLES SCRIBNER'S SONS/*NEW YORK*

FOR

Barbara, Bob, and Jim

Library of Congress Cataloging in Publication Data

August, Eugene R 1935–
  John Stuart Mill.

  Bibliography: p. 263
  Includes index.
  1. Mill, John Stuart, 1806–1873.
B1607.A95   192   75–12649
ISBN 0–684–14232–5

1 3 5 7 9 11 13 15 17 19 H/C 20 18 16 14 12 10 8 6 4 2

PRINTED IN THE UNITED STATES OF AMERICA

❈ CONTENTS ❈

CONTENTS

❋ ILLUSTRATIONS ❋

ILLUSTRATIONS

❈ PREFACE ❈

THE following pages are addressed primarily to the general reader rather than the specialist. They are intended for those who have felt the lure of Mill's splendid mind, and who wish to know more about a thinker at once so timely and so timeless. They are intended for those who have heard something of Mill's life—perhaps of his extraordinary education at home or of his attachment to a liberated married woman —and who wish to know more about this brilliant, dedicated activist in the cause of human betterment.

Still, these pages may be of some interest to specialists as well. So vast is the range of Mill's thought that most scholars necessarily confine themselves to a single segment of it, and may therefore welcome a book discussing works normally outside their purview. Certainly John M. Robson's recent review of works about Mill—in *Victorian Prose: A Guide to Research*—leaves little doubt that most of them are specialist studies; introductions to Mill which take a broader view of his work are conspicuously scarce.

The unifying thread of this book lies in its view of Mill as thinker-artist who fuses logic and imagination to depict a vision of the world. If I have devoted what seems to be an inordinate amount of space to Mill's essays on poetry, that is partly because his views on poetry help to illuminate his own practice as prose writer.

Most of the chapters provide a guided tour to one of Mill's major works, pointing out the significant features of argument and art, describing their interrelatedness. Each chapter frames the discussion with a biographical and historical narrative. These frames are necessarily brief and simplified, as any specialist will readily recognize, but a full account of Mill's intellectual heritage or of the development of philosophy since his day is beyond the scope of this book. Rather, the brief accounts here are intended to provide the general reader with a concise introduction to Mill's life and times. Such information, however sketchy, often illuminates what is happening within the work being discussed. And the primary focus of this book is upon the works themselves, upon what they say and how they say it.

Such a plan involves several difficulties, in addition to the well-nigh insurmountable one of trying to discuss intelligently Mill's contributions in a half-dozen different disciplines. The question of which are Mill's "major" works is apt to occasion considerable disagreement, once one gets beyond listing *A System of Logic, The Principles of Political Economy, On Liberty,* and *Utilitarianism.* I can only hope that the reader will recognize that some selection had to be made here, and that the present choices at least represent most of the principal areas enriched by Mill's mind. I conclude, incidentally, that *On Social Freedom,* published after Mill's death and sometimes attributed to him, has been convincingly shown to be by another hand.

In general this book explores Mill's works in the chronological order in which they were first published, a procedure perhaps open to objections. For one thing, works written close together in time were sometimes published at widely different intervals. *On Liberty* and "Nature," for example, were both written in the 1850s, though the former appeared in 1859, and the latter not until 1874. Moreover, works like the *Logic* and *The Principles of Political Economy* were altered significantly in their later editions. Still, discussing each work at the time of its initial publication involves the fewest confusions, especially when the specifics of each work's composition, publication, and revisions (if any) are spelled out in the appropriate chapter. Unless otherwise noted, however, this book discusses Mill's final revised version of the work. Whenever possible, the text used here is that of the excellent *Collected Works of John Stuart Mill* now being published by the University of Toronto Press.

Because this is a book for the general reader, the scholarly apparatus of footnotes has been dispensed with, although an annotated list of works by and about Mill has been included for those desiring a guide to further reading. I have tried mightily to avoid jargon or technical terms from any of the disciplines touched upon. Though the word "persona" appears intermittently throughout the book, it is essential to my treatment of Mill's artistry, and I believe it is adequately defined in the introductory chapter. Also, I have rejected the formal language of scholarly discourse as inappropriate for this occasion. The diction used here is deliberately informal, at times colloquial, as befitting a book addressed to a wider audience.

In a number of cases I have deliberately refrained from attempting final answers to disputed matters of Mill's thought. Instead, I have indicated the nature of the disagreements over these live issues, and left their ultimate settlement to experts in the appropriate fields. Similarly, I have attempted no definitive answers to certain biographical matters where no such answers seem to me to be forthcoming from the available evidence. In particular, the controversial questions of precisely how brilliant a woman Harriet Taylor was and exactly how much she contributed to Mill's thought receive no absolute answers here—though I have hazarded an occasional guess on these and other matters. Likewise, any psychological or Freudian readings between the lines of Mill's prose should be regarded as possibilities rather than hard and fast truths. The book is not always neutral on controversial matters, however. In a number of cases where I feel that reliable scholars have made a strong defense of Mill against his critics, I have incorporated their arguments into my discussion.

Though nowhere in this book do I argue at length for the overall coherence of Mill's thought, the reader will readily sense my agreement with those scholars who find unity in Mill's diversity. The case for this unity has been ably argued elsewhere, and those interested should consult the annotated list at the end of the book, particularly the works of John M. Robson, Alan Ryan, and C. L. Ten.

In writing this book I have incurred numerous debts of gratitude, and would like to express my thanks:

To the National Endowment for the Humanities, for a Younger Humanist Fellowship which enabled me to devote a full year to the study of Mill; to the University of Dayton Research Council for three summer research grants, which enabled me to do additional work on Mill; to B. J. Bedard, Chairman of English at the University of Dayton, for helping me over many an obstacle to writing and research; to Robert Montavon and the staff of the University of Dayton Library for their readiness and skill in obtaining hard-to-get books, articles, and manuscripts; to Robert Greene and D. J. Yankovic for reading sections of this book and commenting helpfully on Mill's philosophy and economics, respectively; and to Alice G. Vines for her insights as historian and her special generosity as colleague and friend. To Richard C. Tobias and F. E. Mineka I am especially indebted for stimulating and perceptive comments on the early drafts of this book. Needless to say, any errors or misjudgments in the final version are not the responsibility of these readers, but of the author.

Thanks are also due to J. B. Schneewind for sending an early draft of his forthcoming article on Mill's *Utilitarianism;* to F. A. Hayek and Michael Laine for sending photographs in their possession; to Deborah Anderson for her cheerfulness and skill in typing my tangled manuscripts; to Patricia Cristol for her encouraging and perceptive editing; and finally to my wife, Barbara, whose unflagging patience and help has prompted me more than once to label this a "joint production."

JSM

James Mill. From a drawing by Perugini.

CHAPTER ONE

INTRODUCTION

The highest problem of every art is, by means of appearances, to produce the illusion of a loftier reality.
—GOETHE, *Truth and Poetry*

 IN May 1820 James Mill took his eldest son for a walk in Hyde Park. For the first time in his life, the almost-thirteen-year-old lad was about to leave the walled-off environment of his father's house for an extended visit to southern France. Before the boy departed, his father had decided to reveal a well-kept secret.

As he mingled with people, James solemnly warned his son, he would discover that he was singularly different from other youths his age. He would find that he was strikingly better educated, better able to think for himself, better informed on intellectual and political matters. In brief, he would find that, in matters of the mind, he was years ahead of his peers.

Slowly it began to dawn upon the boy how extraordinary his education at home had been. Here was his first inkling that he had acquired the equivalent of a university education at an age when most students had not even begun theirs. He must also have sensed how sheltered his life had been. Had other children been so rigorously sealed off from playmates as he had been? It was most unlikely that other boys spent their leisure hours as he did, reading weighty tomes and disputing impertinently with his father's friends. And surely not every eldest son in the land employed much of the day instructing younger sisters and brothers in the knowledge imparted to him by their father.

All these wild surmises must have shaken the boy considerably. His father had always been so sharply critical, had always demanded so much more than he could perform, that the boy had acquired the distinct impression that he was rather backward. And now to be told that he was a prodigy! But whatever elation he may have felt on this occasion was short-lived, for James Mill soon reverted to his usual, more-than-Roman sternness. "He wound up by saying," the son recalled many years later, "that whatever I knew more than others, could not be ascribed to any merit in me, but to the very unusual advantage which had fallen to my lot, of having a father who was able to teach me, and willing to give the necessary trouble and time; that it was no matter of praise to me, if I knew more than those who had not had a similar advantage, but the deepest disgrace to me if I did not." No doubt the impressionable youngster treasured up this paternal admonition along with everything else he had been told, and set off for France on the next day dutifully determined to be his father's son in thought and feeling.

It was an impossible resolve. In the years to come the boy's life would take strange and startling turns, and of these swervings his father would know little, suspect much, and never fully fathom. Initially, the youth would be a devoted follower of his father's thought, an active campaigner in his father's causes. But before he was twenty-one he would suffer a crushing emotional collapse, and afterward he would go lusting after strange philosophical gods. From what his father would have regarded as the merest intellectual and emotional ragtags, he would reconstruct his life and thought, adding new and exotic truths to the utilitarian ones he had been taught. He would discover the sunlight of poetry and feeling, and like Plato's cave dweller he would return to proclaim his newfound perceptions to a frequently incredulous, perturbed audience. But there would be sympathetic listeners too, and he would rise to become an influential writer and editor. Strangest of all, he would conduct a twenty-year, entirely innocent love affair with another man's wife, claiming to derive from this liaison the greatest insights of his career. He would even enter Parliament in later years, one of the few instances in history of a genuine philosopher to grace the halls of Westminster Palace. But, most significant of all, he would produce a body of writings that would forever extend and enrich the thought and feeling of the Western world.

So varied was the genius of John Stuart Mill that it is now impossible to contain him under a single label. The term used above—"philosopher"—does scant justice to his astonishing diversity of achievement. For the modern university student, one of Mill's works is likely to be required reading in any of a dozen different courses ranging from economics to religion, from literature to logic. Indeed, a single work like *On Liberty* may turn up on reading lists in a half-dozen disciplines as varied as political science, philosophy, history, and the social sciences. For Mill was the last great "Renaissance mind" of Western thought, imperially taking all knowledge for his province. He was also the first great interdisciplinary mind of the modern world, forging links among the various fields of learning to which he contributed so brilliantly. To a world beset by multiplicity of knowledge and narrow specialisms, Mill remains the grand instructive example of intellectual integration.

By all odds he should have been a sickly bookworm living in libraries and grinding out pedantic treatises for squinting academics. But nothing could be further from the truth. Through most of his life he throve in the give-and-take polemical world of Victorian journalism and politics, supporting himself all the while with a position at East India House. Despite this necessary drain on his time and energy, he yet managed to be both activist and intellectual, a triumphant example that action and thought need not be divorced from each other. Even his most seemingly theoretical works sported a keen practical edge, and in later years he carried his arguments for social reform into the House of Commons itself. All his life he was a controversial writer whose essays and books were apt to ignite firestorms of protest and kindle glowing enthusiasm. Nor to this day can they be safely relegated to the library back shelves; they continue to be centers of disagreement and trumpet calls to action, as well as enduring sources of humane inspiration.

Indeed, on the score of success, Mill's works seem to have had it both ways. They have spread their influence imperceptibly over later generations until their ideas and attitudes are now part of the intellectual air we breathe. In short, they are recognized classics of modern thought. Yet their full richness has never been wholly explored or exploited, and so they are still apt to startle the reader with their originality and relevance. And while they seem all lucidity and logic, their effect upon readers' emotions has been often uncommonly powerful. For the truth is that Mill, besides being an intellectual giant, was an impressive literary artist as well.

So decisively has Mill entered the mainstream of modern thought that his voice can still be heard echoing from a hundred different places, from court chambers to feminist rallies. For forty years after his death he held sway over liberal thought as no other person did, and despite attempts to eclipse his reputation, his name is still one to conjure with. Whatever disagreements may arise about some aspects of his thought, he remains the world's most convincing spokesman for the supreme moral value of liberty to human growth.

Though a classic, Mill is hardly a dusty one. Instead, his insights are frequently as fresh as the morning newspaper. He preached women's liberation more than a century ago, defended racial equality with a vigor few modern liberals can match, and championed the environment long before ecological concerns began grabbing headlines. On world population, on big government and big business, on international nonintervention, he is astonishingly pertinent. Whether the subject is no-growth economics or humanist religion, Mill seems to have explored it long before our most advanced thinkers.

But Mill is more than a thinker; he is an artist who shapes his vision imaginatively, who speaks to us through a carefully controlled voice that embodies his finest ideals. Whatever label is attached to such an artist—whether he is called prophet or sage or poet—surely Plato stands as a supreme instance of the type. Unwilling to leave the case for virtue to argument alone, Plato depicted it creatively in the character of Socrates, whose voice still charms our minds and hearts at this distance of twenty-five-hundred years.

Having been practically weaned on Plato's argument and art, John Mill grew to emulate them in his own writings.

But this view of Mill is unorthodox, and so central to what follows that it had best be explored at length.

Mill a poet?

In many quarters the very idea will smack of extravagance, not to say willful perversity. After all, haven't Mill's critics regaled the public for the past century with hilarious quips about his "steam-engine" mind and his "power-loom" prose? Even sympathetic commentators have been known to bestow a passing condescension upon his "flat undistinguished tone of voice," or note with a certain dismay his "serviceable" prose—"clear, plain, nontechnical, and direct," but completely devoid of the literary charms of Thomas Carlyle or John Ruskin. Furthermore, didn't Mill himself confide to Carlyle in 1833 that he was "not in the least a poet, in any sense"? And in the same letter didn't he say that "the same person may be poet and logician, but he cannot be both in the same composition"? So that should settle it: Mill must be a logician in his compositions, leaving poetry to the likes of Carlyle and Ruskin. His writings can then be safely pigeonholed as "literature of fact" not "literature of the imaginative sense of fact." And Mill himself can be comfortably caricatured (especially by those who resent his influence) as a hidebound thinker, rather small, pinched, and pedantic.

But the real John Stuart Mill cannot be so easily dismissed. If he is such a bore, how then to account for his extraordinary impact upon his own and succeeding generations? Undoubtedly, he was one of the livelier controversialists of his day, alternately reviled as Antichrist and revered as the Saint of Rationalism. Nor has the history of later reactions to his works been a quiet one. And despite their frequently running into critical heavy weather, his writings survive as a rallying cry for activists, a seedbed for thinkers, and a source of inspiration for those who cherish reason and tolerance.

Nor can Mill's staying power be credited solely to his "thought," for the excitement his work generates goes beyond that. Pick up one of his works, and what happens? For the first few paragraphs the direst predictions of the steam-engine critics may seem to be coming true. But read on, and almost imperceptibly one's interest begins to quicken. There is, of course, the spectacle of that superb intellect surveying the world of thought, a spectacle to intrigue anyone with the least inclination to the life of the mind. Next, one begins to notice the subtle prescience of the man. How clearly he foresaw the modern world, how splendidly he speaks to our times as well as his own. Soon, however, one senses that the creative resources of language have come into play, that Mill is not merely arguing his case but shaping it imaginatively. Without a ripple disturbing the calm surface of the prose, a powerful emotional undertow begins sweeping the reader along. Suddenly Mill is no longer examining an intellectual puzzle; he is engaged in a struggle for civilization itself. The forces of oppression and ignorance have been summoned up, and stand ranked against the well-being of humanity, against the individual yearning to perfect his own unique being. This is no academic discussion; it is a decisive battle in the war for human betterment. And finally—it is the most important revelation of all—the reader finds himself in the presence of a man whose courage and character are an exalted image of clear-headed magnanimity. "Heart speaks to heart," as Mill's contemporary J. H. Newman put it. Upon closing the book, the reader discovers that somehow—mysteriously, subtly—his heart, as well as his head, has been spoken to.

But how can this be? How can producing such an effect be squared with Mill's remark to Carlyle that the same person cannot be both logician and poet in the same composition? Of course it cannot. But then, on examination, Mill's remark turns out to be a momentary aberration of insight which he rapidly rejected. "Poetry is higher than Logic," Mill wrote at the end of that same letter, "and . . . the union of the two is Philosophy." Before long, he was seeking a voice for that "philosophy," a voice which would combine poetry and logic in the same composition.

Indeed, in the very year of the letter to Carlyle, Mill's "Remarks on Bentham's Philosophy" contained an insight which would undermine his belief in logic and poetry's incompatibility. Discussing the demoralizing effect that Jeremy Bentham's work is apt to have on a dispirited reader, Mill observes:

> It is by a sort of sympathetic contagion, or inspiration, that a noble mind assimilates other minds to itself; and no one was ever inspired by one whose inspiration was not sufficient to give him faith in the possibility of making others feel what *he* feels.

A really inspired moralist, Mill says, will inspire his audience as Socrates, Plato, and Jesus did. It was only a matter of time before this clue would lead Mill to discover that the great moralists inspired their audience by blending logic and poetry. The leading case in point, of course, was Plato.

It is now 1834, a year after the letter to Carlyle. Mill is publishing in a small journal, *The Monthly Repository*, his abstracts of some Platonic dialogues. For the most part he does not comment on them, but to the *Gorgias* he appends this crucial note, which must be quoted at length:

> But no arguments which Plato urges have power to make those love or desire virtue, who do not already; nor is this ever to be effected through the intellect, but through the imagination and the affections.
>
> The love of virtue, and every other noble feeling, is not communicated by reasoning, but caught by inspiration or sympathy from those who already have it; and its nurse and foster-mother is Admiration. We acquire it from those we love and reverence, especially from those whom we earliest love and reverence; from our ideal of those, whether in past

or in present times, whose lives and characters have been the mirrors of all noble qualities; and lastly, from those who, as poets or artists, can clothe those feelings in the most beautiful forms, and breathe them into us through our imagination and our sensations. It is thus that Plato has deserved the title of a great moral writer. Christ did not argue about virtue, but commanded it; Plato, when he argues about it, argues for the most part inconclusively, but he resembles Christ in the love which he inspires for it, and in the stern resolution never to swerve from it, which those who can relish his writings naturally feel when perusing them.

There it is. Mill has found his theory of ethical art. In order to win people to an ideal vision of moral greatness, argument alone does not suffice. Only a person who embodies the vision can move another person to embrace it. "Argument may show what general regulation of the desires, or what particular course of conduct, virtue requires," Mill writes in the same note, "but the understanding has no inducements which it can bring to the aid of one who has not yet determined whether he will endeavor to live virtuously or no." Such inducements come from persons, not arguments. In ethical writings the inducements must come from imaginatively realized characters, like Plato's Socrates and the Christ portrayed in the Gospels.

This time the insight was no momentary aberration. It was a perception that, once grasped, Mill never abandoned. More than thirty years later he was reiterating it as firmly as ever in a review of George Grote's study of Plato. A dialogue like *Gorgias*, Mill says, works its magic "not by instructing the understanding, but by working on the feelings and the imagination." The Socrates portrayed there wins his case for virtue, not by proving it, but by embodying it: "He inspires heroism, because he shows himself a hero." And two years later Mill was proclaiming to the students of St. Andrews that "we may imbibe exalted feelings from Plato, or Demosthenes, or Tacitus, but it is in so far as those great men are not solely philosophers, or orators, or historians, but poets and artists." If this is Mill's opinion, can his practice be far behind?

Looking at the matter from another angle, we can see how Mill disliked rejecting opposites as incompatible. He much preferred reconciling them. He was a great synthesizer of contraries. He inveighed against half-thinkers who coveted their own partial truths and denied everybody else's. He tried to harmonize the demands of reason with those of feeling, the claims of authority with those of liberty, the progressivism of Bentham with the traditionalism of Coleridge. Above all, he strove to fuse the poetic insights of the woman he loved with his own systematic rationalism. Indeed, he viewed his affair with her as a grand symbolic myth in which she was the Artist, he the Scientist; in which she supplied the emotional insights, he the logical framework. And the works which she helped him to compose he called "joint productions"—by which quaint term he surely pointed to their fusion of her poetry and his logic.

It should come as little surprise, then, if those works exhibit an imaginative as well as a logical dimension. Of course, a page of Mill rarely resembles a page of Carlyle or Ruskin, where headlong emotion is apt to pulse with insistent rhythms or erupt into elaborate metaphor and allusion. But such a style would have been absurdly inappropriate for Mill. He prized strong feeling, but insisted that it not become a law unto itself and disregard the demands of reason. To such a writer a different style was imperative—a style at once more restrained and ordered, a style in which feeling and logic were adroitly balanced against each other. And such a style Mill evolved.

Each of Mill's major works, as the following chapters will attempt to demonstrate, displays a range of discreet artistic techniques designed to clarify his perceptions, illustrate his arguments, and shape the reader's responses to both. Moreover, each work is creatively adapted to Mill's ultimate moral goal—the general improvement of humanity through the perfection of each person's unique individuality. In each work Mill gives us a heightened picture of himself, an idealized version of what his own unique individuality would be like if carried to perfection. In short, he gives us something similar to Plato's idealized portrait of Socrates—an imaginatively realized person who inspires us, a heart that speaks to our heart.

In the technical language of literary criticism, Mill creates a superb *persona,* that is, the image of himself which emerges from the very texture of his prose.

Surely this is no very esoteric matter. Style is the man, and the persona is the man whom style reveals. In writing almost anything, the writer unavoidably imprints on the work an impression of himself as identifiable as his fingerprints. The bad writer unwittingly exposes himself; the skillful writer artfully reveals himself—and in such a way as to complement the purpose of his work. How incongruous, for example, for an intemperate writer to be arguing for moderation. In such a case, writer and argument are working at cross-purposes.

But in Mill, as in any skillful writer, persona and argument reinforce each other. Indeed (to risk a McLuhanism) the persona *is* the argument. Mill's persona is an image of a perfected self, and such perfected selves are the ultimate conclusions toward which all his arguments lead. Like Plato's Socrates, Mill is thus transformed by art into an idealized voice, into an inspiring person who moves the reader to admire and imitate.

The question of how faithfully these portraits reproduce their originals is interesting but really of secondary importance. Most likely the portraits are near enough to be recognizable, but ultimately they are intended not as copies of the actual but as working models of the ideal. The most important thing for Plato and Mill is that the reader catch the spirit of these ideal portraits, and be moved to realize a similar greatness in his own character.

To read Mill, then, is to encounter not only a matchless intellect, but a magnificent person as well.

CHAPTER TWO

FATHER AND SON

For I have recoiled
From showing as it is the monster birth
Engendered by these too industrious times.
Let few words paint it: 'tis a child, no child,
But a dwarf man.

—WILLIAM WORDSWORTH,
The Prelude, V, 291–95 (1805–6)

 TO many people in the early 1820s, teenage John Stuart Mill seemed to have sprung full-grown from his father's brain, much as the mythic Athena reputedly catapulted from Zeus's head, fully armed with his wisdom. The impression was accurate, as Mill admits in his *Autobiography*—where his father looms very large indeed, and his mother is not even mentioned. Evidently, to understand Mill, we must know something of his redoubtable father.

James Mill owed his good fortune to early intensive education. Born in 1773, the first child of a humble cobbler and his proud wife, James grew up in a Scottish hamlet so tiny that had it disappeared into the highland fog like Brigadoon, practically nobody would have missed it. Hardly the place to breed a gentleman of distinction, but Mill's mother, whose family had known better days, was determined to do just that. Accordingly, young James was sent off to the parish school as soon as he was able to toddle the two miles to get there. While his younger brother and sister drudged about shop and field, James was kept aristocratically isolated from all occupations but his studies. Later he was boarded at Montrose Academy, to the great indignation of the family's homespun neighbors. Under these favored conditions, the youth's genius flowered, and when Sir John and Lady Jane Stuart needed a tutor for their daughter, the parish minister recommended the local scholar. Usually aloof and severe, James could be charming when occasion demanded. On this occasion, he so bedazzled the Stuarts that they agreed to help finance his studies for the ministry at Edinburgh University.

James was in his element at last. Enraptured by Dugald Stewart's sublime lectures on moral philosophy, he cultivated an enduring interest that he would pass on to his eldest son. If other lecturers were less than sublime, there was always private reading to fall back on—although James's would have struck the devout as a trifle fast for someone aspiring to the cloth. Large helpings of Rousseau, Voltaire, David Hume—skeptics all—were to abet his later defection from the faith. Above all, however, was Plato, another philosophic passion that James would bequeath to his son. Licensed to preach in 1798, James's first sermon in the family parish church agreeably unnerved the mother who had sacrificed so much to lift him from rustic obscurity. Soon after, she succumbed to tuberculosis—another, more ominous legacy that James would transmit to his son.

For all his education (or perhaps because of it), James could find no suitable employment in Scotland and so struck out for London. He soon had a modest income from periodical writing and editing, enough to marry pretty Harriet Burrow in 1805 and move into No. 12 Rodney Terrace, Pentonville, where little John Stuart Mill duly arrived on 20 May 1806. Greater financial security would depend upon a firmer literary reputation; hence, James left his editing to produce a history of British India, estimating that the family had sufficient funds to skimp along for the three years necessary to complete the book. Then —success and a fairly comfortable, very proper middle-class existence. But one event reduced the neat scheme to shambles. In 1808 James Mill met Jeremy Bentham.

Bentham was an improbable character by anybody's standards. In 1808 he was close to sixty and growing younger every year. Like Merlin come to life again, he possessed an old man's head and a boy's heart. Beneath his shoulder-length locks, intellectual acumen and sheer dottiness ran riot in an orgy of crisp logic and warm sentiment. His skepticism was all Hume, his benevolence pure Pickwick. Physically, he resembled a British version of Benjamin Franklin, and indeed he shared that gentleman's fondness for tinkering with scientific apparatus. To little John Stuart Mill, the old man must have seemed his philosophical fairy godfather. In many ways he was.

Jeremy Bentham. Portrait by H. W. Pickersgill.

Bentham had not always been so lighthearted, though. Born in 1748 he too was the product of early education. His father, a crusty attorney determined to achieve respectability through his son, undertook Jeremy's training himself. Luckily, the boy was a prodigy, plowing through whole histories at three and plunging into Latin at four. Sent off to Westminster School at seven, he matriculated at Oxford at twelve. Both schools repelled him: Westminster was all brutality and brownie points, Oxford all port and prejudice. Required by the university to subscribe to the Church of England's Thirty-Nine Articles of faith, he had his doubts and mentioned them. A university official thundered at the impertinence. Terrorized, Jeremy signed—and ended up a lifelong foe of organized religion.

After Oxford, Bentham went from bad to worse, that is, to the law courts. There he witnessed a distressing parade of eighteenth-century squalor and a legal system in which confusion and costliness vied with each other as the leading characteristic. Incredibly, the whole farrago was being eulogized by William Blackstone as the quintessence of justice and reason. Bentham sensed that his mission was not to practice law but to reform it.

In his first naïve attempts, he actually believed that ignorance alone prevented magistrates from improving the system. All he had to do, he felt, was point out its shortcomings. Being soon disabused of this fantasy, he stumbled upon the notion that perhaps those in power are motivated by self-interest. If so, then government needed to be reformed along with law. Come to think of it, ethics itself could use a complete overhaul. A sizable program, but in 1792 Bentham inherited a small fortune and so could devote full time to it. Efficiency, however, was not his forte. His methods of composition were as entangled as the legal system he was trying to simplify, and as the years passed his style flowered into exotic unreadableness. It took a stout-hearted editor to get anything of Bentham's into print. His important *Introduction to the Principles of Morals and Legislation* was stalled for nine years before appearing in 1789, and then was upstaged by the French Revolution. He was constantly distracted—planning model prisons, envisioning model schools, and pottering with scientific projects like an ice house called a Frigidarium. More dubiously, in *Auto-icon, or the Uses of the Dead to the Living*, he suggested that, with proper embalming and a little varnish, corpses might be pressed into service as edifying outdoor statuary: "If a country gentleman have rows of trees leading to his dwelling, the auto-icons of his family might alternate with the trees."

Understandably, when James Mill met him in 1808, Bentham was still pretty much of a prophet without honor in his own country.

Understandable but regrettable, because for all its eccentricities Bentham's thought contained a solid core of important ideas that would significantly affect English and continental philosophy, to say nothing of their centrality to John Mill's thinking. Above all, Bentham saw the need to get ethics onto a more scientific and secular footing. When passing moral judgments, people were always appealing to some vague "moral sense," or "natural law," or "eternal Rule of Right." But such oracles were notoriously inconsistent in their pronouncements. Attacking the problem more scientifically, Bentham looked to the facts of human existence—and saw man under the governance of two sovereign masters, pain and pleasure. Pleasure interpreted broadly was happiness, the highest good of human existence. Thus, Bentham arrived at his most important formulation, the principle of utility or (more aptly) the greatest happiness principle: "It is the greatest happiness of the greatest number that is the measure of right and wrong."

But there was a catch: men always acted in their own self-interest. How to persuade them to seek the greatest happiness of the greatest number? By the "Duty-and-Interest-Juncture-Producing-Principle." In other words, by arranging society in such a way that a man's public duty and private interests would coincide. Through education, law, public opinion, and so on, a society can arrange its sanctions so that duty provides the pleasure that self-interest seeks. With none of the rigmarole of religious controversy, here was a handy guide to good legislation and jurisprudence, to say nothing of ethics and education.

Moreover, the principle of utility admitted of systematic application. Fiercely opposed to acting off the moral cuff, Bentham devised an ingenious "felicific calculus" for assessing any pleasurable activity in terms of seven considerations: its intensity, its duration, its certainty or uncertainty, its immediacy or remoteness, its ability to produce additional pleasures, its freedom from bad after effects, and its extent, that is, the number of people affected by it. To lodge the calculus firmly in the reader's mind, Bentham did what any advertiser would—resorted to a jingle:

> Intense, long, certain, speedy, fruitful, pure—
> *Such marks in* pleasures *and in* pains *endure.*
> *Such pleasures seek, if* private *be thy end:*
> *If it be* public, *wide let them* extend.

FATHER AND SON

Such pains *avoid, whichever be thy view:*
If pains must *come, let them* extend *to few.*

Hardly up to the standard of "Thirty days hath September," but it did enumerate succinctly the main considerations underpinning Bentham's whole fabric of morals and legislation.

To be sure, Bentham had not invented utility, and it contained difficulties he skated right over, but his writings gave it a memorable formulation and applied it to government and jurisprudence with head-spinning directness. Consider, for example, the political implications. Once awakened to the self-interest of "Judge & Co.," Bentham saw that the greatest happiness principle could be achieved only if government were made answerable to the greatest number of people. Such a radical conclusion jolted the Tory-bred Bentham, but he looked it squarely in the eye. True, the excesses of the French Revolution gave him pause, but by 1808 he was clearly ready for radicalism.

The meeting of Bentham and James Mill set up shock waves that reverberated down the century, but the immediate repercussions were felt in the fragile Mill household. Having concluded in disgust that his wife was as empty-headed as she was pretty, James installed himself as Bentham's lieutenant and heir-apparent, and spent considerable time away from home. His keen disappointment with his wife as intellectual companion could hardly have escaped the notice of wide-eyed little John, and may help to explain his own quest for a woman he considered his intellectual compeer. The domestic situation further deteriorated under the strain of increasing family size. In all, James fathered nine children—an alarming total for a man acquainted with the gloomy population prophet Thomas Malthus. Hitherto discreet about his radical views, James began trumpeting them abroad, thereby curtailing his small income from *Edinburgh Review* articles. (A Whig journal, the *Edinburgh* did not take kindly to low radicalism.) Nor did the *History of British India* help at all: as James initially knew next to nothing about the topic, the book took twelve years to complete instead of the estimated three. Predictably, the home atmosphere became perfectly electrical, with James raging, Harriet tearful, and the children cowering.

Bentham helped when he could. On the grounds of his house at No. 2 Queen Square Place was a cottage once occupied by no less a personage than John Milton. Into this shrine he shunted the Mills in 1810, but its general dankness soon drove them to higher ground at Newington Green. Four years later Bentham tried again, this time leasing a nearby house (No. 1 Queen Square Place), then subleasing it to James at reduced cost. Here in the heart of Westminster John Stuart Mill lived from his eighth to his twenty-fourth year. During the summer Bentham carried off the whole family to his country retreats, first at Barrow Green House in the Surrey Hills, and later at Ford Abbey, a splendid architectural pile in rural Devonshire. These excursions, sometimes six months long, eased the domestic strain considerably.

And what of John himself? At two, he was already catching significant glances from his father and Bentham. "If I were to die any time before this poor boy is a man," James confided to Jeremy, "one of the things that would pinch me most sorely, would be, the being obliged to leave his mind unmade to the degree of excellence of which I hope to make it." In brief, John had been selected to be "a successor worthy of both of us." To fill this portentous role he would need special training, and so began one of history's most famous educations.

James undertook it himself, allowing no grass to grow under John's baby feet. At three the boy was already memorizing Greek words and translating Aesop. During the next four years, he worked his way through a spate of Greek authors, including the whole of Herodotus and parts of Xenophon, Diogenes Laertius, Lucian, and Isocrates. During the same years, besides being introduced to mathematics, he devoured biographies and histories in English, as well as the more usual diversions like *Robinson Crusoe* and *Don Quixote*. Nor did he just read them; he took notes and reported daily to his father as the two of them sped through the green lanes of Hornsey during James's morning constitutional.

John was later to insist that any normal child could duplicate his early intellectual feats, and he may be right. His father apparently introduced him to reading and Greek just as he was passing through that sensitive period when the child possesses enormous powers for acquiring language. From this base James constructed John's entire education, creating a lifelong habit of reading and self-instruction.

Between eight and twelve, the boy's educational pace quickened. Adding Latin to his repertoire, he polished off a mind-boggling array of ancient classics, as well as a small library of works in English. He read up on higher mathematics, experimental science, and logic. In 1817, when James's *History of British India* was at last crawling into print, John absorbed it all by reading proof. Next it was economics, with John drawing up an abstract of David Ricardo's newly published

No. 1 Queen Square, Westminster. Residence of the Mill family from 1814 to 1830, from John's eighth to his twenty-fourth year. The Mills' garden joined that of Bentham's house at No. 2 Queen Square Place. The Mill house is now 40 Queen Anne's Gate, headquarters of the National Trust.

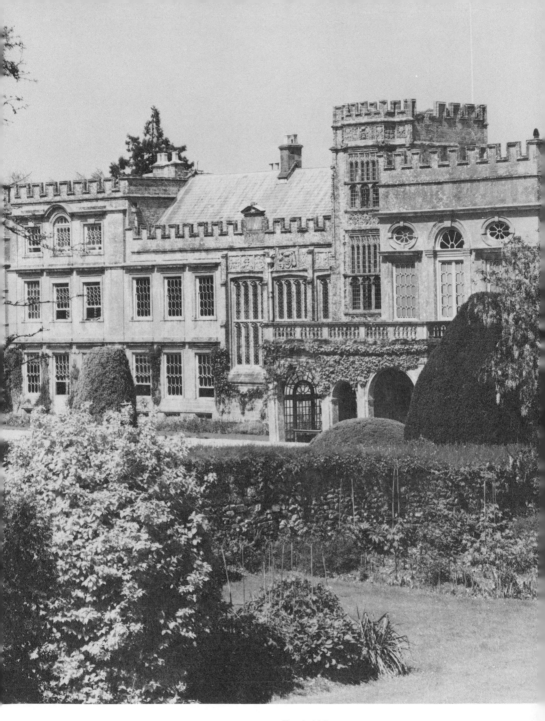

Ford Abbey

and quite formidable *Principles of Political Economy and Taxation.* Meanwhile, he was instructing his younger sisters and brothers, being held responsible for their progress as well as his own. By 1820 (he was then nearly fourteen) his lessons with his father were over. He had gained, he said in his *Autobiography,* "an advantage of a quarter of a century over my cotemporaries."

All was not gain, however. In some ways John was cruelly retarded. Protected from the "corrupting influence" of children his own age, his sense of play shriveled, his motor ability atrophied. To the end of his days he had trouble tying a cravat. Amid the frosty factuality of James's tutelage, his son's poetic and religious sensibilities withered aborning. It was an education of fear, almost at times of hate. No physical punishment was used, but James's scorching sarcasm was worse. The psychosexual damage, no doubt extensive, constricted the boy's ability to love. So severely dominated was John that he always remained slow to act on his own unless performing for some authority figure—his father, his wife, his stepdaughter. Small wonder, then, that he once remarked: "I never was a boy; never played at cricket: it is better to let Nature have her own way."

The country interludes helped. Not that James permitted any holidays from study, but the surroundings nourished John's starved imagination. Especially Ford Abbey, a marvelous old country retreat in which ornamental Tudor work alternated with Inigo Jones additions. Its airy rooms enabled John to look up from his books and gaze across the rolling hills of rural England. The walks were gloriously leafy, tame deer roamed the park, and trout caught in the river Axe swam in the fish ponds. Often he could listen dreamily as Bentham poured out melodies upon the abbey organ.

And then there was the trip to France in 1820–21. His formal lessons over, it was time to see something of the world. Family finances ruled out the Grand Tour, but Sir Samuel Bentham (Jeremy's younger brother) and his family were staying in southern France. They invited him to visit. John's journal shows us the fourteen-year-old boy pluckily making his way through Paris to Pompignan. At first he maintains a fearful regimen of study, as if his father's glaring eye were still upon him. But the Benthams, it seems, are forever on the move, and the incessant packing and unpacking throw him off schedule. Though vexed when all the books are boxed up, he is forced to relax, begins to laugh at the family charabanc whose wheel keeps rolling off, and is soon agog over a traveling circus. Lady Bentham, as competent as his own mother is ineffectual, begins to put some polish to his rough exterior; the eldest son, George, introduces him to the joys of botanizing; and, most marvelous, the Pyrenees transport him into Wordsworthian raptures. When the family has at last settled at Montpellier, John is taking university courses and making friends with a French student of his own age. He returns to England with an enduring relish for French thought and politics, botany, and picturesque mountain scenery. And he has tasted freedom. About this particular installment in his education, John always spoke enthusiastically.

The England John returned to in 1821 was stewing in discontent. Ever since the 1780s the country had been Tory-dominated in sheer reaction to events across the channel. The French Revolution of 1789 had degenerated into the Reign of Terror, to be followed by the crowning of Napoleon as emperor and his military campaigns across Europe. After a declaration of war in 1793, England was occasionally faced with the possibility of a French invasion. It was a situation to muddle the loyalties of the most committed radical. But with the Napoleonic wars over in 1815, English liberals were ready to get on with reform at home. Conservatives were not. Repression became all too familiar. To radicals, the "Peterloo Massacre" of 1819, with government troops charging peacefully assembled citizens, typified Tory recalcitrance.

The backlash could hardly have come at a worse moment: early nineteenth-century England sorely needed creative government. For the past fifty years, the country had been industrializing—the first nation in the world to do so. Simultaneously, a swelling population seemed to threaten the basis of civilized life with sheer numbers. Eventually industry would cope with mass population needs, but meanwhile England was confronted with problems both unprecedented and critical. As control of the land reverted to a wealthy few, workers streamed into industrial boom towns that mushroomed without planning or sanitation. Only the nightmare genius of a Dickens or a Doré could adequately depict the fetid slums that evolved. Work conditions (when work could be found) were harrowing: men, women, children sweated twelve to sixteen hours a day in factories and mines —the work dulling, degrading, unsafe. Pay was minimal, and the Napoleonic wars had left a cruel legacy of inflation and unemployment. Worse, industrialist and worker had no legitimate voice in government, for voting rights had not followed economic and population shifts, but remained in the old agricultural strongholds. Thus, sprawl-

Gustave Doré, *Wentworth Street, Whitechapel*. Perhaps more vividly than any other artist, Doré depicted the horrors of the Victorian slum—its overcrowding, filth, poverty, hunger, and despair. The slums sketched by Doré in the seventies differed little from those of a half-century earlier.

ing industrial centers like Manchester, Birmingham, Leeds, and Shef-field elected no members to Parliament, but Old Sarum (with seven inhabitants), Gatton (with only six houses), and Dunwich (almost completely awash in the encroaching North Sea) each returned two members. Consequently, Parliament was largely the private preserve of wealthy landowners and their allies in the Church and courts, with government power used mostly for self-serving purposes. The most glaring case in point were the Corn Laws which kept English wheat prices exorbitantly high.

With Tory backlash driving industrialist and worker into each other's arms, the tide for parliamentary reform had begun to swell by 1821. Thus arose that extraordinary band of reformists later known as the Philosophical Radicals—with Bentham as patriarchal figurehead, James Mill as commander-in-chief, and son John as aide-de-camp. In the ranks could be found notable reformists like Francis Place, the indefatigable tailor of Charing Cross, the economist Ricardo as head of the party's countinghouse wing, and the methodical jurist John Austin, whose high-powered wife Sarah took John in tow much as Lady Bentham had done. Ready and eager to propound the gospel according to utility, the radicals lacked a suitable organ for evangelizing. The big journals were out of the question. The Whig *Edinburgh Review*, fitful and tepid in its liberalism, merely traded ponderous feints with two truculently Tory journals—the Wagnerian *Quarterly Review* and its more nimble and vitriolic magazine counterpart, *Blackwood's*. None of the three would touch genuine political reform at all. The only solution was a radical review. Thus, in 1824, with the help of Bentham's money, the *Westminster Review* was born. Its pages found no reformer more enthusiastic than young John Mill.

Indeed, John had developed into a formidable teenage activist since 1821. After the heady French interlude, he was soon put back on the utilitarian straight and narrow when his father had him read a redaction of Bentham's thought by the Swiss disciple Etienne Dumont. At last, in French translation, Bentham spoke out loud and bold. John was transfixed. In the first flush of enthusiasm, he discovered he now had "opinions; a creed, a doctrine, a philosophy; in one among the best senses of the word, a religion." He also had a mission—to be a utilitarian reformer of the world. With implacable fervor he rushed out to organize debate societies and study groups, fire off letters to the newspapers, and even prepare the master's *Rationale of Judicial Evidence* for the press—no mean task, given Bentham's rococo methods of composition. Meanwhile, his father had found employment for him: in 1820 the directors of East India House, impressed by the *History of British India*, had offered a position to James, who later procured a minor post for John. Lifetime financial security was within grasp, but John's youthful zealotry nearly wrecked the arrangement at the outset.

According to one version of the story, seventeen-year-old John was walking to work one morning when he spied a bundle of grimy rags in St. James Park. Investigating, he discovered an abandoned infant, strangled. Shaken, John continued on his way, only to pass the Old Bailey, where several criminals had been left hanging by their necks. John was stunned into desperation. What could be done, now, to prevent these horrors? Francis Place had the answer: unwanted children and crime (really caused by overpopulation) required an identical solution—contraception. It was a subject in which Place, the father of fifteen children, took an understandably keen interest. He had spelled out the techniques of a French method in several handbills, one entitled "To the Married of Both Sexes of the Working People." Gathering up the tracts, Mill and a friend (possibly William Ellis) sped through London strewing copies—to working women principally, for they were the chief victims and the information most concerned them. Nabbed by the police, Mill and his accomplice were hauled off to Bow Street, where they defended themselves so warmly that the magistrate remanded them to the Lord Mayor. The details are uncertain, but this official seems to have sentenced them to fourteen days in jail for attempting to defile the purity of English womanhood. Thinking better of the matter, he released them in a day or two. James had the affair hushed up, but shortly afterward John was unrepentantly penning letters on population control to a radical paper called the *Black Dwarf.*

These years of youthful propagandism showed off Mill's training to great advantage. After all, the main point had not been to teach Greek at three but to form a rational mind keyed to utilitarian ethics. To this end, the education had been long on logic, short on imagination. And it showed: John was a brilliant activist, but (it began to be whispered) he was also something of a stick—or rather, a reasoning machine programmed with his father's favorite opinions. Start a conversation, and Mill ground logic. And then one devastating day in the autumn of 1826 the machine broke down—unexpectedly, instantaneously, irrevocably.

Mill records the event memorably in the *Autobiography:*

> I was in a dull state of nerves, . . . the state, I should think, in which converts to Methodism usually are, when smitten by their first "conviction of sin." In this frame of mind it occurred to me to put the question directly to myself, "Suppose that all your objects in life were realized; that all the changes in institutions and opinions which you are looking

forward to, could be completely effected at this very instant: would this be a great joy and happiness to you?" And an irrepressible self-consciousness distinctly answered, "No!" At this my heart sank within me: the whole foundation on which my life was constructed fell down.

To find no happiness in the greatest happiness principle! To Bentham it would be inconceivable, to James Mill rank heresy. John had no one to turn to. Outwardly he went through the motions of existence; inwardly he contemplated suicide. Then, just as suddenly, the spell was broken:

> I was reading, accidentally, Marmontel's Memoirs, and came to the passage which relates his father's death, the distressed position of the family, and the sudden inspiration by which he, then a mere boy, felt and made them feel that he would be everything to them—would supply the place of all that they had lost. A vivid conception of the scene and its feelings came over me, and I was moved to tears. From this moment my burthen grew lighter. . . . I was no longer hopeless: I was not a stock or stone.

Six months of despair were over. John began to live again.

What had caused the spectacular mental crisis? Overwork, no doubt. The absence of love, probably. A repressed hatred for his dominating father, quite possibly. (Freudians cite Mill's reaction to the father's death in the Memoirs.) Mill himself blamed his one-sided education: by overstressing analysis, it had eroded the feelings, the very motive power needed to strive for human betterment. John would have to complete his education, but first he needed to replenish his emotions. The effort would transform him forever: the youthful propaganda machine would disappear into the philosopher of many-sidedness. Out of the ashes of his mental crisis would rise a phoenix of rare plumage indeed.

Instinctively John turned to the arts—first music, then poetry. A volume of Wordsworth's lyrics brought healing balm, and soon he was gazing at sunsets over tranquil waters. So grateful was he that when a Benthamite friend dismissed the poet derisively, John stunned his Debating Society with a resounding defense of Wordsworth in particular and poetic imagination in general. The orthodox utilitarians blinked in disbelief. But worse news was on the way. John was becoming alarmingly friendly with John Sterling and F. D. Maurice, two disciples of the archconservative oracle Samuel Taylor Coleridge. He was even reading Coleridge and allowing himself to be whisked off occasionally to Highgate to listen to the old sage himself. There, where smoke-palled London was but a smudge glimpsed through suburban greenery, the battle-scarred transcendentalist drifted through the garden or sat enthroned indoors, entrancing young disciples with rambling soliloquies on German metaphysics or with bright visions of English society harmonized through regenerated ancient institutions. John began reading the Germans, Goethe especially, and even made some sense of those *Edinburgh* articles on German thought by Thomas Carlyle—articles which his father would always anathematize as insane rhapsodies. For the first time in his life John was investigating the enemy camp from within, and discovering in amazement that truth was to be found there too.

Of course this new enthusiasm had to be hushed up at home. James Mill was not one to take lightly his son's defection from the Benthamite standard. Moreover, John guessed he would never again be precisely what James had in mind when he began teaching him Greek at three. Suspecting something, hurt by his son's secretiveness, James nevertheless remained stringently silent while John sneaked off to explore an intoxicating new world of heretical speculation.

On the philosophical battlefield of John's day, two main camps—empiricist and idealist—faced off against each other, with epistemology (the nature and limits of man's knowledge) as the main bone of contention. After all, ultimate questions could not be decided until some agreement had been reached on man's ability to answer them. Besides, discussions on epistemology had a way of getting around to the ultimate reality that man apprehends, always a lively topic for philosophers to tussle over.

The empiricist tradition was a hardy one in British philosophy, claiming such earlier heavyweights as John Locke and David Hume, with Bentham and James Mill as contemporary standard-bearers. In this tradition the mind of the newborn child is a *tabula rasa*, a blank page on which external reality writes impressions through the child's senses. Eventually, from a multitude of such impressions, the mind begins to reflect, noting for example some things as alike or unlike. From various red objects, the mind arrives at an idea of redness. Seeing A always followed by B, the mind associates them in a cause-effect relationship. Thus, knowledge derives from sense impressions and reflection. The tradition acquired important ethical overtones from

David Hartley, who saw man's moral awareness emerging from the pleasures and pains associated with certain experiences. From Hartley's associationism, it was but a short leap to Bentham's greatest happiness principle and to James Mill's thoroughgoing educational plan to form the rationally moral man by training the child to associate duty and happiness. The mind, as described by empiricists, was somewhat mechanical and passive, recording sense impressions and constructing from them more complex ideas, rather like a computer programmed by external reality and solving problems with the data. As an account of mind and world, empiricism was scientific, secular, sane.

But enter the idealists' world, and you discovered things undreamed of by empiricist philosophers. The British idealist tradition, though flaring more fitfully than the empiricist one, had lately been stoked up by German transcendentalists, most notably Immanuel Kant, whose thought had set off philosophic fireworks in Coleridge's teeming brain. To the idealist or intuitionist, the mind is active and dynamic, half creating the reality it perceives by imposing its own innate ideas upon external stimuli. Thus, an object is seen as beautiful because the mind apprehends (sometimes only dimly) an ideal Beauty within itself. If the mind to empiricists was something of a machine, to intuitionists it was like a creative artist shaping his materials to some half-understood inner vision of a greater reality. Further, intuitionists distinguished between the scientific Understanding *(Verstand)*, which deals with sense experience, and the intuitive Reason *(Vernunft)*, which perceives truths unverifiable in sense experience. Thus, mind is fitted to a world in which physical appearances mask spiritual or ideal reality. In this world, good and evil are matters not of toting up pleasures and pains, but of intuitive awareness of basic moral realities, such as: we have a free will, we have a conscience, we need to harmonize the two. In short, intuitionist reality contained a whole other dimension, the spiritual or ideal, that empiricists either denied or felt it profitless to explore. While empiricists explained the world rationally, intuitionists walked amid its marvels and mysteries.

The whole controversy might have been safely left to the philosophers except that its implications radiated in all directions—into ethics, business, politics, art, education. Indeed, the debate was but one skirmish in the larger battle raging between the powerful tradition of eighteenth-century rationalism and the surging new sensibilities of Romanticism. In the confused alarms of struggle and flight, the reasons of the head were ranged against the reasons of the heart, Greek revival temples fought for ground against Gothic revival churches, poetry of statement disputed with lyricism, religious skeptics quarreled with Oxford Tractarians, while neoclassical and Romantic landscapists flung the paintpot at each other.

But while everybody was choosing sides in the melee, John was discovering that truth must be gently culled from opposing camps. His insight was reinforced by a stir over his father's *Essay on Government*. Although the tract had been around since 1820, reform fever had caught up with it only in 1828, during one of its many reprintings. The essay's opening was pure Benthamism: the end of government is the greatest happiness of the greatest number, all men act in their own self-interest, only representative government can secure the greatest happiness. After this headlong radical start, the essay pulled up abruptly. Apparently universal suffrage was untidy, and James veered away sharply to consider whose voting rights were expendable. No point in enfranchising those whose interests were already covered by others, so James crossed off the list all women and children, as well as all males under forty. Though James's prose is a marvel of muddiness on the point, the lower classes apparently could be enfranchised because they were sure to be guided in their voting habits by "the middle rank" of society—not, mind you, by the aristocrat or the rich industrialist. So, suffrage should extend at least to "the middle rank," that is, to those exemplary heads of households who were "the chief source of all that has exalted and refined human nature." In brief, the James Mills of society were surety against democratic anarchy.

This, however, was more radical than even reformist Tories and Whigs would allow. Accordingly, the Whig *Edinburgh* brought up its heaviest artillery in Thomas Babington Macaulay's ponderous parallelisms. Sonorously sarcastic, Macaulay insisted (unkindest cut of all) that James Mill's method was unscientific. Instead of utilizing historical fact, Mill deduced his conclusions from sweeping generalizations about human nature—a charge that uncomfortably resembled the one Benthamites were always flinging at their intuitionist opponents.

John Mill was dumbfounded. Turning to his father's essay, he found that Macaulay was right. Though here and there nodding to historical evidence, James was forever intoning phrases like "the fundamental principles of human nature." And then there were his dismaying opinions about women's voting rights. But John saw, with some relief, that Macaulay was wrong in believing that political theory could be put on the same footing with the physical sciences where observation

Thomas Babington Macaulay. Portrait by J. Partridge.

of past events yielded universal laws. Macaulay had simply overlooked the complexities of human behavior, which is not always predictable from past events. Whatever the solution, it lay with neither his father nor Macaulay, who each clutched his portion of truth and refused to acknowledge anyone else's. More than ever John was convinced: synthesizing partial truths was the philosopher's most pertinent business.

So he listened to everybody—from conservative intuitionists to Saint-Simonians, members of a strange new French sect. These were perhaps the happiest years of John's life: in the process of reeducating himself, he was constructing a new self upon the old. Despite minor lapses into melancholia, John was at his most sociable, making friends everywhere—friends like William Johnson Fox, the expansive Unitarian minister whose congregation included the affable, if somewhat heavy-footed merchant John Taylor, and his pretty young wife, Harriet, whose enormous dark eyes flashed hidden insights from a quick, questioning mind. John talked to them all, enthusiastically taking for his motto Goethe's "many-sidedness." Never again would he be strait-jacketed into party doctrine. Though Gustave d'Eichthal, the Saint-Simonian missionary to the British Isles, tried mightily to bag young Mill for his sect, John successfully eluded capture. His role would be to mediate between conflicting truths, to speak not for party dogma but for critical open-mindedness.

Meanwhile, England had more than its share of party conflict: indeed, the struggle for parliamentary reform was threatening to explode at any moment into full-scale revolution. In July 1830 the French government of Charles X was toppled; would England be next? (John Mill sped to Paris to see what a real revolution looked like, sending back reports to his father who had two of them printed in the radical weekly *Examiner*.) For the next two years England would crackle with political tension: would it be reform or revolution?

In the midst of the uproar, a new voice was heard—in another *Examiner* series entitled *The Spirit of the Age* running from January to May 1831. True, the voice was barely audible in the general tumult, but it was, and is, worth listening to. Here, perhaps for the first time, we catch the voice of the young radical who had sea-changed into a genuine human philosopher. No longer is it the voice of James Mill's son; it is now the voice of John Stuart Mill.

CHAPTER THREE

ZEITGEIST:

The Spirit of the Age

Wandering between two worlds, one dead,
The other powerless to be born.
—MATTHEW ARNOLD,
"Stanzas from the Grande Chartreuse," 85–86

 THE Spirit of the Age may come as a shock to those who think of Mill simply as a spokesman for freedom of thought. Consider, for example, this forcible monition from the articles:

But if you once persuade an ignorant or a half-instructed person, that he ought to assert his liberty of thought, discard all authority, and—I do not say *use* his own judgment, for that he never can do too much—but *trust* solely to his own judgment, and receive and reject opinions according to his own views of the evidence;—if, in short, you teach to all the lesson of *indifferency*, . . . the merest trifle will suffice to unsettle and perplex their minds.

Mill even finds a word of praise (albeit a qualified one) for the medieval Catholic Church and feudal barons. Clearly, something new has been added to the old Benthamite formula.

However tempting, it will not do to pass off *The Spirit of the Age* as a youthful indiscretion. Mill later fancied the style too lumbering for a newspaper like the *Examiner*, but modern readers will hardly concur: compared with subsequent weightier works, the *Spirit* is easy reading indeed. Perhaps, as Mill said, the series was badly timed, what with reform bill rumblings overpowering all lesser noises. Still, the work's philosophical speculations are adroitly linked with the political tremors of the day. Furthermore, the series often looks disconcertingly like a concise preface to Mill's later work. In it are contained many of his subsequent preoccupations—fitting political questions into historical context, adjusting the conflicting claims of liberty and authority, searching for a method in the social sciences, and synthesizing the half-truths of party zealots. Even the artistry anticipates maturer works—the writer's moderate "voice" poised between conflicting extremes, the interweaving of key words and images, the careful matching of thought and structure within the essay. Above all, the *Spirit* shows Mill as a philosopher awakening people to a fuller vision of reality through insight and argument. Few would now dispute F. A. Hayek's 1942 decision to resurrect *The Spirit of the Age* because "it deserves to be rescued from the oblivion in which it has rested for over a hundred years."

When Mill's *Spirit of the Age* appeared, British society had already reached the advanced stages of acute future shock. Anxious pulse-takings of the national health had been commonplace for several years. To Conservatives like Robert Southey the life signs were fading fast, while most Liberals argued that a judicious dose of government reform would revive the patient swiftly. To the independent mystic Thomas Carlyle the signs of the times indicated that the patient was in danger of losing his human heart and replacing it with a mechanical substitute. "The spirit of the age" was on everybody's lips—to radicals as a rallying cry, to reactionaries as a malediction. The spirit demands a reform bill, cried Liberals. The spirit demands only to be put down, replied Conservatives. To both parties, the French Revolution of 1830 came as a prime manifestation of the spirit of the age—for better or for worse. In the December *Blackwood's* conservative David Robinson refused to worship the age's unholy spirit, while in the *Examiner* of 2 January 1831 radical editor Albany Fonblanque was hailing 1830 as "The Year One of the People's Cause." The following week the *Examiner* featured Part One of Mill's *Spirit of the Age*, the rest of the five-part series appearing intermittently until ended by Mill with the May 29 installment. The articles thus ventured out into a world of political pandemonium in which "the spirit of the age" was a somewhat harried watchword.

Trust Mill to do something more philosophical with the term. Brushing aside both eulogy and abuse, he proposes a systematic inquiry into the nature of the embattled age. Practical politicians and party zealots will no doubt groan at the suggestion, but Mill has persuasive reasons. Only through such inquiry, he argues, can people truly know what is happening in the present; only thus can they intelligently act for the future. Nor does such inquiry prevent their taking sides; rather, it clarifies which side to take. Indeed, Mill in the *Spirit* shows precisely how to go about it.

Calmly, he examines the tumultuous times:

> The first of the leading peculiarities of the present age is, that it is an age of transition. Mankind have outgrown old institutions and old doctrines, and have not yet acquired new ones.

Consequently, society is fractured into men of the past, with their death's grip on the old ways, and men of the present, rambunctiously pushing for change. More, the generation gap yawns distressingly between young and old, with elderly wisdom obsolete and youthful enthusiasm unseasoned. And however comforting to think so, the increase of knowledge among the masses is not what has discredited the past—the "useful knowledge" being diffused to the multitude hardly qualifying as profundity. Rather, it is greater freedom of discussion that has helped people shuck off old errors, and in the process has left them naked of any positive convictions whatsoever. This lack, however, is no deterrent to their collecting into wrangling camps, vociferously proclaiming their half-truths. With no viable authorities in the field, the uninstructed proceed to think for themselves—with frequently grotesque results. Happily, in the physical sciences the instructed are listened to, but no such attentiveness is apparent in politics or ethics. The moldy establishments of Church and State no longer put the fittest men into power; on the contrary, they now impede the process.

Dismal as this prospect at first seems, Mill argues in Part Three that it is just part of humanity's growing-up process. In short, Mill has acquired a philosophy of history. Studied judiciously, history reveals a succession of natural and transitional ages. In the natural age worldly power and moral influence are exercised by the fittest persons in the society. The result is a harmonious culture in which people operate within the structures available rather than in defiance of them. The prevailing creeds are believed in, and rulers usually foster progress. Civilization either dawdles dreamily or advances smoothly, undisturbed by gigantic convulsions in morals or politics.

Such natural societies can be of two kinds. In the first, the fittest persons are selected for power, as in the best ancient republics (Athens, Sparta, Rome) or in the modern republic of early-nineteenth-century United States. In the second kind, possession of power tends to call forth leadership ability. Mill cites Europe in the Middle Ages and "small societies of barbarous people," such as Highland clans. In these cases power is often inherited, the future ruler being bred to his station. Moreover, as the leader-to-be soon realizes that his survival depends upon know-how, he generally bestirs himself to acquire it. The republican kind of natural society, however, can be more flexible, because people can choose new rulers to suit new conditions. The other society carries the seeds of its own destruction: once locked into power, a ruler or ruling class can be left behind by change, thereby throwing the whole society into decline.

And so, Mill observes, societies enter upon transitional periods— where power and ability are sundered, with no easy way to nudge the fittest into power or the unfit out of office. Consequently, drastic reform and revolution become the order of the day. People have outgrown their old political and religious creeds, and a spirit of critical skepticism jubilantly sets about demolishing the orderly house of received opinion.

Such, Mill says, has been the situation in Europe since the Renaissance and Reformation. Once fit for authority, the wealthier classes "have retrograded in all the higher qualities of mind," until now they represent an unfit minority wielding political and moral influence. The point is made by a delicious juxtaposition of names: "Think, good heavens! that Sir John Elliott, and John Hampden, and Sir John Colepepper, and Sir William Wentworth, were *country gentlemen*—and think who are the parliamentary leaders of that class in our own day: a Knatchbull, a Bankes, a Gooch, a Lethbridge!" Meanwhile, genuine leadership ability has been accumulating (in England anyway) among the middle classes (presumably James Mill's "middle rank"), and the first big step toward a new natural age would be granting this group a share of power. Thus, what starts out in *The Spirit of the Age* as a sweeping historical survey transforms itself at series' end into a rousing argument for practical political reform:

Now, the men of hereditary wealth . . . must, therefore, be divested of the monopoly of worldly power, ere the most virtuous and best instructed of the nation will acquire that ascendancy over the opinions and feelings of the rest, by which alone England can emerge from this crisis of transition, and enter once again into a natural state of society.

So Mill's spirit of the age ends up demanding reform too. What then, one may ask, has been gained by all the philosophical inquiry? Simply the inestimable difference between an unthinking response to the latest political breezes and a rational cooperation with changing conditions that is based upon thoughtful study of history.

Striking though it is, Mill's concept of transitional and natural ages is not original. It was at the time current coin among French and German intellectuals, though cultural lag and British insularity had all but prevented its crossing the channel. Mill got the idea mostly from the Saint-Simonians, who talked of "critical" and "organic" ages. Possibly also of French origin (Mill had been dipping into Auguste Comte's early work) was the *Spirit*'s parallel between society's evolution and that of the sciences. The physical sciences, having fought through a transitional phase, had at last reached a natural phase where their credibility was widely accepted. "The physical sciences, therefore . . . , are continually *growing*, but never *changing*: in every age they receive indeed mighty improvements, but for them the age of transition is past." A similar deliverance of the social and moral sciences is now about to take place. Then perhaps European society will stumble after them into the final natural age.

To some modern ears, dividing history into alternating transitional and natural periods may sound too neat. But it would be unwise to dismiss the theory lightly. For one thing, it depicts humanity as a developing species, in sharp contrast to earlier theories of mankind as essentially static. The theory also changes history from a nasty account of oppression by sinister interests into a record of fuller civilization gradually unfolding itself in time. In brief, the new history reveals a pattern of progress. And consequently it has an enormously bracing effect upon humanity's mental health. With or without theological overtones, it offers hope for the future; it lends meaning to the work of bettering the world. Certainly, its importance for the nineteenth century can scarcely be overestimated: rare is the eminent Victorian uncommitted to some version of human progress achieved through alternating periods of struggle and harmony. Nor has modern skepticism succeeded in dimming the idea's basic luster. Belief in progress, historian John Bowles notes, "is still dominant today. We fight our wars, we organise our welfare state, democratic or communist, for the benefit of generations unborn. This outlook is still, in spite of the catastrophes of the last half century, spreading about the planet."

Furthermore, the succession of natural and transitional periods, whether or not derived explicitly from Mill, is now a widely recognized feature in the landscape of modern consciousness. Here, for example, is American historian Eric F. Goldman being interviewed on the turbulent decade following President Kennedy's 1963 assassination:

> I would describe the years as a period of important transition.
>
> What I mean is this: I think 100 years from now historians will find that those years fit into a kind of cycle in our national life—consensus, the shattering of consensus, the formation of a new consensus. It has happened again and again.
>
> In a decade of transition, an old consensus on basic issues disintegrates, and we develop a new one. . . .
>
> It seems to me that we had developed one of these consensuses in very powerful form in the mid-1950s. We generally shared certain attitudes. . . .
>
> And then the cycle operated, as it has operated in the past: The consensus flew apart. We became two nations in our attitudes towards basic issues, and there was a very serious clash. But gradually, in ways not too discernible, Americans began moving towards a new consensus.

Minor variations aside, it is the pattern of history traced by Mill in his 1831 articles.

In any event, the outlook involved Mill in some sharp departures from old-line Benthamism. Eighteenth-century radical philosophers bewailed history as such an appalling record of crimes and misfortunes that they were often eager to forget it altogether. "Happy is the nation without a history," proclaimed Cesare Beccaria, one of Bentham's tutelary deities. So Mill's persistent reliance upon historical theory in *The Spirit of the Age* represents a clear victory for the Germano-Coleridgeans. Certainly the theory has the great advantage of allowing Mill to appreciate past ages and cultures, while fully recognizing their inadequacy for the present. "Human nature must proceed step by step, in politics as well as in physics," says Mill, refusing to decry the ancients for not having annual Parliaments, universal suffrage, and vote by ballot. He even manages to announce that the Middle Ages had the best form of government and moral leadership possible at the time—an opinion guaranteed to set radical teeth on edge. And if James Mill ever read the anonymously published *Spirit*, he might well have taken umbrage at its critique of his method of reaching conclusions from general principles of static human nature.

Most important, however, is Mill's tinkering with Bentham's concept of utility. In his own sometimes bizarre way, Bentham was absolutely committed to the greatest happiness of people—pretty much as they were. But in Mill's modernized view, human beings are evolving creatures whose greatest happiness lies in developing their humanity to its fullest. The shift in emphasis is at once slight and decisive. Utility begins to mean improvement rather than hedonistic happiness. Or, as Mill proclaimed memorably in *Utilitarianism:* "It is better to be a human being dissatisfied than a pig satisfied."

Equally momentous, Mill's historical relativism led him to a certain amount of philosophical relativism—a point to remember when the subject of his "inconsistencies" arises. Mill believed that an expanding intellect must always rearrange its philosophical furniture to accommodate a new truth. Also, the true and desirable position for one age might not be so for another; accordingly, a philosopher aiming at human improvement might have to stress that portion of the truth needed most by his times.

Such ideas help to account for his surprising views on freedom of discussion in *The Spirit of the Age*. Mill allows that, yes, such freedom is necessary—in an age of transition, when legitimate authorities no longer exist. "Learn, and think for yourself, is reasonable advice for the day," he grants. But the advice has its pitfalls: too often the results are skepticism and arrogance firmly grounded on ignorance. Not that Mill takes a dim view of the common man's ability to learn; it is just that, in the press of everyday life with a living to be earned, most people lack—and perhaps always will lack—the leisure and training to cultivate even one area of knowledge, let alone several. Necessarily, then, most people must take their opinions from authorities who, it is to be fervently hoped, are reliable. In the coming natural age this will be the case: "The first men of the age will one day join hands and be agreed." In such case, however, less value must be placed upon everybody's thinking and speaking *ex cathedra* for himself.

Whatever its philosophical implications, Mill's theory of history gives *The Spirit of the Age* its dominant artistic pattern. In his historical dialectic, one set of extremes engenders an opposite set, the two eventually merging into grander synthesis. As times change, for example, the opinions and sentiments of a natural age become outlandishly outdated and thus extremist. During the transitional age, opposition takes to the barricades with extremist reactions. When the sound and fury have subsided, the best of the two extremes have mingled themselves into a new natural age. "I looked forward," Mill recalls in the *Autobiography*, "through the present age of loud disputes but generally weak convictions, to a future which shall unite the best qualities of the critical with the best qualities of the organic periods." Briefly, the pattern is an early version of thesis creating antithesis, followed by synthesis.

Presenting this pattern artistically was complicated by the essay's being published serially (like many a Victorian novel), its five parts appearing in seven installments, with Parts Three and Five each cut into two segments. Such publication compels an author to recapitulate or otherwise prod his reader about what went before. The subtler the reminder, the better. Throughout the series Mill elects to restate his ideas in varied format, repeating key words, images, and themes as memory-joggers. In particular, varied repetitions of the thesis-antithesis-synthesis pattern are used as low-keyed reminders of Mill's central point about historical development.

For example, *The Spirit of the Age* repeatedly evokes the synthesizing mind of Mill's persona. If the transitional age is the problem, the open-minded persona is the solution. Little time is lost establishing this persona as a median between two extremes. Early on, Mill describes Tory reactions to the spirit of the age, specifically Robert Southey's low moans in *Colloquies on the Progress and Prospects of Society* and David Robinson's hoarse defiance in *Blackwood's Magazine*. On the other hand, the jubilant huzzahs of liberals, Mill says, can be heard reverberating from any popular newspaper—perhaps a glance at Fonblanque's dithyrambs in the previous issue of the *Examiner*. At this point Mill openly enters the essay himself, dismissing "all this indiscriminate eulogy and abuse," to conduct his philosophical inquiry into the turmoil of the times. After the sound and fury, the voice of sweetness and light.

Part Two of the *Spirit*, coming along two weeks later, nudges the forgetful reader about the persona by means of a lengthy simile involving a lost caravan in which two sets of guides are squabbling about how to proceed. "While these two contending parties are measuring their sophistries against one another," the travelers would do well to heed "the man who is capable of other ideas than those of his age"—in short, a philosopher like Mill who sees beyond the age's factional half-truths. Skillfully the well-balanced persona is insinuated again, early in Part Three:

> It is the object of the present paper . . . to demonstrate, that the changes in the visible structure of society which are manifestly approaching, and which so many anticipate with dread, and so many with hope of a nature far different from that which I feel, are the means by which we are to be carried through our present transitional state, and the human mind is to resume its quiet and regular onward course.

Once again, extremist nay- and yea-sayers are followed by Mill's more discriminating persona.

Surely the most significant version of the pattern occurs in Part Three when Mill assesses the half-truths of his father and Macaulay —though neither man is named. First, he castigates Macaulay as a veneer-deep historian babbling about induction without having thought much about it. But, ever so gingerly, he also reproves those like his father "who build their philosophy of politics upon what they term the universal principles of human nature." And here Mill pinpoints a permanent weakness in his father's thought: the elder Mill kept imagining that John Bull was Everyman, that the rest of humanity was exactly like eighteenth-century Englishmen. Consequently, he was forever attempting to spin universal theories of humankind from merely English threads. With Macaulay and the elder Mill representing the extremes, John's persona reenters the essay to establish the tolerant mean. The whole passage briskly dramatizes Mill's determination to transcend both the Benthamites and their critics.

Open-mindedness like the persona's is the remedy for a transitional age—that is the *Spirit*'s main point. To demonstrate it imaginatively, Mill depicts his age as wandering in the desert, badly in need of a philosophical Moses to point out the promised land. The essay teems with references to roads, paths, journeys, caravans, and travels. Even Homer's much-enduring Ulysses makes a cameo appearance, a perfect image of the beleaguered traveler struggling homeward.

Amid the age's confused wanderings, the perfect guide would be someone capable of seeing beyond present conflicts. The point is dramatized by a liberal sprinkling of references to eyes, seeing, and guides. Naturally, Mill's persona is exactly the kind of guide needed. "The best guide is not he who, when people are in the right path, merely praises it, but he who shows them the pitfalls and the precipices by which it is endangered; and of which, as long as they were in the wrong road, it was not so necessary that they should be warned." That is precisely Mill's role in *The Spirit of the Age.*

So the transitional age is on its way, precariously, toward a new and perhaps final natural age, where growth without revolution will reign. Meanwhile, power and ability are still strangers to each other, and further philosophical inquiry, Mill insists, were best curtailed during the knockabout efforts to reform the situation.

> But "fit audience," even "though few," cannot be found for such discussions, at a moment when the interests of the day and of the hour naturally and properly engross every mind. The sequel of these papers must therefore be postponed until the interval of repose, after the present bustle and tumult. I shall resume my subject as early as possible after the passing of the Reform Bill.

There is a time to think and a time to act. Mill accepts the rhythm just as he accepted the rhythm of natural and transitional ages. Thus, by series' end, contemporary chaos has assumed meaning and fitness in the pattern of human progress.

In his acceptance of present turmoil, in his abrupt turning from speculation, the *Spirit's* persona somewhat resembles the fictional speaker of "Locksley Hall," Alfred Tennyson's brilliant portrait of the angry young man of the 1830s. Bidding a long farewell to the hall, his childhood home and symbol of old England, the youthful speaker relinquishes the past by turning to the future. Meanwhile, the storm cloud of the nineteenth century gathers ominously above the hall:

> *Let it fall on Locksley Hall, with rain or hail, or fire or snow;*
> *For the mighty wind arises, roaring seaward, and I go.*

Though hardly qualifying as nostalgia for merrie England, Mill's respect for the past does not blind him to the need for change, though change destroys forever the glory that has been. He too accepts (and much more readily than Tennyson's young man) the storm cloud threatening old England; he too goes his way as it descends.

John Doyle, *New Reform Coach*, 17 June 1832. With a confident Lord Grey holding the
reins and a nervous King William inside, the coach of reform government gathers
precarious momentum. Atop the coach, Irishman Dan O'Connell exuberantly waves his
shillelagh, while portly John Bull points in derision to Wellington who has been left
behind expostulating about the coach's discarded drag chain.

This confidence, one suspects, was born of the mental crisis. Indeed,
Mill's portrait of the age in 1831 resembles his own crisis writ large.
Language parallels between the *Autobiography* and the *Spirit* certainly
suggest as much: in the *Autobiography* the crisis is called Mill's "years
of transition." And the language describing the onset of the crisis
("But the time came when I awakened . . . as from a dream") repeats
the *Spirit*'s account of England's future shock: "Thousands awoke as
from a dream." Though terrifying, his awakening from Benthamite slumbers had led him to the Germano-Coleridgean half of the
truth and toward synthesis. On a larger scale, the age was experiencing similar waking frights, and was also moving toward synthesis.

The Spirit of the Age closes with a program and a promise:

> But it greatly imports us to obtain a far deeper insight into the futurity
> which awaits us, and into the means by which the blessings of that
> futurity may be best improved, and its dangers avoided.

It was to this subject that Mill pledged to return once the Reform Bill
had passed. But the struggle for reform proved more protracted than
anticipated, and he never resumed the series. However, he did not
break his promise. In all the articles, books, letters that later streamed
from his pen, he kept returning to his subject—the future of humanity
and how best to secure its blessings.

As Mill saw, the momentum of reform was sweeping all other interests before it. When the new Parliament elected after George IV's
death had convened in autumn 1830, the conservative Duke of Wellington (the hero of Waterloo and now Prime Minister) had staunchly
refused to yield ground on reform. "No surrender!" he cried, as if in
the midst of battle. He soon was. Discontented agricultural workers,
led by a fictitious Captain Swing, burned hay ricks, sacked farmers'
homes, and generally terrorized the south of England. When Wellington resigned over an issue unrelated to reform, the liberal Whig Lord
Grey formed a coalition ministry, and on 1 March 1831 introduced a
reform bill—which squeaked through the House of Commons by one
vote and then became entangled in committee. At Grey's request, King
William IV dissolved Parliament, and in the ensuing general election,
reformist elements won heavily. It was during this flurry of reform
excitement that Mill canceled *The Spirit of the Age.*

But the reform question was not to be settled easily. Lord Grey's
second reform bill swept through Commons on September 22 but was
thrown out by the House of Lords on October 8. This time the whole
nation felt the shock of recoil. In London a monster rally organized
by Francis Place seemed to portend a state of siege. Rioting erupted
in Worcester, Bath, and Derby. In Bristol a mob held the city for two
days, sacking jails, the Mansion House, and the Bishop's Palace. Those
bishops who had voted against the bill in Lords were hooted by
crowds: Wellington's windows were broken, and the Duke of Cumber-
land was dragged from his horse. The borough-mongering Duke of
Newcastle was a natural target: having evicted two hundred residents
of Newark for failing to vote according to his wishes, he had silenced
cavilers by imperiously quoting scripture—"Have I not a right to do

what I like with my own?" In short order, he was attacked by a London mob, and his castle at Nottingham put to the torch.

On December 12 Lord Grey tried again, introducing a third bill, which soon passed Commons. The nation was in an ugly mood: the question making the rounds was no longer "What will the Lords do?" but "What will be done with the Lords?" Backs to the wall, the Lords passed the second reading of the bill by nine votes on 13 April 1832. But all was not over yet. In a death-rattle ploy, Tories attempted to doctor the bill in early May. Grey and his cabinet resigned in a huff, and in the ominous crisis that followed King William besought Wellington to come up with a watered-down bill that would satisfy Lords. Meanwhile, the country teetered on the brink of revolution. Factories shut down while everyone flocked to mass meetings; there was talk of armed rebellion, of not paying taxes. The militia was alerted. With the activist's sure sense of the appropriate gesture, Francis Place had London placarded with:

TO STOP THE

DUKE

GO FOR

GOLD

An immediate run on the banks brought a nervous deputation from the City to the King's doorstep. Wellington could not form a government, and the exasperated William reinstated Lord Grey, who had taken care to extract the King's agreement to create new reform-prone peers should the Lords again reject the bill. With this final bit of arm twisting, the Lords at last approved the bill on 4 June. Three days later it received royal assent.

Bonfires of triumph blazed all about the countryside. Up in Lincolnshire the news arrived in the dead of night, but the Tennyson brothers and sisters rushed out anyway to ring the church bells madly, to the great indigation of the Tory parson. Wellington merely groaned: "The waters of destruction have burst the gates of the temple."

Not quite. The new bill was hardly the anarchistic thing that its enemies had proclaimed. Nor was it the cure-all that many of its supporters had hoped. It enfranchised about half of the middle class, but workers were yet without the vote. Some redistricting was achieved, but the big industrial centers were still underrepresented.

Commercial interests began to carry some weight in government. Despite the election of some leading Radicals, working-class interests remained largely beyond the parliamentary pale. But an enormously important psychological point had been made. The form of British government was no longer sacrosanct: it could be modified to meet change.

And what role did Mill play in these historic events? Probably a small one. "Until the whole of the existing institutions of society are leveled with the ground," he scribbled furiously to John Sterling, "there will be nothing for a wise man to do which the most pigheaded fool cannot do much better than he." So he apparently remained on the political sidelines, waiting for reactionary and reformist to do their worst. Besides, all his emotional energies were being directed elsewhere. He was in fact perched on his own personal powder keg.

In his letters the first hint of what had been happening appears in this storm-tossed item of summer 1832, the original in wildly operatic French:

> Blessed be the hand which wrote these letters! She has written to me —it is enough; although I realize it is only to bid me an eternal farewell.
>
> This farewell, she must not believe I accept it. Her path and mine have parted, she has said it: but they can, they must meet again. Whenever, wherever that may be, she will find me always as I have been, as I am still.
>
> She shall be obeyed: my letters will not trouble her tranquility, nor pour another drop into the cup of sorrows. She shall be obeyed, for the reasons she gives,—she would be, even if she had limited herself to telling me her wishes. To obey her is a necessity for me.
>
> She will not refuse, I hope, the offering of these small flowers, which I have brought for her from New Forest. Give them to her if necessary as if from you.

John Stuart Mill had finally fallen in love—with John Taylor's wife.

Harriet Taylor (ca. 1834)

CHAPTER FOUR

LOGICIAN IN ORDINARY:

Four Essays on Poetry

Do not all charms fly
At the mere touch of cold philosophy?
—JOHN KEATS, *Lamia*, 229–30

 HARRIET always elicited strong reactions. Taylor doted upon her, Mill worshiped her. Others, less entranced, saw only a spoiled, would-be bluestocking. The Carlyles were alternately attracted and repelled. To those who knew of the Mill affair, she was an item of gossip. And then, in 1873, Mill's encomiums to her in his posthumous *Autobiography* touched off a forensic free-for-all whose dust has not settled yet. Was she really the paragon of poetry and intellect he depicted? For over a century, assessors of her personality have snapped at each other in disagreement, and the question of her intellectual contributions can still reduce even the soberest discussion of Mill's thought to unseemly acrimony.

A year and a half younger than Mill, Harriet Hardy was born in 1807 at Walworth, the middle child of seven. Her early years are clouded from view (as so much about her is), but apparently emotions ran high in the Hardy family, with the father domineering and difficult, and the mother and two daughters forming a mutually exasperating triangle. Nevertheless, Harriet acquired the usual accomplishments, including a zest for religious controversy. In 1826 eighteen-year-old Harriet married John Taylor, then about thirty, a well-to-do wholesale druggist with radical leanings. The couple settled at 4 Christopher Street, Finsbury Circus, near South Place Unitarian chapel, where Taylor was a leading member of the congregation. For a few years Harriet was content with her role as bride and mother of two sons. But the tranquility was not to last.

She had made a respectable marriage and only later discovered its drawbacks. Sexual lovemaking had come as an unpleasant shock, but worse was the tedium of life as a businessman's household ornament. Her husband, twelve years her senior, was preparing for a comfortable snooze through middle age. She was in her early twenties, awakening to new ideas, seething with questions, enraptured with poetry, and perceiving that Taylor's radicalism was as sluggish as complacent conservatism. Taught that marriage was the shining end-all of woman's existence, she found herself a doll rattling the bars of her dollhouse.

Legend has it that Harriet confided her troubles to the South Place minister William Johnson Fox—who was prepared to commiserate, his own marriage of ten years having gradually turned to ashes. Ensnarled in the situation was Fox's feverishly gifted ward, Eliza Flower, whose affection had helped dispel his marital miseries. Did the dubious example of his own case prompt the suggestion that Harriet have a talk with John Mill? However it came about, one evening in summer 1830, John found himself a dinner guest at the Taylors', looking across table at Harriet's enormous dark eyes. What did those eyes see? A young man of twenty-four, good-looking in an earnest underfed sort of way; a brilliant intellectual reaching out for the warmth of poetry; and, best of all, a devotee of women's rights, desperately lonely for someone to share his dream of human improvement.

It was only a matter of time before the high winds of passion were gusting at gale force. For the next three years the Taylor household fairly hummed with fervid notes and high-voltage emotions. Harriet could bring herself to part with neither husband nor lover, and so the three settled down to a thoroughly respectable version of the *ménage à trois*, with John Taylor conveniently dining out a lot and John Mill calling during specified visiting hours. The affair was entirely platonic; after Helen Taylor's birth in 1831, the marriage apparently became so.

The question of Harriet's influence being the thorny thing it is, suffice it to say that during their early relationship, Mill's thought

Wordsworth on Helvellyn. Portrait by Benjamin Robert Haydon, 1842.

branched out most notably in two directions. He pondered the nature of poetry and the dangers to individualism posed by democratic society. On the latter topic, his "On Genius" (*Monthly Repository*, October 1832) hymned the Greek ideal of the inquiring mind so eloquently that, were it not for a sudden demur in the final paragraph, the essay might be taken for a complete recantation of *The Spirit of the Age*'s fear of independent thinking. A fuller exposition, "Civilization—Signs of the Times" (*London and Westminster Review*, April 1836) depicted the modern individual disappearing into the group—the committee, the union, the corporation. That cooperative effort is a sign of civilization Mill recognized, but he also foresaw, with chilling accuracy, the resulting intellectual and moral enervation. Possible solutions, he ventured, lay in more sensitive organizations and finer education. For all its calmness, the essay remains disturbingly pertinent.

Harriet's parallel fears for the individual found expression in two unpublished essays, on (significantly) toleration and divorce. And on the subject of poetry she must have invigorated Mill's thought considerably. Her great poetic passion was Shelley's cloud-misted radical verse, to which she occasionally did the honor of an imitation:

> *Whence comest thou, sweet wind?*
> *Didst take thy phantom form*
> *'Mid the depth of the forest trees?*
> *Or spring, new born,*
> *Of the fragrant morn,*
> *'Mong the far-off Indian seas?*

Enraptured, Mill began to see her as his completing counterpart, a being of sure and noble feeling, whose perceptions were as quick as his logic was cautious. In brief, she was the quintessential poet.

In the early thirties, however, there were a couple of contenders for her laurels. One, of course, was Wordsworth, whose verse had charmed away Mill's mental crisis with mountain scenery and tranquilizing emotion. In summer 1831, while all England wrangled about reform, Mill escaped on a walking tour to the Lake District, crowning the pilgrimage with reverential visits to the old poet in his sanctuary at Rydal Mount. Mill even kept a journal replete with detailed descriptions of picturesque views:

The beck, or torrent, which makes the Rydal falls, is the finest specimen of its kind which I ever saw. The bed, or trough through which it rushes, seems as if it had been chiselled several feet deep in the living rock; the sides of the ghyll are green, and richly wooded, but over the stream the rock is laid bare, and shows itself in crags above and slabs and fragments below, superior in wildness to everything I have seen of this class. The falls are only in a stream of this character like the most brilliant passages in a fine piece of music. The stream is all waterfalls.

Though reading for all the world like a stray leaf from Ruskin or Gerard Manley Hopkins, the passage is indeed Mill's—and an eye-opening illustration of just how romantic this "steam-engine intellect" could be.

Equally enthusiastic about Wordsworth himself, Mill declared him even more amiable and tolerant than his poetry promised. This, at a time when radical abhorrence of Wordsworth could be summed up nicely in lines that Browning would later fling at him:

> *Shakespeare was of us, Milton was for us,*
> *Burns, Shelley, were with us,—they watch from their graves!*
> *He alone breaks from the van and the freemen,*
> *—He alone sinks to the rear and the slaves!*
> *"The Lost Leader," 11. 13–16*

But Mill knew that when radical reforms were won, the world would still need Wordsworth's healing emotion.

The following autumn a third poet bedazzled Mill's eyes—although Thomas Carlyle saw himself more as prophet than anything else. Clutching the manuscript of *Sartor Resartus* like the Tables of the Law, he had descended upon London from his Scottish mountaintop, primarily to search out a publisher for the new dispensation. But while there, he also desired to survey a possible disciple in the "new mystic" who had written those articles on the spirit of the age.

Carlyle's election to prophecy had not come easily; nothing in his life ever did. Born in 1795 into a Scottish household where even the Kirk was found wanting in moral earnestness, young Tom at thirteen was marched off to Edinburgh to study for the ministry. There, in a repeat of James Mill's fate, he read the skeptics and saw his religious beliefs crumble. Meanwhile, his pious old mother kept writing things like: "Have you got through the Bible yet? If you have, read it again." Years of bitter poverty and mental torment followed, as Carlyle dragged from job to job, trying to find the purpose of any work in a purposeless universe. It was only after a massive mystical experience in 1822 or '23 that he began to exorcise his demon of *angst*. Then, even his earthly lot began to prosper: in 1826 he married Jane Baillie Welsh (aptly described as "that brilliant mocking-bird of genius whom he was to love and quarrel with till her death"), and his *Edinburgh Review* articles brought a modicum of fame. But literary success was not for Carlyle. Casting all aside, he and Jane retreated to Craigenputtock, an isolated Dumfriesshire farm, where he could listen to the divine voice. Evidently it was a choice location for this pursuit: in the interval between gales the silence was so profound that Jane could hear the sheep munching a quarter mile away.

Here amid the bleak splendors of the Scottish lowlands, Carlyle at last discerned that he was to be prophet to an age of unbelief, preaching a message to redeem the perplexed world from the same doubts that had paralyzed his own life. Six years Carlyle spent in the Craigenputtock wilderness, maturing his message, poring over the German transcendentalists, and muttering wrathfully at utilitarian materialism. How significant, then, when word reached him through his brother John that the arch-utilitarian's eldest son had defected from the camp, was known to weep over Wordsworth's poetry, and was the author of those mystical articles on the spirit of the age. So young Mill too had learned the barrenness of Benthamite profit-and-loss philosophy! Thus, high on Carlyle's list of London curiosities to inspect was John Stuart Mill.

Philosopher and prophet met at the Austins' house in September 1831, and Mill—ever seeking many-sidedness—listened attentively to the Scotch prophet's great organ peals of laughter and invective. It was an age of transition, Carlyle proclaimed, with orthodox Christianity dead, and the faith of the future not yet born. Caught in the trough between two waves of faith, the present generation wondered whether God had died, whether humanity might not soon follow Him to the grave. But no, Carlyle thundered, God was not dead; just the old-time creeds were. Eventually, humanity's better understanding of the universe would enable it to weave a new faith in which to clothe the divine mystery.

All this—and much, much more—he had embedded in the darkly gleaming prose of *Sartor Resartus* (The Tailor Retailored). Mill was permitted to peruse the sacred text and came away blinking. But on a second reading—as *Sartor* appeared serially in *Fraser's Magazine*—he recognized its poetic genius.

For a while Mill's docile friendship convinced Carlyle he had landed a disciple. When he and Jane moved to London in 1834, ensconcing themselves in the now-famous house on Cheyne Row, Mill's friendly visits were as certain as the church bells. And with Mill's aid, Carlyle embarked upon his next major oracle. After five months' work Book I of *The French Revolution* was completed. Carlyle lent the manuscript to Mill—with the disastrous result that it was accidentally burned as scrap while in his keeping. Horrified, Mill gathered up Harriet Taylor and dashed to Cheyne Row to confess the catastrophe. Superbly compassionate, Carlyle comforted his thunderstruck friend and agreed to accept his financial help while rewriting the book. The finished work was splendid, and Mill in 1837 heralded it handsomely in the *London and Westminster Review* as nothing less than an epic poem.

But why was Mill's ear so partial to poets during the 1830s?

Healed by art and emotion following the mental crisis, he needed to reconcile feeling and logic, to bring poetry into the utilitarian scheme of things. Given Bentham's coolness toward the muse, he had his work cut out. Insofar as poetry afforded pleasure, Bentham judged it worthy. But then his demurs began. If other amusement—a game of push-pin, for example—afforded more pleasure, it was then worthier. Push-pin was at least innocent, Bentham sniffed; "it were well could the same always be asserted of poetry." Poetry, then, was a vehicle of (sometimes suspect) pleasure—but never of truth, to which empirical observation and rational discourse held exclusive rights. "Indeed, between poetry and truth there is a natural opposition: false morals, fictitious nature." Poetry was constructed of fictions, lies. And it was forever stimulating emotions that beclouded reason, thereby rendering its devotees prone to prejudice and passion. No, poetry was something a rational man would not want to meddle with.

James Mill quite agreed. Glancing from his drudging wife to the nine hungry mouths at table, he too had definite reservations about passion. Forewarned is forearmed, so he had trained John to suspect strong emotion and passionate literature. So spectacularly had he succeeded at this task that, in John's 1824 literary debut in the *Westminster*, even Shakespeare lost points for being short on radicalism and long on ribaldry. Not that John's training ignored literature, but James gave very precise reasons for assigning verses: some things were expressed more forcibly in verse, most people unduly prized a jingle; *ergo*, anyone wishing to sway public opinion had better court the muse—perfunctorily. It was an aesthetic of breathtaking utility.

Nor were Bentham and James Mill alone in their strictures. They merely stated technological society's suspicion of feeling and imagination. Then, as today, practical people doubted poetry's practicality, puritans its purity, and scientists its truth. It was Mill's achievement to break through these prejudices—but then he had the task of expanding his philosophical framework to include his new awareness.

He can be seen groping his way in a series of articles and reviews of the 1830s, to which his correspondence with Carlyle provides valuable running commentary. In particular, four articles deserve close attention for their pertinence to his progress: "What Is Poetry?" and "The Two Kinds of Poetry" (*Monthly Repository*, January and November 1833, respectively), a review of Tennyson's poems (*London Review*, July 1835), and the review of Carlyle's *French Revolution* (*London and Westminster Review*, July 1837). Since the original texts, rather than the revised ones, tell most about his development, they are the subjects of the following examination. In these essays Mill can be glimpsed piecing together a utilitarian rationale of poetry and defining his own role in relation to the artist. More broadly, he is attempting to justify feeling and art in a scientific, secular world.

In "What Is Poetry?" Mill takes aim at the Benthamite charge that poetry is untrue. Happily hoisting the old utilitarian with his own petard, Mill uses Bentham's method to undercut his accusation.

The method is described in Mill's "Bentham" of 1838: "He begins by placing before himself the whole of the field of inquiry to which the particular question belongs, and divides down till he arrives at the thing he is in search of; and thus by successively rejecting all which is not the thing, he gradually works out a definition of what it is." Precisely Mill's tactic here. Starting off with the question "What is poetry?" he systematically isolates poetry from science, narrative, drama, description, and eloquence. Turning from literature, Mill extracts the pure poetry from music, painting, sculpture, and architecture. Along the way he defines poetry and implicitly defends its truth.

Though using Bentham's method, Mill is quick to dissociate himself from Benthamite narrowness. Establishing himself as someone who has felt poetry's power, he rejects the facile notion that poetry is merely verse writing. No; people correctly sense that poetry is "the better part of all art whatever, and of real life too." And though a half-philosopher may sneer at such notions, a practitioner of "philosophy carried to its highest point" (like our author) will humbly follow up popular wisdom, much as an irrigation ditch will regularize and aid the flow of natural streams. Having beamed ingratiatingly through the essay's first four paragraphs, Mill begins his "modest inquiry."

The "dividing down" process now continues uninterrupted throughout the essay. Along the way, it emerges that pure poetry is associated with the inner world of feeling; everything else has to do with the outer world of empirical fact.

Thus, poetry is easily distinguished from science and its matter-of-fact literature. And though poetry may exist in a novel, Mill insists that the narrative and poetic elements can be readily isolated: narrative describes the incidences of outer life, poetry the feelings of inner life. Children and puerile adults (like Bentham, one suspects) appreciate stories and novels; grown-up people with deep feelings (like Harriet, one gathers) appreciate poetry. Of course, drama can also combine the two elements, but again discerning adults can distinguish them. Thus, Shakespeare's stories appeal to the many, his poetry to the few. Nor can poetry be confused with description, though there is descriptive poetry. Description gives the look of something; poetry gives one's feelings about it. So poetry will distort outward reality to convey the inward reality of the poet's response.

Poetry is thought tinged by feeling—but then so is eloquence, and everybody senses a difference between the two. Mill pinpoints it in a famous passage arguing that "eloquence is *heard*, poetry is *overheard*":

Eloquence supposes an audience; the peculiarity of poetry appears to us to lie in the poet's utter unconsciousness of a listener. Poetry is feeling confessing itself to itself, in moments of solitude, and bodying itself forth in symbols which are the nearest possible representations of the feeling in the exact shape in which it exists in the poet's mind. Eloquence is feeling pouring itself forth to other minds, courting their sympathy, or endeavoring to influence their belief, or move them to passion or to action.

The conclusion: "All poetry is of the nature of soliloquy." And here, of course, Mill clinches his point about poetry's truth: as expression of the inner world of feeling, poetry can be just as "true" as empirical observation and logic.

Passing from literature to vocal music, Mill contrasts the outspoken passions of Rossini's operas with the more poetic soliloquies of Mozart's, citing "Dove sono" from *The Marriage of Figaro*. The same distinction holds in folk songs; witness the vigorous oratory of "Scots wha hae wi' Wallace bled" and the affecting poetry of "My Heart's in the Highlands." In instrumental music, any snappy military symphony or march will exemplify musical oratory, while the gloomy grandeur of Beethoven's *Egmont* overture epitomizes the poetry. In portraits and landscapes, the canvases of Lawrence and Turner are poetry: they do not mirror reality but transform it into images embodying emotionally powerful ideas, like grandeur, melancholy, solemnity. Such ideas transmit the painter's feelings and evoke similar ones from sensitive beholders.

Having got the critical bit between his teeth, Mill paces the gallery, bestowing praise on Rembrandt's "Peasant Girl," harrumphing at Rubens's "fat, frowzy Dutch Venuses," basking in the glow of Claude and Rosa landscapes, and railing at turgid narrative in French historical canvases. Turning to architecture, he notes the airy solidity of Greek temples embodying the ancient idea of majesty, the loftiness of Gothic cathedrals crystallizing medieval awe. The trouble with modern architecture, he says (anticipating Ruskin), is that it ransacks Greek and medieval styles without possessing any of their informing ideas and emotions. His critical romp over, Mill concludes: "All art, therefore, in proportion as it produces its effects by an appeal to the emotions partakes of poetry, unless it partakes of oratory, or of narrative."

Ending apologetically, Mill confesses his speculations are less a finished theory of poetry than a desperate stab at one. Philosophic inquiry into the subject being in such a primitive state (especially among utilitarians), he hopes only to spark thought on the subject.

He had reason to be uneasy. The feeling most often celebrated in the essay as the height of poetic emotion is a lugubrious affair indeed— lovelessness, isolation, general melancholy. Mill seems to have converted the deepest emotion of his mental crisis into a touchstone for pure poetry. Countess Almaviva lamenting her lost love in "Dove sono" is the operatic counterpart of those lovelorn Tennyson ladies— Mariana, the Lady of Shalott, Oenone—who attracted Mill's attention as images of his own emotional state during the crisis. Significantly, "My Heart's in the Highlands" becomes "the lament of a prisoner in a solitary cell, ourselves listening, unseen, in the next." Dreaming of far-off mountain glory, Mill and unseen singer share (without really communicating) a lonely sorrow, and pure poetry becomes "the very soul of melancholy exhaling itself in solitude." Clearly, the essay's idea of poetic emotion is thoroughly depressing.

Likewise, poetry's role in life is claustrophobic. In fact, that invisible singer warbling to himself in solitary confinement *is* Mill's poet, locked away from the outer world of human activity. It is clear now why the chief technique in the essay is one of isolation, why the dominant mood is lonely melancholy: poetry, by Mill's definition, is emotion hermetically sealed off from the outside world of progress and struggle. By essay's end, thought and feeling, action and emotion, are solidly walled off from each other. Poetry has been resolutely exiled to that outlying district depicted by W. H. Auden:

> For poetry makes nothing happen: it survives
> In the valley of its saying where executives
> Would never want to tamper; it flows south
> From ranches of isolation and the busy griefs,
> Raw towns that we believe and die in; it survives,
> A way of happening, a mouth.
> "In Memory of W. B. Yeats," ll. 36–41

Yes, Mill has clinched his point about poetry's "truth" to inner emotion, but the victory is decidedly Pyrrhic when it requires converting poetry into a hothouse bloom.

The essay's last word is "use," and a strange note it strikes too. What *is* the use of this poetry? How does it contribute to humanity's improvement? Presumably, by nourishing the emotions and thereby staving off mental crises—though nowhere in the essay does Mill say so. And is pure poetry the most useful form? Inevitably, Mill would ask.

Unsurprisingly, then, even before the essay appeared in print, he was grumbling about its inadequacies and writing to Carlyle for insight on the subject.

Anxious to rectify the shortcomings of "What Is Poetry?" Mill went all out for his next effort on the subject. So much so that "The Two Kinds of Poetry" is in danger of intellectual overload, with ideas flying thick enough to send an unwary reader scurrying for cover.

Mill's most evident aim this time is to distinguish between "born poets" and poets by cultivation. How is it that some people are naturally poetic? How do others, not naturally endowed, manage to pass for the genuine article? The explanation requires a refining of associationist psychology, after which Shelley and Wordsworth are entered as illustrations of the difference. Following some hints that natural poetic temperament can be combined with intellection, the discussion closes with further division: in the present transitional age, poets are uncompromising worshipers of either past or future. Thus, the dominant structure of the essay is division by contrast: natural poet disjoined from cultivated poet, feeling from thought—though brief instances of union appear within the essay. But at least poetry is no longer relegated to isolation; now it plays a larger role in human progress.

Again Mill starts with a nugget of popular wisdom, this one dating from ancient times—*Nascitur poëta* ("a poet is born, not made"). As Antiquus, the name appended to the article, he might be expected to defend ancient wisdom against all modern comers, but manifestly the author is no such partisan. His object is to clarify and complete the proverb's partial truth—his first love being truth, not the past. (Any reader so unsubtle as to miss the hint will have it restated emphatically by the essay's final footnote, where Antiquus declares himself "a writer who attempts to look both ways," toward past and future.)

Mill will say this for the ancients, however: they lived in a natural age, unlike the present transitional one. Writers then were busy producing works of genius, instead of just criticizing them. Mill wastes no time exploring the remark's implications, but hurries on to ask and answer a now-familiar question: "What *is* poetry, but the thoughts and words in which emotion spontaneously embodies itself?" The element of isolation is conspicuously absent from the definition, though poetry remains the expression of deep feeling. Thus, on occasion everyone is a poet. But some people are habitually so—and not just the verse writers, Mill insists. Indeed, some people writing passable verse are not naturally poets at all. No; natural poets are people with a different mental cast, says Mill, plunging into a thicket of associationist psychology.

His thinking on the matter had been lately triggered by some comments of James Martineau in the *Monthly Repository*—a classic example of how a few stray hints could fire Mill's mind. Discussing the philosopher Joseph Priestley, Martineau wondered aloud whether associationists had not glossed over the reason for divergent mental types. Since sensations were received by the mind either simultaneously or successively, might that be a clue to mental differences? In minds where simultaneity dominated, wouldn't sensitivity to physical reality hold sway? Wouldn't the sensations be more vivid? And in the minds whose forte was successiveness, wouldn't sensitivity to events, to causes and effects, predominate? And if so, is this the reason why some people are poetic, others scientific? To dramatize the two mental types, Martineau contrasted Mrs. Barbauld and Dr. Priestley as poet and logician, a contrast sure to capture Mill's attention. "Perhaps each was right, except in condemning the notions of the other," Martineau observed tolerantly, thereby endearing himself further to Mill. "We throw out these brief hints with diffidence," Martineau concluded. "They can be of no further use, than to suggest something better than themselves to more competent thinkers."

Never one to miss a cue like that, Mill takes up where Martineau had left off. "Whom, then, shall we call poets?" he asks, replying: "Those who are so constituted, that emotions are the links of association by which their ideas . . . are connected together." Here, then, is the associationist crux of the matter: in naturally poetic minds, sensations and ideas are linked together by emotion. Less poetic minds associate things because they occur together chronologically or because they fit into categories constructed by the understanding. In an uncultivated mind, for instance, a fact will be remembered because it got itself linked to some minor event occurring at the same time. The scientist or businessman will group ideas together into more sophisticated categories and will associate them accordingly. In these minds, the prosaic understanding holds ascendancy. But in the natural poet's mind objects and thoughts will be linked together by feeling. A sunset will call up a feeling of awe and thus the idea of grandeur. Though other minds occasionally operate this way, poets' minds habitually do.

With terms like "intuitive truths," "Imagination," and "Fancy" floating about in the discussion, it looks alarmingly as if Mill has sailed off the utilitarian map into transcendentalist *terra incognita*. But a closer look shows him safely coasting phenomenalist waters. Mill's poet has his insights, but Mill insists that he examine them to see (first) whether they are genuine intuitions or "only a process of inference completed in a single instant" and (second) whether they are timeless truths or temporal errors. In short, Mill still rejects *a priori* epistemology. His poet has no intuitive grasp of transcendental realities, and only "matured and perfected intellect" can verify his earthly insights as valid. Nor is the poet's unique emotional endowment any substitute for intellectual culture; indeed, his full-sailed emotionalism requires greater philosophical ballast. And not even poets can live by intuition alone. The very meaning of the language necessary to their art, for example, depends upon information gleaned from judicious study and experience. For all its Wordsworthian-Coleridgean ring, Mill's Imagination in the essay is not a faculty for dealing with metaphysical reality; it is a mechanism for unifying fragments supplied by earthbound Fancy. (Fancy apparently supplies images and thoughts already associated by feeling; Imagination simply assembles them into unified wholes.) In rebelling against utilitarian narrowness, Mill was not about to jettison utilitarian discernment.

The associationist mini-course over, Mill elaborates upon the essay's central dichotomy: the distinction between natural poet and poet of culture. The first, with feeling holding ideas and images together in solution, pours forth the emotional overflow in a lyrical torrent of pictures and passions. The poet who has cultivated feeling (but whose mind is not naturally poetic) decks out his thought in a thin outer garment of feeling. In the natural poet, feeling outsings thought; in the other, thought outtalks feeling.

To illustrate, Mill summons up Shelley and Wordsworth—and before long has raised them to symbolic images of contrasting mental types. (One of his happiest techniques, to be used supremely in contrasting articles on Bentham and Coleridge.) Wordsworth's poetry is more thoughtful; indeed, the emotion seems dragged in as a sort of afterthought. His poetry is never exuberant, does not even seem spontaneous. It is essentially unlyrical. And lyric poetry, Mill says (taking the Romantic view), is the earliest, most emotional, and therefore most truly poetic poetry. In contrast to stolid Wordsworth, Shelley trills away from excess of feeling, undistracted by connected thought, extravagantly strewing about sensuous imagery from a seemingly bottomless cornucopia of mental associations.

Though admirable, each is but half of Mill's ideal poet-philosopher who holds the reins on both galloping passion and plodding thought. To prevent our overvaluing either poet, Mill slyly laces his essay with ironic allusions to their works, echoing Wordsworth's Preface to *Lyrical Ballads* to show that Wordsworth is not a natural poet, transforming images from Shelley's poems to underscore his intellectual flightiness. In particular, Wordsworth's well-known remark, "For all good poetry is the spontaneous overflow of powerful feelings," comes back to haunt him here: "On the other hand, Wordsworth's poetry is never bounding, never ebullient; has little even of the appearance of spontaneousness; the well is never so full that it overflows." Indeed, Mill's whole essay is awash with images of spontaneously overflowing water, nearly all of them rinsing away Wordsworth's claims to natural poetry. And Shelley's famous simile from the ambitious elegy *Adonais*,

> *Life, like a dome of many-colored glass,*
> *Stains the white radiance of Eternity,*
> *Until Death tramples it to fragments,*

is converted by Mill into: "his more ambitious compositions too often resemble the scattered fragments of a mirror; colors brilliant as life, single images without end, but no picture."

Mill now makes his pitch for the poet-philosopher. The philosopher cannot make himself a natural poet; he cannot change the association-ist bent of his mind. But the natural poet can make himself a philoso-pher, because (Bentham to the contrary) "the poetic laws of association are by no means incompatible with the more ordinary laws." Philoso-phy, it seems, can result from emotion recollected in tranquility. Un-fortunately, contemporary education (Mill seems to have at least one eye on his own) represses strong feeling when it should train up corrective powers of mind. Given this situation, the poet were better not educated at all. Not, as some of his critics charge, that Mill prefers his poets ignorant. The ideal—when it can be had—is still the poet-philosopher: "Whether the superiority will naturally be on the side of the logician-poet or of the mere poet . . . is too obvious in principle to need statement."

After this speedy glimpse of poetic-philosophic union, the essay closes with renewed division. In the present transitional age, genuine poets (whose emotions necessarily run high) are either resolutely radi-cal or rabidly conservative: "Those who have any individuality of character, if they are not before their age, are almost sure to be behind it." But the essay is not permitted an entirely gloomy ending. In a final footnote, Antiquus turns up with his dual regard for past and future, a quick final image of reconciliation.

Strong contrasts dominate this essay, because Mill sees his age as a sharply divided one. But not a hopelessly divided one: future unity is glimpsed as images of synthesis flash by like subliminal messages.

Crowded to capacity as it already is, "The Two Kinds of Poetry" offers more—some intriguing biographical hints. Certainly, this trib-ute to Wordsworth came straight out of Mill's experience:

> But he has not labored in vain: he has exercised, and continues to exer-
> cise, a powerful, and mostly a highly beneficial influence over the forma-
> tion and growth of not a few of the most cultivated and vigorous of the
> youthful minds of our time, over whose heads poetry of the opposite

Percy Bysshe Shelley. Portrait by A. Curran.

description would have flown, for want of an original organization, physical and mental, in sympathy with it.

Further, Wordsworth and Shelley bear strong resemblances to John and Harriet. Mill sees Wordsworth as "the poet of unpoetic natures" like himself. And certainly Mill's persona, a philosopher cultivating feeling, resembles Wordsworth as poet of culture to whom feeling is not spontaneous. Conversely, Shelley's poetry appeals to naturally poetic people like Harriet. "I have often compared her, as she was at this time, to Shelley," Mill notes in the *Autobiography*, "but in thought and intellect, Shelley, so far as his powers were developed in his short life, was but a child compared with what she ultimately became." What she ultimately became (for Mill anyway) was the poet-philosopher he envisions briefly in this essay.

Thus, along with everything else, "The Two Kinds of Poetry"—written only three years after John and Harriet had met—contains the

Alfred Tennyson. Portrait by Samuel Laurence (ca. 1840).

basic plot outline of their life-long relationship as Mill would act it out and depict it in the *Autobiography*. He was to be the philosopher cherishing emotion, she was to become the philosopher-poet, their works were to be (so far as he was able to achieve it) "joint productions" of logic and poetry.

Perhaps from the start, their affair was to Mill a sacred myth in the Religion of Humanity.

Though freighted to the hull, "The Two Kinds of Poetry" was originally intended as mere tugboat to an oceangoing appraisal of Tennyson's early poems. Mercifully, Mill disjoined his critiques and launched "Tennyson's Poems" separately in 1835.

At the time Alfred Tennyson, fresh from the Lincolnshire wolds, was still nursing emotional wounds resulting from the sudden death of his worshiped friend Arthur Hallam. A comparative unknown, Tennyson had yet managed to draw rapier thrusts from *Blackwood's* and an Olympian thunderbolt from the *Quarterly*, both journals having an unfortunate record of disparaging young talent. But Mill sensed a kindred spirit in the poet, and in his review Tennyson emerges as the poet-philosopher in bud.

The review is divided into three sections. First, Mill's persona is sketched in, then Tennyson's qualifications as natural poet are substantiated, and finally Mill offers him advice for becoming a poet-philosopher. In this last section Mill unveils an out-and-out moral aesthetic. No more poetry of isolation. Poetry must be wedded to philosophy to effect the improvement of humanity. Or as a friend once cautioned Tennyson: "Alfred, we cannot live by Art."

Before discussing Tennyson, Mill gingerly introduces himself—a necessary task given the situation. It was one thing to discuss poetic theory for the *Monthly Repository*'s artistically tolerant readers; it was something else to review two volumes of lyrical flights for the grim-mouthed Benthamites who scrutinized the *London Review*. Shrewdly, Mill first discusses Tennyson's previous reviewers. Depicting the *Blackwood's* man as exhibitionist and the *Quarterly*'s as reactionary, Mill quietly shows himself soberly liberal. Besides, to radical readers, anyone—even a poet—attacked by Tory journals couldn't be all bad.

With the reader thus won over, Mill now presents Tennyson as natural poet. Clearly, Tennyson knows strong feeling, especially that most poetic feeling of all to Mill—isolated lovelessness. Further, he can transform such feeling into symbols; witness "Mariana," "The Lady of Shalott," and "Oenone"—all quoted in the review. So far, Tennyson meets the basic requirement of "What Is Poetry?"

But Mill has larger demands now, and Tennyson promises to meet them too. For one thing his poems do not just picture emotional and poetic isolation, they show its futility—as Mill demonstrates with long extracts. In the review the Lady of Shalott drifts down to Camelot, an image of natural poet escaping stagnant isolation, even at the cost of destroying herself as natural poet. The speaker of "The New Year's Eve," once "wild" and "overflowing" like the natural poet, now dies repenting her Shelleyan shallowness. And by praising "The Palace of Art," Mill points the reader to its Soul nauseated by artistic isolation, cured by a dose of fellow feeling with humanity. Obviously, this poet knows the emotional poverty of trying to live by Art alone.

He shows additional promise, however. He can transform ideal human characteristics into symbols—and, best of all, into symbols that resemble Harriet Taylor. In her "swanlike stateliness," Tennyson's Elëanor reveals "thought folded over thought" in her "large eyes."

Quite overpowered, the male speaker of the poem can only worship: "In thee all passion becomes passionless." The very vagueness of Tennyson's description is a virtue to Mill. "The loveliness of a graceful woman," he sighs, "words cannot make us see, but only feel. The individual expressions in the poem . . . may not always bear a minute analysis; but ought they to be subjected to it?" It was ever his way in portraying Harriet. The *Autobiography*'s abstractions make us feel her presence, not see her form. And if the expressions will not always bear a minute analysis, ought they to be subjected to it?

And finally Tennyson's genius is maturing, as improvements in his latest poems show. Although reach exceeds grasp in "The Palace of Art," the poem clearly aims at philosophic truth. With a logician's coaching Tennyson might yet develop into a full-fledged poet-philosopher.

On this cue Mill openly enters the essay to offer direct advice to the poet. Beginning as usual with psychology, he again summarizes what the poet owes to nature, what to nurture—the same ground covered in "The Two Kinds of Poetry," only this time nurture has seized more of it. To nature the poet owes his finer senses and thus his more vivid sensations (though here "practice does even more than nature"), as well as his more intense pleasures and pains. In this way, his mind is predisposed to "poetic associations." But whether he will make anything worthwhile from this associationist raw material depends entirely upon culture—upon education, self-cultivation, intellectual and moral growth. Though appearing briefly in "The Two Kinds of Poetry," this crucial *caveat* here mushrooms to the point where Shelley, natural poet *par excellence*, is roundly scolded for forfeiting "the noblest end of poetry as an intellectual pursuit, that of acting upon the desires and characters of mankind through their emotions, to raise them towards the perfection of their nature."

Certainly a novel twist to Bentham's scruples about poetry's morality. And a far cry from Mill's earlier idea of true poetry as feeling bemoaning itself in solitude. Here is poetry (indeed all serious art) stepping into the vacuum caused by religion's demise—a point caught by Alexander Bain: "He seemed to look upon Poetry as a Religion, or rather as Religion and Philosophy in one." Here is poetry whose highest object is "to incorporate the everlasting reason of man in forms visible to his sense, and suitable to it." Scrapping Romantic and Benthamite dogma about poetry and logic's incompatibility, Mill proclaims: "Every great poet, every poet who has extensively or permanently influenced mankind, has been a great thinker. . . ." Indeed his most urgent advice to Tennyson is to "cultivate, and with no half devotion, philosophy as well as poetry."

Two more pieces of advice follow. Tennyson should guard against "embracing as truth, not the conclusions which are recommended by the strongest evidence, but those which have the most poetical appearance;—not those which arise from the deductions of impartial reason, but those which are most captivating to an imagination, biassed perhaps by education and conventional associations." In short: don't become another Romantic reactionary. And finally Tennyson must improve his craft.

In this review Mill begins to close the gap between poetry and life, feeling and thought, that had yawned so dismally in earlier essays. Fittingly, Tennyson as potential poet-philosopher dominates the review and appears as closing image, ascending toward "the high place in our poetic literature for which so many of the qualifications are already his own."

Two years later, in 1837, Mill presented *London and Westminster* readers with a portrait of a more accomplished poet-philosopher in his review of *The French Revolution* by Thomas Carlyle.

It was a name guaranteed to raise the hackles on any self-respecting Benthamite. Wasn't Carlyle that lunatic Scotsman whose frenzied prose foamed with German transcendentalisms? And didn't his writings (whisper it not in Westminster!) occasionally take in vain the names of Bentham and James Mill? It was bad enough having Tennyson's dreamery commended in the organ of Philosophical Radicalism, but the French Revolution, confound it, was supposed to be history! Hardly the proper study for half-mad visionaries with possible conservative leanings.

Obviously, Mill had a formidable rhetorical task in hand, but he rose to it willingly. In fact, he saw it as his mission, as he explained to Carlyle himself five years earlier:

> My vocation, as far as I yet see, lies in a humbler sphere; I am rather fitted to be a logical expounder than an artist. You I look upon as an artist, and perhaps the only genuine one now living in this country: . . . Yet it is something not inconsiderable (in an age in which the understanding is more cultivated and developed than any of the other

faculties, and is the only faculty which men do not habitually distrust) if one could address them through the understanding, and ostensibly with little besides mere logical apparatus, yet in a spirit higher than was ever inspired by mere logic, and in such sort that their understandings shall at least have to be *reconciled* to those truths, which even then will not be *felt* until they shall have been breathed upon by the breath of the artist.

A year later his vocation was still running in his mind. The poet may have trouble reaching prosaic audiences; he may be hissed offstage "for want of a Logician in Ordinary, to supply a logical commentary on his intuitive truths."

And that is precisely Mill's task here. In the review Carlyle is the artist to be mediated to an unpoetic audience by Mill as Logician in Ordinary. Also (a point broached with utmost tact in Mill's letters to Carlyle) the logician on occasion serves as Arbiter in Ordinary, testing the soundness of the artist's vision.

Recommending Carlyle to Benthamites requires bold measures, at least initially. "This is not so much a history, as an epic poem; and notwithstanding, or even in consequence of this, the truest of histories," Mill bugles in an opening paradox sure to jolt readers attuned to Benthamite doctrine about poetry's falseness. After this opening trumpet blast, Mill soothes jangled nerves by allowing that Carlyle's style *is* a bit startling. It is sure to be instantly decried, Mill hints slyly, by reactionaries ready to decry anything new and considerable. More tolerant types will judge more slowly and (on the whole) more favorably. Once the reader sees what Carlyle is about, the style will be judged excellent. True, Carlyle does have an annoying habit of muttering about "mystery" and "infinitude," but the broad-minded will overlook these transcendental grubs in humanist amber.

To clarify just what Carlyle is about, Mill starts a careful buildup to his achievement. He introduces David Hume, as a historian who gives the skeleton of events without flesh and blood:

> Does any reader feel, after having read Hume's history, that he can now picture to himself what human life was, among the Anglo-Saxons? how an Anglo-Saxon would have acted in any supposable case? what were his joys, his sorrows, his hopes and fears, his ideas and opinions on any of the great and small matters of human interest?

Gibbon, to take another case, does occasionally try for more imaginative history, but with meager success: his scenes are about as historically convincing as the opera-house ballets. Advancing on the problem from the opposite direction, dramatist Friedrich von Schiller provides vivid scenes aplenty, but his history is muddled with fiction.

Carlyle, however, combines historical accuracy with poetic imagination. No mere chronicler, he projects himself imaginatively into history's events and re-creates them for the reader to experience vicariously. Fusing fact and emotional sense of fact, Carlyle's history is truer —better history because it gives the poetry (the emotional facts) of events, better poetry (more emotionally stirring) because its events really happened. Turning Bentham inside out, Mill grants to fact a greater poetic potential than fiction.

Having braced the reader for the shock of Carlyle's epic voice, Mill lets him hear it—in judicious snippets from *The French Revolution.* The effect is magical. In a trice, the corruption and collapse of French aristocracy are conjured up before our eyes by Carlyle's prose. French republicanism limps into view briefly, succeeded by a whirlwind of violence driving all restraint before it. However impressive the excerpts, their success here owes much to Mill's good offices.

Poetry, one notes in passing, is still associated in Mill's mind with emotion, but not just lonely dejection. In the *French Revolution* selections, all sorts of emotions run rampant—and not in solitude either. Instead of mourning the far-off Highlands, feeling seems to have burst its prison bars at last and gone ranging the streets in fierce pursuit of social justice.

For any Benthamite sniffing suspiciously for reactionism, Mill offers further assurance: Carlyle's opinions are not crucial to the book, because his re-creation of events allows the reader to devise his own interpretation. Besides, the opinions themselves might be recommended—with a caution or two—to radical consideration. French aristocracy, as Carlyle sees it, had grown incompetent, and moderate republicans were unable to salvage the social order before a deluge of horrors descended upon them.

Having served thus far as the artist's logician in ordinary, Mill now claims equal rights for logic, slapping the wrists of Carlylean presumption:

Thomas Carlyle. Portrait by Sir John Everett Millais.

His own method being that of the artist, not of the man of science—
working as he does by figuring things to himself as wholes, not dissecting them into their parts—he appears, though perhaps it is but appear-

ance, to entertain something like a contempt for the opposite method; and to go as much too far in his distrust of analysis and generalization, as others (the Constitutional party, for instance, in the French Revolution) went too far in their reliance upon it.

Though it *is* unsafe to dogmatize about human nature while failing to check what people actually do (one of James Mill's fatal predilections, though of course his son does not say so here), still, it would be equally risky to dispense with general theory altogether. Once again Mill blends the half-truths of his father and Macaulay: "To start from a theory, but not to see the object through the theory; to bring light with us, but also to receive other light from whencesoever it comes; such is the part of the philosopher, of the true practical *seer* or person of insight."

Further, Carlyle underrates representative government. Granted, it is not a substitute for communal faith in men or principles, but (given such faith) it serves better than other forms of government. And at least it is government by consent, not constraint.

His reservations stated, Mill hastily reassumes the role of Carlyle's evangel to the rationalists. With the essay drawing to a close, he makes a final furious bid for reader sympathy. Carlyle's compassion, he avers, is truly catholic, some of his aphorisms deserve to live forever, and (given his artistic purpose) his style is superbly appropriate. Redoubling his efforts, Mill remarks that conservatives who once hooted Wordsworth and Coleridge would no doubt abuse Carlyle; indeed, those who attack him are just the sort who would denounce Milton's great liberal tract the *Areopagitica* were it first appearing now. Clearly, Mill is determined to leave no stone of persuasion unturned.

Carlyle is given the last word, in a passage shrewdly selected to pique radical interest. Likening French misgovernance to British misrule in Ireland, Carlyle solemnly exhorts Englishmen to go and do otherwise before another revolution blazes.

His work of mediation over, Mill confidently steps aside. A poet-philosopher of Carlyle's stature can now win his own hearing.

Mill's achievement in the four essays is considerable. His utilitarian background had bequeathed him a generous allotment of all those suspicions about art that thrive, with awesome vitality, to the present day. To workaday minds then and now, art is a frill with no role in the real business of the world. At worst, art is for would-be aristocrats parading their pretensions. At best, art is popular entertainment; the more escapist, the better. Whenever it tries for truth, art becomes depressing and arty. Truth is what the scientist, not the artist, says.

In the teeth of philistine prejudice Mill offers a cogent apologia for what he calls "poetry"—an apologia all the more impressive for not straying seriously from hard-headed utilitarian principles.

From first to last he champions the validity of emotion itself and of art's importance in this realm. If he initially locks away "poetry" from worldly concerns, he later makes ample amends by liberating it from the moated grange of morbid self-consciousness and drawing it into the busy marts of philosophic thought and action. The imprisoned singer of "My Heart's in the Highlands," Shelley, Tennyson, Carlyle —all phases of poet evolving into poet-philosopher—represent stages in Mill's progressive liberation of feeling. His goal ultimately becomes the intelligent cultivation of strong feeling, the thoughtful harnessing of strenuous emotion to noble aims.

And with modern depersonalization waiting in the wings of history, Mill deploys the artist as defender of life's emotional dimension. Carlyle in *The French Revolution*, for example, never forgets what historian and scientist occasionally seem to: that life is experienced by the whole man, thinking and feeling; that people are neither abstractions nor statistical digits; that the naked ape, in one corner of his heart, yearns to perfect himself.

Not that Mill grants the artist any special metaphysical vision; far from it. (Indeed, some critics have never forgiven him for withholding it.) Always, he insists that the artist's intuition must be tested by the thinker's logic, the philosopher's investigations. But given this guidance, the artist can do what the thinker-philosopher cannot: he can envision ideal humanity in vivid symbol, thereby awakening our noblest feelings and giving us the emotional strength to strive toward human perfection. He can offer a secular age at least something of what religion once offered a believing one.

For all their richness, the four essays on poetry did not mark the extent of Mill's interest in art during the 1830s. In the *Examiner*, for example, he was frequently breaking into eulogies over Eliza Flower's songs, and in the *London and Westminster* he kept sifting poets of nostalgia like Alfred de Vigny and Richard Monckton Milnes. These poor souls, born into one age and surviving into another, consoled themselves amid the rubble of the past with elegies and conservatism. Having suffered something of the same fate, Mill was remarkably sympathetic.

The *Pauline* debacle was something else. In a thundering gust of anticipation, young Robert Browning had descended upon his old friend Fox with copies of his new poem *Pauline*. After supplying the expected panegyric in the *Monthly Repository*, Fox passed on the poem to Mill in hopes of getting it reviewed elsewhere. But Mill neither liked the poem nor could place his review. Worse, his copy of *Pauline* —complete with unflattering comments—found its way back to Browning who was sufficiently stung to lament: "Only this crab remains of the shapely Tree of Life in this Fool's Paradise of mine."

In later years, as other subjects occupied Mill's attention, his comments on art slacked off, but never ceased completely. In letters, in his 1854 diary, in the splendid St. Andrews address of 1867, he again discoursed on poetry and art. Finally, in Harriet's portrait in the *Autobiography*, he symbolized the perfect poet-philosopher.

Meanwhile, his life had settled into an exhausting routine of kaleidoscopic activities. His literary output was enormous: he seemed to be writing about everything for every radical journal in sight, besides composing the massive *System of Logic* and carrying on extensive correspondence. India House promoted him, but greater salary meant more responsibility. Though the very pink of Victorian propriety, the Harriet affair brought inevitable stresses and strains. His father accused him of coveting another man's wife (Mill stood his ground), his friend Roebuck insisted he was ruining his career (Mill immediately demoted him to ex-friend), and society in general disapproved (Mill ignored it as best he could). Carlyle, furious that a woman had made off with his disciple, erupted (out of Mill's earshot) and resolved to see less of him. Luckily for the lovers, John Taylor proved a most tractable husband.

On top of all this, Mill had agreed in 1834 to become editor in all but name of a new radical journal, *London Review*. (Mill's position at India House put curbs on his political activities.) After its reform bill triumph, the radical *Westminster* had fallen on evil days under John Bowring and Col. Perronet Thompson. Bowring, who set both Mills' teeth on edge, was Bentham's literary executor, gracing the master's memory with a questionable edition of his works, as well as what Leslie Stephen called "the worst biography in the language." Meanwhile, Parliament's newly elected Radicals were frittering away the future with private disagreements. Somehow they had to be forged into effective political unity. To Mill the only resort was a journal of enlightened utilitarianism—hence, the *London Review*.

Ominously, however, his life began to resemble another prelude to another mental crisis. Predictably, his health failed; in April 1836 he was ordered off to Brighton for recovery. By mid-June he was back in London, still unwell and bracing himself for one of the most searing emotional experiences of his life. All spring his father had been dangerously ill. Now it was clear he would not recover.

CHAPTER FIVE

COMPLETING COUNTERPARTS:
"Bentham" and "Coleridge"

Without Contraries is no progression.
—WILLIAM BLAKE,
The Marriage of Heaven and Hell

 JAMES MILL'S death on 23 June 1836 precipitated a crisis in his son's life, surpassing even the terrifying mental breakdown of a decade earlier. Called down to Mickleham to help Mill through a trying weekend a month after the funeral, Carlyle—his friendship already on the wane—described Mill with graphic cruelty: "His eyes go twinkling and jerking with wild lights and twitches; his head is bald, his face brown and dry . . . He seemed to me to be withering or withered into the miserablest metaphysical *scrae* [old shoe]." In truth, Mill was desperately ill. Besides the startling facial twitches and eye tics, his head and stomach ached periodically, and his lungs were badly infected. Even a three-month holiday in southern Europe failed to restore him. No doubt, overwork had contributed to the breakdown, but the subconsciously desired death of his father also must have overwhelmed him with guilt feelings that found expression in physical debilities. In despair, he even talked of giving up his position with East India Company.

Instead he fought back to his feet with characteristic doggedness. He assumed his father's household tasks and pitched into the backlogged work at India House. He continued seeing Harriet and remained as editor of the *London Review*, now merged with the old *Westminster Review* and retitled the *London and Westminster Review*. When Sir William Molesworth would no longer finance it, Mill in 1837 took on the burden of ownership. By main force he attempted to mold the review into an instrument of enlightened radical reform. In defiance of the old-guard Philosophical Radicals, he opened its pages to his own wider interests and to suspect writers like Carlyle and Sterling. No longer restrained by his father's presence, he now expressed himself freely on formerly taboo topics—including his unvarnished opinion of Bentham contained in a superb essay of 1838. It was Mill's first masterpiece.

After a long life dedicated to legal and political reforms, the kindly, eccentric Bentham had died in 1832, having lived just long enough to rejoice in the passage of the epoch-making reform bill that owed so much to his exertions. Ever the utilitarian, Bentham had ordered his body dissected for scientific study. Accordingly, it was carted off to the Webb Street School of Anatomy where his friend Dr. Southwood Smith delivered a eulogy over it before cutting it up. Later, again on Bentham's instructions, the skeleton was stuffed and clothed, seated in a chair, and fitted with a wax-works head. The auto-icon eventually found a home in a glass case at University College library, Bentham's actual head lying on the floor between his feet. In the best English tradition, Bentham's ghost is reported to roam the library halls at night.

Even before the Webb Street episode, Mill's laudatory obituary had appeared in the *Examiner*. But his more critical views of Bentham's philosophy soon after found their way into print as an anonymous appendix to Edward Lytton Bulwer's *England and the English* (1833). "I do not acknowledge it, nor mean to do so," Mill said at the time, no doubt fearing the thunderclap at home should his father discover who had written it.

When the full-length essay "Bentham" appeared in the August 1838 issue of the *London and Westminster*, it caused something of a sensation and a scandal, having been written at the height of Mill's recoil from Benthamism. Demand for it was so heavy that the review went into a second edition, the essay itself soon after appearing separately as a pamphlet. Orthodox Benthamites were angered or puzzled; everyone

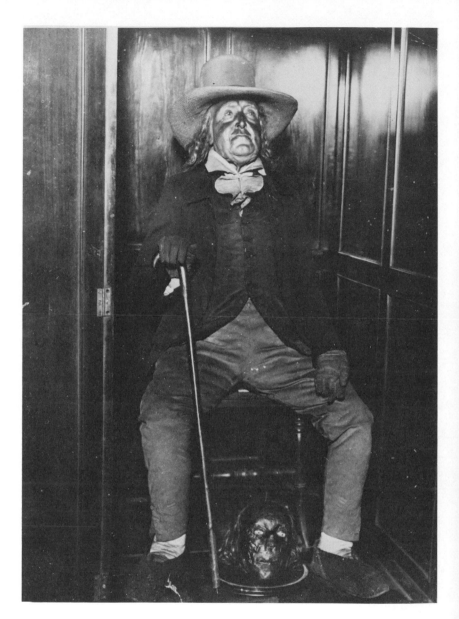

The Bentham auto-icon

else was intrigued by this eminently readable assessment of the sometimes unreadable old reformer. The essay's importance has been recognized right up to the present, even more so since 1950, when F. R.

COMPLETING COUNTERPARTS

Leavis prescribed "Bentham" and its companion piece "Coleridge" as current classics for the literary student.

"Bentham" opens with a splendid prose overture introducing Bentham and Coleridge as the two great seminal minds of their age—and incidentally introducing John Mill as one of the superb prose writers of his own. With great concision, he takes a panoramic view of early nineteenth-century thought, tracing its two main streams back to their sources in Bentham and Coleridge. The two men are depicted as almost archetypal examples of Progressive and Conservative, the one forever at war with the established order, the other insisting upon the values inherent in it. "To Bentham," Mill writes, "it was given to discern more particularly those truths with which existing doctrines and institutions were at variance; to Coleridge, the neglected truths which lay *in* them." Intelligently reconciling the views of these two men, he suggests, is the most important task of modern thinkers—a task Mill proceeds to undertake in this first of two remarkable essays.

Leaving Coleridge for a later time, Mill portrays Bentham as the great subversive thinker of his time, the great questioner of things established, following in the tracks of Voltaire and David Hume. Like a warrior charging into battle, Bentham pitched into the complacent aristocracy, the arrogant established Church, and (above all) the corrupt legal profession of his day. Besides denouncing judicial wrongs, he ridiculed the absurdity of basing law upon precedent—or, more exactly, the usages of a feudal society—rather than some enlightened idea of what modern law was supposed to accomplish, such as the greatest happiness of the greatest number. But Bentham did more than slash away at old institutions; he also introduced a method of precision into questions of ethics and law. This method Mill calls "the method of detail" or "the exhaustive method of classification," which divides wholes into parts, abstractions into things, classes into individuals. Above all, it separates questions into workable segments, subjecting vague generalities to rigorous analysis in order to expose their meaning or their emptiness. Such a method Bentham made mandatory for all future moral and political speculation, and this, says Mill, "is nothing less than a revolution in philosophy."

Up to this point in the essay, Bentham has been portrayed as that most appealing of modern heroes—the morally sensitive individual opposing the forces of a corrupt society. Suddenly the essay takes a dramatic turn. The opening paragraph of the third section begins innocently enough:

> It will naturally be presumed that of the fruits of this great philosophical improvement some portion at least will have been reaped by its author. Armed with such a potent instrument, and wielding it with such singleness of aim; cultivating the field of practical philosophy with such unwearied and such consistent use of a method right in itself, and not adopted by his predecessors; it cannot be but that Bentham by his own inquiries must have accomplished something considerable. And so, it will be found, he has; something not only considerable but extraordinary; . . .

In midsentence, the tone shifts abruptly:

> though but little compared with what he has left undone, and far short of what his sanguine and almost boyish fancy made him flatter himself that he had accomplished.

The swift reversal from eulogy to stricture heralds what is to come and repeats in miniature the essay's overall pattern of anticlimax. The reformer's accomplishments will be greatly qualified, the hero's moral innocence exposed as mere shallowness.

Later sections of the essay have a way of undoing earlier praise. At first, Bentham is lauded as the great questioner of things established; later, Mill points out that things established often contain great wisdom unseen by narrow thinkers. At first Bentham is shown attacking vague generalities; later, he is shown oblivious to the possibility that such generalities contain "the whole unanalysed experience of the human race." The praise of Bentham as both positive and negative thinker is lost in the dispraise of him as a thinker who could see only half the truth. Bentham's ability to think precisely is undercut by his inability to think comprehensively. At first, Bentham is praised for introducing the exhaustive method into politics and morals; then Mill points out that the method is as old as philosophy, and Plato (whom Bentham had disparaged) "does everything by it." What Mill gives with one hand, he whisks away with the other.

The original image of Bentham is already in tatters, but Mill's assessments grow increasingly stringent and personal, despite an assurance that his criticism of Bentham has ended. Bentham could be so clear-sighted, Mill continues, only because he was so narrow-minded, so impervious to "many-sidedness"—that openness to differing viewpoints that Mill had come to value so. "Bentham failed in deriving light from other minds," Mill curtly announces. Indeed, this line of criticism finds Mill at his most abrupt and aphoristic. "Nobody's synthesis can be more complete than his analysis," he snaps at one point. And again: "A man of clear ideas errs grievously if he imagines that whatever is seen confusedly does not exist." Moreover, Bentham lived out his life in perfect physical and mental health, a condition Mill finds almost irritating and certainly limiting. If only Bentham had experienced a mental crisis, if he had even had the imagination to understand such self-consciousness, he might have awakened to a juster estimate of what human nature really is. But he never did. The limitations of the philosophy, Mill concludes, are rooted in the limitations of the man—and Bentham never grew up.

Turning from the man to his philosophy again, Mill discovers this fatal childishness in Bentham's theory of human life: "Man, that most complex being, is a very simple one in his eyes." In fact, Bentham sees people as children pursuing pleasure, avoiding pain, and motivated by various kinds of self-interest. He never sees people as capable of pursuing spiritual perfection as an end in itself, regardless of external rewards and punishments. (Bentham had never met a Harriet Taylor, was most likely the thought at the back of Mill's mind.) Likewise, society to Bentham was an aggregate of self-interested children who could be restrained from jostling each other too much by hopes and fears derived from sources of authority—the law, religion, and public opinion. But he never saw that in a progressive society national character can be cultivated just as the mature individual can cultivate himself. Ultimately, Mill objects to Bentham's vision of man because it denies the existence of grown-up people who are capable of directing their own development.

Not that Mill has any delusions about the number of grown-up people in any given society. But precisely because they would be such a small minority, they needed to be protected from the tyranny of the mediocre majority. And here Mill again faults Bentham. Not content with enthroning the majority as sovereign, Bentham exhausted his ingenuity to prevent minorities from exercising even the slightest influence on public policy. Mill's impressive vindication of minority opposition to majority rule merits quotation at length:

There must, we know, be some paramount power in society; and that the majority should be that power, is on the whole right, not as being just in itself, but as being less unjust than any other footing on which the matter can be placed. But it is necessary that the institutions of society should make provision for keeping up, in some form or other, as a corrective to partial views, and a shelter for freedom of thought and individuality of character, a perpetual and standing Opposition to the will of the majority. All countries which have long continued progressive, or been durably great, have been so because there has been an organized opposition to the ruling power, of whatever kind that power was: plebians to patricians, clergy to kings, freethinkers to clergy, kings to barons, commons to king and aristocracy. Almost all the greatest men who ever lived have formed part of such an Opposition. Wherever some such quarrel has not been going on—wherever it has been terminated by the complete victory of one of the contending principles, and no new contest has taken the place of the old—society has either hardened into Chinese stationariness, or fallen into dissolution. A centre of resistance, round which all the moral and social elements which the ruling power views with disfavour may cluster themselves, and behind whose bulwarks they may find shelter from the attempts of that power to hunt them out of existence, is as necessary where the opinion of the majority is sovereign, as where the ruling power is a hierarchy or an aristocracy. Where no such *point d'appui* exists, there the human race will inevitably degenerate; and the question, whether the United States, for instance, will in time sink into another China (also a most commercial and industrious nation), resolves itself, to us, into the question, whether such a centre of resistance will gradually evolve itself or not.

For Bentham majority rule was enough; for Mill even that could pose a threat to human improvement.

In the essay's concluding pages, Mill seems intent upon driving the final nail into the coffin of Benthamite ethics. At last broaching the subject of Bentham's "principle of utility" or "the greatest happiness principle," Mill breezes past it with disarming nonchalance: yes, the principle is valid up to a point, but then what did Bentham really know of human happiness and misery? Almost before we realize it, Mill is arguing with Bentham for being preoccupied with the morality of acts, while overlooking their aesthetic and sympathetic aspects: Bentham asked only whether actions were right or wrong, never whether they were admirable or lovable.

Reserving the worst for last, Mill plunges into a scathing review of Bentham's peculiar opinions on poetry, trotting out the old utilitarian's most outrageous statements on the topic: "Quantity of pleasure being equal, push-pin is as good as poetry," and "All poetry is misrepresentation." With all the ardor of a recent convert, Mill springs to the defense of imaginative writing—and indeed of all serious art. Such art does misrepresent, Mill says, but only so that we may feel truth more forcibly. The difference between the two views of art is still recognizable. Like the tired businessman or the ordinary televiewer, Bentham sees art as entertainment or amusement, not to be confused with the hard facts of reality. Mill sees art as a vehicle for making truth impressive and for nourishing man's noblest feelings. As such, art could play a crucial role in Mill's ethic; it did not enter into Bentham's at all.

Resuming a more equable tone of voice, Mill concludes the essay by granting Bentham "an indisputable place among the great intellectual benefactors of mankind." A final footnote, however, undercuts even this tribute: Bentham is seen as "a pettish child" needing to be excused from his immaturities.

"Bentham" itself illustrates Mill's theory of art, its prose imaginatively conveying Mill's vision of Bentham's inadequacies. The essay is laced with anticlimax. Figurative language, for example, at first portrays Bentham as an impressive father figure, a great teacher, a hero, and even a god. But then Mill undermines this exalted image by showing Bentham as inadequate in all these roles. The great "seminal" mind of his age, the "father of English innovation," is unmasked at last as a peevish boy. Employing another tactic of anticlimax, Mill originally praises Bentham as a positive as well as a negative thinker, but soon Bentham's positive contributions are reduced almost to nullity, and Mill keeps discussing him in negative terms: "The truths which are *not* Bentham's, which his philosophy takes *no* account of, are many and important; but his *non*-recognition of them does *not* put them out of existence" (my italics). Whole paragraphs of this kind of negativized prose, lurking throughout the essay, are guaranteed to blight any lingering faith in Bentham's positive traits. By such means, anticlimax conveys Mill's central truth about Bentham: his promise was mighty, his performance middling.

For all its manhandling of the old reformer, "Bentham" has its positive vision too, a vision embodied in the very texture of Mill's prose. Reading the essay, we find ourselves in the presence of a thinker more comprehensive than Bentham could have been, a thinker who can survey, appreciate, and even reconcile two such diverse minds as Bentham and Coleridge. Coolly correcting Bentham's shortcomings with insights garnered from the opposite philosophical camp, Mill's persona becomes a dynamic image of the complete thinker that the essay speaks of: "Almost all rich veins of original and striking speculation have been opened by systematic half-thinkers: though whether these new thoughts drive out others as good, or are peacefully superadded to them, depends on whether these half-thinkers are or are not followed in the same track by complete thinkers." In this way, too, "Bentham" becomes a tribute to the great utilitarian: systematic half-thinker that he was, he was also the necessary forerunner of the kind of whole thinker whose voice we hear as we read Mill's prose.

Undaunted by outcries over "Bentham," Mill prepared to beard the lion once again, this time with a full-length assessment of Coleridge designed to trumpet his fame to narrow utilitarians. Published in 1840, the essay demonstrated triumphantly that "Bentham" was no accidental achievement. In "Coleridge" the artistry is surer, the intellectual tolerance greater, and the repudiation of hard-line ideology more persuasive than ever.

Like "Bentham," "Coleridge" begins with a splendid proem poising the two philosophers against each other in the eternal struggle between progress and order. But the introduction to "Coleridge" is a fuller, richer, more sustained restatement of the theme, as if Mill were exulting in his power to better even the extraordinary opening of "Bentham." The names of Coleridge and Bentham are immediately invoked together and are repeatedly interwoven thereafter: "It is hardly possible to speak of Coleridge, and his position among cotemporaries, without reverting to Bentham: they are connected by two of the closest bonds of association—resemblance and contrast." They resembled each other by refusing to philosophize off the cuff, by insisting upon first principles, and by giving priority to theories of how the mind acquired knowledge. Both were great questioners of the establishment.

But here the resemblances end. Bentham saw institutions as corrupt and wanted to reorganize them upon new principles; Coleridge saw the same thing and wanted to reconstitute them upon their original idea and purpose. Bentham stood outside things established and questioned whether they promoted the greatest happiness; Coleridge imaginatively entered into the spirit of things established, asked what

Samuel Taylor Coleridge. Portrait by Washington Allston, 1814.

original function they served, and how they could be purified to serve that function again. "By Bentham, beyond all others," Mill writes, "men have been led to ask themselves, in regard to any ancient or received opinion, Is it true? and by Coleridge, What is the meaning of it?" Bentham becomes, in Mill's view, the perfected image of eighteenth-century revolutionary thought, Coleridge of the conservative reaction to revolutionary anarchy. Each sees what the other does not, but each is the other's "completing counterpart." However much they may disagree, their conclusions "will in the end be found not hostile, but supplementary, to one another." In Mill's introduction, Bentham and Coleridge are antithetical forces poised in creative tension.

Amplifying the need to balance conflicting truths, Mill works two minor variations upon the theme, in both cases demonstrating his singular ability to focus on modern issues. First, he contrasts the worshiper of technological civilization with the lover of freedom and nature. The one sees the improvements wrought by industry, the other the terrible price paid for such progress. Simple-minded allegiance to one or the other view will not solve the dilemma, Mill says; both views must be given their due. Second, he contrasts the supporter of aristocracy with his republican opponent, the first seeing the need for a cultivated class to guide the average sensual man toward greater humanity, the other the need to protect him from exploitation by more advantaged classes. Reconciling this pair of contraries was to become a central preoccupation of Mill's later thought—and indeed of much modern political philosophy.

Mill's prologue establishes the basic rhythm that pulsates through the entire essay. One extreme creates its opposite, the two finally merging in fruitful balance. The extreme of Bentham creates the extreme of Coleridge, the two partial minds meeting in the eclectic mind of Mill as it is depicted in the essay. "Whoever could master the premises and combine the methods of both [Bentham and Coleridge], would possess the entire English philosophy of their age," Mill writes, sounding like someone who has done just that. Bentham, Coleridge, Mill—the pattern resembles that of thesis, antithesis, synthesis; or perhaps more exactly that of action, reaction, tentative balance. "Thus every excess in either direction," Mill explains, "determines a corresponding reaction; improvement consisting only in this, that the oscillation, each time, departs rather less widely from the centre, and an ever-increasing tendency is manifested to settle finally in it." As we read "Coleridge," we see the same configuration repeated—an action opposed by its reaction and righted by an intellect poised between them.

Poised, but not undecided. As Mill explores various contraries in the essay, tolerance does not prevent judgment. On the crucial question of epistemology, Mill firmly opts for the empiricism of Locke and Bentham over Coleridge's intuitionism. On political economy, Coleridge writes "like an arrant driveller." Nevertheless, the dominant tone is one of warm approval toward Coleridge's ideas. "I was writing for Radicals and Liberals," Mill explains in the *Autobiography*, "and it was my business to dwell most on that in writers of a different school, from the knowledge of which they might derive most improvement." "Coleridge" is the work of a brilliant devil's advocate.

Still another clue to the essay's meaning lies in Mill's observation that Bentham asked, Is it true? and Coleridge, What does it mean? As might be expected, Mill asks both questions. Is the Germano-Coleridgean philosophy true? No, at least its theory of mind isn't. But what does it mean? For radicals, that is indeed *the* question to ponder. The bulk of the essay is Mill's answer.

First, Mill surveys continental eighteenth-century radicalism, the heritage of Bentham and James Mill. His critique is relevant to much revolutionary thought before and since. Believing that man is inherently good, that institutions only corrupt him, that the one thing needful is the destruction of establishments, the radicals unleashed "the natural tendency of mankind to anarchy." But that "inherent" goodness of man, Mill argues, was instilled largely by the very institutions the radicals were busy decrying. However corrupt these institutions may have become, they at one time served an indispensable social purpose that reformers ignore at their peril. This section of the essay, opening with radicalism dominant in eighteenth-century Europe, closes with allusions to revolutionary chaos—the section's structure thus becoming a symbol of radicalism's grim course on the continent.

Turning from action to reaction, Mill notes that conservatives corrected the radicals' error: they at least saw the need for appraising the past, for understanding why institutions had existed, for evolving a philosophy of history—a point since made quotable by George Santayana: "Those who cannot remember the past are doomed to repeat it."

So much for the continent; England was another matter. Here the spirit of indolent compromise, loath to mediate between opposites, had patched up an impossible settlement. The Church, neither destroyed nor reformed, was simply converted into an expensive, irrelevant establishment. Government mismanagement was made bearable only by a policy of governing as little as possible. Christianity was debased into Bibliolatry; secular philosophy into a crude doctrine of virtue as self-interest. Inevitably, the situation created extremists, "two sorts of men —the one demanding the extinction of the institutions and creeds which had hitherto existed; the other that they be made a reality: the one pressing the new doctrines to their utmost consequences; the other reasserting the best meaning and purposes of the old. The first type attained its greatest height in Bentham; the last in Coleridge."

True to the essay's basic pattern, the extremes are followed by moderation. Bentham and Coleridge are followed by Mill. "We hold that these two sorts of men," says Mill, stepping between them with his white flag, "who seem to be, and believe themselves to be, enemies, are in reality allies. The powers they wield are opposite poles of one great force of progression." To demonstrate, Mill proceeds to pull radical rabbits out of the Coleridgean hat. By pointing out what institutions once existed for, Coleridge provides a principle for reforming them or (if beyond reform) a reason for destroying them. In its role as state-supported institution, the Church, according to Coleridge, should be a vehicle of national education and culture, not religious sectarianism. Instead of being a club for the privileged, Parliament should be constituted so as to maintain a balance between the forces of progress and permanence. As if this weren't heresy enough to Tory prejudices, the state may legitimately interfere with the landed aristo-crat's predilection for doing as he likes with his own: landed property is a trust from the nation, and the state may legitimately intervene should that trust be abused. With conservatives like Coleridge around, the liberal cause need never despair. Even in ethics, Coleridge managed to sanction utility (up to a point) by fixing the "outward" object of virtue as "the greatest producible sum of happiness of all men." And whatever one made of his philosophy of religion, his aver-sion to literal-minded Biblicism showed he was no lover of supersti-tion. By essay's end, two points are manifestly clear: liberals have no monopoly on reform, and the conservative method of reform is fre-quently preferable.

Mill's survey of Coleridgean thought is an astonishing performance on many counts, none more so than the degree of admiration that irradiates the essay. An important clue to the reason for this hero worship can be found in the very passage in which Mill is dissenting most baldly from Coleridge. He is describing Coleridgean intuitive "Reason": "we see, before we know that we have eyes; but when once this is known to us, we perceive that eyes must have pre-existed to enable us to see." Mill denies the existence of this intuitive faculty that perceives a reality beyond ordinary human experience, but he repeat-edly acknowledges Coleridge's lynxlike ability to see other truths. Words like "eyes," "see," "view," and "insight" are orchestrated like leitmotifs throughout the essay. Mill may question Coleridge's tran-scendental insight, but he celebrates his earthly vision.

How did Coleridge gain this vision? By looking beyond his nose, as Bentham never did. Coleridge exemplified that eclecticism that sees beyond personal bias and party doctrine. "Almost all errors," Mill writes of him, "he holds to be 'truths misunderstood,' 'half-truths taken as the whole,' " the very terms, one notices, used by Mill himself earlier in the essays—and thus another important key to his admiration for Coleridge. Bentham had the better theory of mind; Coleridge the better mind.

The enduring greatness of "Bentham" and "Coleridge" lies not only in their appreciation of two seminal intellects but in their depiction of Mill's own intellect at work. Here is the Victorian "dialogue of the mind with itself" in its most creative and fruitful form. Instead of dispiriting self-questioning, Mill provides the spectacle of a distinguished mind mediating tentatively, and yet confidently, between two seemingly antagonistic modes of thought. Mill's effort to absorb, sift, and unify these two great adversaries is a dramatic portrait of the genuinely open intellect in operation. Here is not the open-mindedness of indifference or indecision. Here, rather, is the open-mindedness that refuses to surrender its critical intelligence to party slogans or simple-minded crusades. Here is the open-mindedness that seeks authentic alternatives, that seeks truth even in the enemy camp —and urges others to go and do likewise. Through much of his life Mill preached such an open-mindedness; in these two essays he triumphantly practices it.

"Coleridge" appeared in the March 1840 issue of the *London and Westminster Review*—the last issue published under Mill's proprietorship. Mill had opened up the review to wider winds of culture but had failed to make it an instrument for consolidating the disparate elements of radicalism into an effective political force. "With considerable expenditure of head and heart," he wrote, "an attempt was made to breathe a living soul into the Radical party—but in vain—there was no making those dry bones live." Also, the review had consistently failed to turn a profit. Not all was failure, however. By a timely review he had saved Carlyle's brilliantly quirky *French Revolution* from an impending Niagara of execration; another opportune article had rescued Lord Durham's enlightened report on Canadian government from a similar fate; and Mill had made Guizot's name known in England. But that, he felt, was the sum total of his accomplishments as proprietor of the review. On March 12, he signed it over to two liberals, Henry Cole and William Hickson. Before the month was out, Mill was in Falmouth watching his nineteen-year-old brother Henry die of tuberculosis.

Far from defeating him, these trials only strengthened Mill's resolve. "But if there be a purpose in this," he wrote shortly after his brother's death, "that purpose it would seem can only be fulfilled in so far as the remainder of my life can be made even more useful than the remainder of his would have been if it had been spared." His mission was still the improvement of humanity, but "the mental regeneration of Europe must precede its social regeneration." As a start Mill got himself accepted as contributor to the Whig *Edinburgh Review.* His father most likely would have blanched, but as far as Mill was concerned the Radical party was defunct, and the Whigs could use the enlightenment.

All the while Mill was working tenaciously on his first full-length book; it was to be his magnificent opening salvo in the campaign for European mental regeneration.

CHAPTER SIX

RATIONAL PROOF:

A System of Logic

The supreme task of the physicist is to arrive at those universal elementary laws from which the cosmos can be built up by pure deduction.
—ALBERT EINSTEIN, *The World As I See It*

 THE salvo bore the formidable title *A System of Logic, Ratiocinative and Deductive, Being a Connected View of the Principles of Evidence and the Methods of Scientific Investigation.* It had taken Mill thirteen years to write the book. Actually, he had been working on it even longer than that.

His first formal introduction to logic had come in 1818, when he was twelve years old. In the general eighteenth-century reaction against things medieval, syllogistic logic had fallen on evil days, being dismissed as so much feudal folderol. Luckily, James Mill shared no such prejudices and perseveringly drilled young John in the sublime intricacies of ratiocination. During his boyhood visit to France, he eagerly jotted down insights from Joseph-Diez Gargonne's lectures on logic as an introduction to the philosophy of science. By the mid-1820s he was heading a discussion group that met at George Grote's house in Threadneedle Street, with the young participants tussling over such items as the *Manuductio ad logicam* by a seventeenth-century Jesuit, Thomas Hobbes's *Computatio sive logica* (1655), and the more recent *Elements of Logic* by Richard Whately, Archbishop of Dublin. In a game effort to restore the dignity of syllogistic deduction, the archbishop went so far as to characterize it as the type and standard of all scientific

(89)

inference—a view Mill endorsed in his 1828 article on the *Elements* for the *Westminster Review*. Mill would later revise his thoughts on the subject, but meanwhile the Threadneedle Street discussions had given him the idea of publishing his own little treatise on deduction.

From such an acorn did the mighty *Logic* grow. In the midst of his ruminations on logic came Macaulay's 1829 attack upon the *Essay on Government*, prompting Mill to realize the error of his father's methodological ways. Geometrical deduction was not a science of causation, so how could James use it validly in matters of history and politics where causation was all? But Macaulay's alternate plan of making the physical sciences the working model for the social sciences was equally unlikely. How could the social scientist conduct experiments like the physical scientist's?

Working on a paper on logic in 1830, Mill suddenly saw that sciences must be either deductive or experimental, depending upon how effects were caused in their particular provinces. Where the addition of one cause to another could easily be traced, as in mechanics, the deductive method would work easily. But in chemistry where two causes, say hydrogen and oxygen, are utterly transformed to result in water, the experimental method would have to be called in. Already Mill's little treatise on deduction was branching out toward distant heights.

Later, possibly in 1831, Mill was reading Dugald Stewart in the garden at Mickleham and was led to speculations that later turned up in Book Two of the *Logic*. Then came ideas to be used in Book One. Meanwhile, other parts of the *Logic* had been taking shape. A chapter on free will and determinism, later fitted into Book Six, had been brewing ever since the mental crisis had made the problem disturbingly personal. Likewise, his speculations on political economy in 1830–31 had forced him to consider methodology in the social sciences, a problem to be spelled out in the *Logic*'s sixth book.

But around 1832 Mill was pulled up short, unable to make anything of induction. According to the *Autobiography*, his logical speculations lay fallow for the next five years.

Those years offered plentiful distractions from logical pursuits. The Harriet affair careened through several crises, and Mill's writing and editorial work for the *Westminster* took a heavy toll of his time. Then his father's death and his own subsequent breakdown suspended his studies altogether. And all the while troublesome matters at India House were simmering fitfully.

Having assumed the task of creating political and social order out of the chaos that was India, the British government chose to rule the vast subcontinent through the East India Company, which operated under the supervision of a governmental Board of Control. Shorn of its commercial monopoly in 1813, the company thereafter consisted of a hierarchy of public officials formulating policy in London to be carried out by administrators on the spot in India. Lodged in the East India House, whose stately Ionic columns soared imposingly above Leadenhall Street, the company staff in the early nineteenth century was increasingly dominated by men like James Mill who saw their task as one of bringing order and learning to a land ravaged by native tyranny and ignorance.

It was a view of British rule that John Stuart Mill, just turned seventeen, brought with him when he joined the company in 1823. And such a vision sustained him through thirty-five years of service at Leadenhall Street. He harbored no grandiose dreams of British imperialism; he was untainted by national chauvinism or racial prejudice. But he saw India as a backward nation incapable of representative government, its people readily preyed upon by native despots. The British mission to India, in his eyes, was to be a civilizing and liberating one, resulting ultimately in India's political independence.

Usually his India House chores were far from taxing. The hours of work, from 10 A.M. to 4 P.M., generally allowed ample time for visits, personal letter writing, and even philosophical composition. Indeed, sizable stretches of the *Logic* and the *Principles of Political Economy* were composed at Leadenhall Street. And the paid vacations were fairly generous. But on occasion the work could pile up, personality clashes could flare into acrimony, and policy differences could lead to testy office politics.

Such was the case in 1834–35 when Anglicists and Orientalists within the company clashed over the question of Indian education. Should English be the language of instruction, or should Arabic and Sanskrit? In the thick of the struggle was none other than Thomas Babington Macaulay, lately arrived in India as member of the Supreme Council. His appointment had been approved by James Mill, who generously overlooked Macaulay's acid attack upon his *Essay on Government*. In his famous "Minute" on Indian education of 2 February 1835, Macaulay spelled out with characteristic vigor the case for English as the language of instruction, a case in which Sir William Bentinck, the governor general, concurred entirely. But back at Leadenhall Street, John Stuart Mill and a body of others did not. In Mill's

East India House, Leadenhall Street. Drawn by Thomas H. Shepherd, engraved by W. Tombleston, 1829.

view, the only way to reach the mass of Indian people was through a corps of educated Indians trained in Eastern languages. On behalf of the Court of Directors, Mill drew up a stiff "Previous Communication" protesting the "Minute," and submitted it to Sir John Cam Hobhouse, president of the Board of Control. A hard-line Anglicist, Hobhouse rejected the paper *in toto*, after scribbling caustic comments into its margins. For better or for worse, English became the language of education in India.

Mill was livid. In an 1837 letter to Henry Taylor, he excoriated Macaulay as "a coxcombical dilettante litterateur who never did a thing for a practical object in his life." And on that furious note he flung himself back into logic.

Induction was the big problem. Everybody talked about formulating general propositions from particular cases, but nobody believed the process could be as systematically certain as the syllogism. Such certainty was just what was needed, Mill felt, but in order to effect such a wonder he would have to take a comprehensive view of scientific methodology. Understandably he paused before this gargantuan task. Then William Whewell's *History of the Inductive Sciences* appeared early in 1837, and gave him a running start. After rereading Sir John Herschel's *Preliminary Discourse on the Study of Natural Philosophy* (1830), Mill plunged into two months of white-heat writing, producing a goodly portion of what later became the extraordinary Book Three of the *Logic*. Then he happened upon the first two volumes of Comte's *Cours de Philosophie Positive* with its further insights into the inductive process.

By 1838 Mill was working on what would become the *Logic*'s fourth and fifth books, and by 1840 he had completed a full draft of the entire work, six hefty books in all. The following year, just as he began the awesome business of rewriting the whole thing, he discovered Whewell's *Philosophy of the Inductive Sciences* (1840), a book which gave him precisely what he needed—someone to disagree with.

If Whewell hadn't existed, Mill would have been forced to invent him. To Mill, Whewell was an arch-intuitionist with a knack for discovering intuitions to uphold the whole Establishment fabric, from unreformed Church and state to unreformed universities. He seemed to be the very embodiment of the intuitionism that Mill so detested. "There never was such an instrument devised," growls the *Autobiography*, "for consecrating all deep seated prejudices." Fired with renewed zeal, Mill rewrote the *Logic*, lacing it with some noticeably polemical passages.

By 1842 the book had already been once rejected before John Parker agreed to publish it. But Mill's rewritings were not over yet. He had just made the acquaintance of a canny young Scot named Alexander Bain who agreed to go over the work from start to finish, with an especially watchful eye on induction. Many of his suggestions Mill incorporated almost verbatim. Then along came the sixth volume of Comte's *Cours*, spurring Mill into a considerable recasting of his own Book Six. At last, in March 1843, the two volumes of Mill's *System of Logic* were ready for the booksellers.

But would they sell? Mill had no high hopes, though he trusted his passages at arms with Whewell would attract some attention. No such luck. To his dismay the *Logic* was greeted with almost total silence from the major reviews. The *Westminster* of course came through with

Bust of William Whewell, D.D.

an effusion from Bain, and quite unexpectedly the *British Critic* printed an amicable dissent from W. G. Ward, an Oxford Movement adherent in the last stages of conversion to Roman Catholicism. But nearly everybody else—including those who disagreed most violently with Mill—seemed temporarily awed into silence. Even Whewell did not muster a reply until 1849.

Nevertheless, the *Logic* began to sell nicely. "How the book came to have, for a work of the kind, so much success," Mill wondered bemusedly, "and what sort of persons composed the bulk of those who have bought, I will not venture to say read, it, I have never thoroughly understood." It was adopted as a text at Oxford—surprisingly, as the university was then in the throes of an Anglo-Catholic revival. At Cambridge—where Whewell reigned as Professor of Moral Philosophy—students about to be quizzed on his pet doctrines began to bone up on them by studying Mill. And the *Logic* was pored over in other places, equally unlikely, from working-men's libraries to rural parsonages.

In all, the *Logic* went through eight editions in Mill's lifetime, and made him nationally famous. Indeed, to many contemporaries he never surpassed the achievement of the *Logic*. Certainly the book formed a natural boundary in British philosophical thought. On the one side, it capped magnificently the late-eighteenth-century tradition of empiricism—though Mill himself disliked the word and preferred a label utilizing "experience." It demonstrated conclusively that the experience philosophy was no mere negative tool for destroying credulity, but a systematic body of thought with positive contributions to make to human knowledge. On the other side, the *Logic* provoked —either by admiration or reaction—many significant developments of later thought.

The book has come under attack on several occasions, most notably perhaps by W. Stanley Jevons in the *Contemporary Review* of 1877–79. Assailing the "disconnected and worthless character" of Mill's thought, Jevons concluded, "Mill's mind was essentially illogical." Though a recent critic replies that Jevons misread Mill "only because his own mind was *essentially illogical*," few would now underrate the contributions to logic of Mill's contemporaries, including Whewell and Jevons, to say nothing of Boole, De Morgan, and Frege.

Nevertheless, Mill's *Logic*—like so much else he wrote—retains a thought-provoking freshness that forestalls attempts to classify it as a relic. For anyone intrepid enough to venture into it, the *Logic* holds a rich store of rewards.

The most technical of all Mill's works, *A System of Logic* yet abounds in subtle and significant drama.

Beginning as a textbook on syllogistic logic, it grows into an intriguing study of scientific method, and ends in a sublime vision of Science and Art conjoined in the cause of human betterment. Starting with the building blocks of terms, the *Logic* erects a solid superstructure crowned by the Art of Life itself. From an introduction which eschews controversy, the book evolves into one in which controversies erupt in the footnotes, then creep into the text, and finally occupy whole chapters. In the course of this survey of the mind's resources for evaluating truth, Mill can be seen reconciling traditional ratiocination with the latest scientific experiments, battling the encroachments of intuitionist theories, and ultimately revealing himself as a humanist philosopher espousing the improvement of humanity.

Indeed, during the course of the *Logic* Mill's persona is metamorphosed from mere logician into comprehensive philosopher. Book One is perhaps the most depersonalized stretch of prose Mill ever wrote. All is formal, correct, mechanical. Yet the final book stands as one of the most powerful in the Mill canon. Whether elucidating the great-man theory or depicting the union of Science and Art, Book Six hums with fervid intensity. In between, Mill's persona grows increasingly human. Little by little, an individualized "I" evolves from the faceless "we" who originally dominates the text. More and more, this "I" pauses to argue with opponents, pay tribute to allies, linger over particularly delicious fallacies, and thrash out a personally vexing philosophic problem. The subject of naming, treated so rigidly and simply in Book One, is reviewed in Book Four in terms revealing the persona's increased awareness of language's complexity, subtlety, and richness. Indeed, the *Logic*'s own language grows progressively more conversational and metaphoric, and eventually rises to the sublime. It is as if the *Logic* were dramatizing Mill's transformation from reasoning machine into humanist philosopher.

Certainly it seems that the logician who begins the book has but an imperfect idea of how the philosopher will finish it. More than one critic has noticed that the preface and introduction do not adequately describe what follows. Insisting that the book will merely systematize other thinkers' speculations, the logician leaves the reader unprepared for the large originality involved in such a synthesis.

By depicting logic as noncontroversial, the introduction gives scant hint of the book's progressively polemical nature. Defined as the science of proof (not belief), logic is supposed to be "common ground on which the partisans of Hartley and of Reid, of Locke and of Kant, may meet and join hands." Perhaps. But the moment the logician insists upon the need to verify our knowledge (regardless of how we think we have arrived at it), he has already parted company with intuitionists who regard their intuitions as sufficient unto themselves, and requiring no logical proof whatsoever. It is difficult to imagine Carlyle, for instance, getting through the introduction without total and vehement disagreement. Nor would many intuitionists feel that logic was common ground after being treated to the barrage of anti-intuitionism that enlivens the later pages of Mill's *Logic*.

On one point, the introduction provides a valuable hint of things to come. The first thing considered in the book is Whately's definition of logic as the science and art of reasoning. The definition is soon rejected (its concept of reasoning is too narrow), but its placement at the start of Mill's study is no accident. From this flawed attempt to unite science and art in logic, the book steadily progresses toward another, fuller union of Science and Art founded upon a truer logic.

Though the usual procedure of logical treatises is to get down to the business of ratiocination after a few preliminary remarks on terms and propositions, Mill's superprecise logician spends the entire first book analyzing such matters. As he sees it, every proposition consists of a subject, a copula, and a predicate—A is B, the world is round, all men are mortal. Taking up subject and predicate, he distinguishes between connotative and nonconnotative terms. Connotative words indicate one or more attributes attaching to what is named. Thus, the word "man" marks the individual so designated with certain attributes, say, animal life, reason, body, a "human" form. Nonconnotative words— like "John" or "whiteness"—name a subject or an attribute, but not both, as connotative terms do.

By this time the logician is nearing the dangerous waters of the much rewritten third chapter, "Of the Things Denoted by Names." As the subject in hand is actually the nature of reality, the intuitionist Scylla and the phenomenalist Charybdis threaten to wreck all impartiality at the discussion's very outset. Tacking carefully, the logician states his own experiential convictions, while stoutly maintaining that, for purposes of logic, the point is moot. Still, he feels most comfortable with an intuitionist like Kant who, while professing belief in things-in-themselves, nevertheless insists that all we can know about them are what we perceive through our senses. (In later editions of the *Logic*, Mill was able to refer readers by footnote to the *Examination of Sir William Hamilton's Philosophy*, where his own phenomenalism is set forth in no uncertain terms.) The logician emerges from these choppy waters, having classified all nameable objects into feelings or states of consciousness, the minds which experience those feelings, the bodies or external objects which excite some of them, and certain attributes of those feelings; specifically, quality, quantity, and relation—for example, their likeness or unlikeness. Despite the siren song of metaphysical controversy, Mill's logician has steered through with his freightage of neatly packaged phenomena.

So it goes throughout Book One. In discussions of propositions, of classification, of definitions, the logician makes straight the philosopher's way. At last, in the final paragraph of Book One, "the philosopher" himself appears, and the preceding technical discussions are adroitly linked with "some of the most profound and most valuable investigations which philosophy presents to us."

The philosopher who begins to emerge in Book Two ("Of Reasoning") resembles Mill's old synthesizing persona. Rejecting the partisans of deductive and inductive procedures, he calmly sets out to unite both methods in a single process of reasoning. Not that he refuses to take sides. On the contrary, whenever an empiricist-intuitionist difference of opinion crops up, he demonstrates an increasing willingness to dabble in polemics. Certainly, his voice becomes progressively humanized: at one point he tosses off a slightly irreverent quip about the Koran, and pauses to tell an anecdote or two. In short, the logician of Book One is beginning to come alive.

The persona's first order of business is to rescue the syllogism from the charge of being pointless question-begging. To illustrate, the classic syllogism will serve:

Major premise:	All men are mortal.
Minor premise:	Socrates is a man.
Conclusion:	Socrates is mortal.

Surely, argued the syllogism's enemies, the conclusion tells us nothing we did not already know when we formulated the major premise. If we know that all men are mortal, then we know Socrates is mortal. So what is the point of decking out the obvious in the trappings of systematic thinking?

The point, Mill replies, is that the conclusion tells us specifically something indistinctly contained in the major premise. To be sure, arriving at such major premises requires induction, or what Mill calls reasoning from known particulars to unknown particulars. But inductive inferences are then translated into shorthand form as major premises, and the syllogism becomes a way of deciphering our notes. Deftly, Mill has established a working relationship between the two kinds of logic. Induction draws the inferences, deduction provides a way of dealing with them accurately. Induction is the logic of truth, deduction the logic of consistency.

Turning to the sciences, Mill argues that the more certain their inductions become, the more readily will they lend themselves to deduction. The overriding aim of every science, as he sees it, is to grow as deductive as possible by means of inductions that progressively simplify the science's major laws. In this way, the science approaches to the certitude of such "exact sciences" as geometry and mathematics.

And with that, Mill throws logical decorum to the winds and plunges headlong into controversy. Geometry and number being intuitionist strongholds, he cannot refrain from a philosophical frontal attack. Because intuitionists pointed to the nonexperiential nature of these sciences, Mill's tactic is to remain unbudgingly empirical about them. Geometry's ideal lines and angles, he insists, derive from our experience of actual lines and angles. An axiom proclaiming that two straight lines cannot enclose a space draws upon ideas put into our minds by experience. Likewise, the abstract numbers of mathematics are abstracted from our experience of concrete things. In short, geometry and mathematics—far from representing intuitive truths—are really inductive sciences.

So hotly contested was this section of the *Logic* that later editions sported a whole new chapter devoted to fending off disputants. But as Book Two concludes in a swirl of polemics, Mill steps nimbly from the battle and calmly prepares for "the philosophic theory of Induction itself."

What now opens up before the reader is the *Logic*'s monumental Book Three, twenty-five massive chapters that form a landmark in Western thought. In the history of logic, Mill's achievement here is sometimes ranked with that of no less a personage than Aristotle, whose formulation of the rules of syllogism transformed deduction into a science. To many, Mill effected a similar miracle with induction, an accomplishment long deemed impossible. As Mill sets about the task, the *Logic* expands into an entire philosophy of scientific method, stunning in its comprehension and potential.

What exactly is induction? Mill begins his answer by viewing it from two slightly different angles. From one direction, it is "the operation of discovering and proving general propositions." From another, it is "the process of indirectly ascertaining individual facts." Not two different kinds of induction, but two aspects of the same process, for "generals are but collections of particulars."

All particulars exist either simultaneously or successively. When one fact precedes another, there may a case of causation, because every phenomenon is produced by an antecedent or set of antecedents. In short, every effect has its cause or causes: such is the universal law of causation. By deciphering individual cases of causation, induction makes possible ever wider general laws that are instances of this universal law. By accumulating such general laws, sciences grow progressively more exact—and increasingly deductive. With ever greater ease, the scientist draws upon a swelling stock of inductive evidence to discover unknowns and predict unpredictables.

But can the business of ascertaining causes be scientifically systematized? Derived in part from Herschel, Mill's classic solution to this problem consists of the Four Methods of Experimental Inquiry—although he seems to have included a fifth one for good measure. The first two are the method of agreement and the method of difference. Next—and this is probably the extra member of the quartet—the joint method of agreement and difference; lastly, the method of residues and the method of concomitant variations.

The method of agreement is summarized in Mill's first canon:

> If two or more instances of the phenomenon under investigation have only one circumstance in common, the circumstance in which alone all the instances agree, is the cause (or effect) of the given phenomenon.

Suppose (to cite J. L. Mackie's example) that we are trying to track down the cause of a certain disease. Suppose we discover that all persons suffering from it do not eat fruit. They seem to have nothing else in common; their ages, places of residence, other dietary habits—all are different. Then we may conclude that the one thing they have in agreement—their dietary lack of fruit—is the cause of the disease.

Mill's second canon describes the method of difference:

> If an instance in which the phenomenon under investigation occurs, and an instance in which it does not occur, have every circumstance in common save one, that one occurring only in the former; the circum-

stance in which alone the two instances differ, is the effect, or the cause, or an indispensable part of the cause, of the phenomenon.

Suppose (to take the same scholar's example) that we find that two pieces of iron have different degrees of hardness. Next, we discover that they have been forged in exactly the same way, except that the harder piece had been dipped, while hot, into water, and that the other had not been. Then, dipping the iron in water is the cause of the extra hardness, or at least an indispensable part of the cause.

The joint method is more complex, and is described in Mill's third canon:

> If two or more instances in which the phenomenon occurs have only one circumstance in common, while two or more instances in which it does not occur have nothing in common save the absence of that circumstance; the circumstance in which alone the two sets of instances differ, is the effect, or the cause, or an indispensable part of the cause, of the phenomenon.

Basically, the joint method attains to greater certainty than the method of agreement. Suppose, to revert to the first example, we have discovered through the method of agreement that people suffering from a certain disease have in common a diet devoid of fruit. But can we be absolutely certain this is the only thing they have in agreement? To strengthen our case, we begin to examine persons who do *not* have the disease. If we find that they all eat fruit regularly, then we can be more certain than before that the lack of fruit is the cause, or at least an indispensable part of the cause, of the disease.

The fourth canon summarizes the method of residues:

> Subduct from any phenomenon such part as is known by previous inductions to be the effect of certain antecedents, and the residue of the phenomenon is the effect of the remaining antecedents.

This is a most useful device for discovering unknown phenomena, as Mill notes. The element lithia, for example, was detected when excess weight was noticed in a sulfate. The sulfate's weight had been calculated from known causes; the excess weight—the residue—was then conjectured to be caused by some unknown element.

Finally, the method of concomitant variations, described in the fifth canon:

> Whatever phenomenon varies in any manner whenever another phenomenon varies in some particular manner, is either a cause or an effect of that phenomenon, or is connected with it through some fact of causation.

Suppose (to take one of Mill's examples) we wish to determine the effects of the moon upon the earth. We cannot remove the moon to see what changes occur on earth. But we can chart the varying positions of the moon, and we can chart such earthly variations as those in the time and place of high tides. And thus we are led to conclude that the moon is wholly or partly the cause of these tides.

Though Mill has defined and illustrated his canons—and in later editions beaten off Whewell's attacks on them—Book Three is not half finished. He has much more say about induction, his speculations ranging from empirical laws to calculation of chance. At the finish the reader is apt to be limp, but Mill's persona crisply concludes "such exposition . . . as the writer has it in his power to furnish."

Moving into Book Four, Mill tidies up from the feast of reason in Book Three, mulling over a number of matters "subsidiary" to induction. More the philosopher than ever, Mill now reconsiders the problems of philosophical language, displaying a breadth of insight that the logician of Book One seemed barely capable of. "The tide of custom first drifts the word on the shore of a particular meaning, then retires and leaves it there": it is a graceful metaphor beyond the reach of the earlier logician. The many-sided tolerance of the "Coleridge" essay once more glows attractively:

> However much we may be able to improve on the conclusions of our forefathers, we ought to be careful not inadvertently to let any of their premises slip through our fingers. It may be good to alter the meaning of a word, but it is bad to let any part of the meaning drop.

Generously impartial, Mill closes with warm praise of Bentham as "the great authority on codification."

A section on fallacies being *de rigueur* for all logic books in Mill's day, Book Five fulfills this obligation with style and ease. Delightful examples of the intellect caught off guard lift this section above the merely perfunctory. Few thinkers are spared—neither Plato nor Coleridge, Descartes nor Bishop Berkeley. But it is all good clean fun, as if Mill were enjoying a gentle laugh after completing his inductive labors and before taking up the rigors of methodology in the social sciences.

Book Six ("On the Logic of the Moral Sciences") rounds out the *Logic*'s overall design so impressively that it is frequently in print as a separate volume. Here Mill demonstrates that, in addition to everything else he may have been—philosopher, political scientist, economist, moralist, poet—he is also one of the first and most perceptive of social scientists. Having broken through to a more complex vision of humanity than old-line Benthamism provided, Mill now goes on to redraw the map of the social sciences and to redefine the greatest happiness principle. A *locus classicus* of Mill's thought and moral vision, Book Six closes the *Logic* with a grand statement of themes that echo throughout Mill's work.

But before he can explore the castle of the social sciences, there is a dragon at the gate to be defeated. The dragon's name is Necessity. If we are going to talk of the human sciences, Mill asks, are we implying that people's behavior is as deterministically caused as that of chemical compounds? If human actions are susceptible to scientific study, doesn't that mean that they are predictable? And if so, what happens to the old belief in free will? If people have no freedom of choice, what happens to their sense of responsibility? How can Mill even talk about moral behavior if people have no freedom of choice in such matters?

Mill's battle with Necessity is fought out in the second chapter of Book Six, an impassioned duel to the finish that reflects his own agonized struggles with despair. Along with everything else that had come storming in upon him after the mental crisis, there was the fear that life was an automatic acting out of unavoidable absurdities. The doctrine of Necessity "weighed on [his] existence like an incubus"— until sometime in the late 1820s when he saw light and wrote out an early version of this key chapter. Strictly speaking, the question of free will is not really the scientist's concern, but Mill at this point in the *Logic* is already assuming the guise of a philosopher-moralist to whom such matters are crucial.

His case against Necessity is so simple that it carries the force of a revelation. What the social scientist predicts is not how people will act, but how they will choose to act. Though antecedents may "cause" a person to choose in a certain way, such antecedents do not rob him of his ability to make the choice. More, among the antecedents causing choices is the person's own character, which he can shape to some extent for better or for worse. Mill rejects outright the Owenite claim that an individual's character is formed *entirely* by his social environment. To some degree he can modify his character—if he desires. And to enkindle that desire is, incidentally, the whole aim of Mill's ethical art.

This major battle over, Mill proceeds to argue that there can be a science of human nature. It will not be an exact one, but then few sciences are at first. As time goes on, it will grow more exact. The laws of the human mind will coalesce into a science of psychology; the laws of character formation will grow into a science which Mill dubs ethology. Though largely nonexistent at the moment, ethology is one of Mill's major *desiderata* for the future.

From the science of human nature, Mill branches off into the social sciences and the main topic of Book Six—how to develop a methodology for them. First, what methods *won't* work? Obviously, the experimental method will be extremely limited. Even Mill's five canons of induction—so useful on other occasions—will be of less help here. On the other hand, James Mill's method of deducing behavior from simplified generalizations about human nature will not work either. Though Mill is tactful in the extreme about exposing the fallacies of "the Bentham school," his rejection of them is quite firm. Once again, he has said no to both Macaulay and his father.

Now he must rise above such partial thinkers. His first solution to the problem in hand is the Concrete Deductive method, which utilizes generalizations drawn not from his father's abstractions, but from the concrete realities of human behavior. Of course, such generalizations will be inexact, but they will show tendencies. In addition, certain social sciences—political economy, for example—can be studied in isolation with more or less success, though their conclusions will always have to be corrected by the other sciences.

Next, there is the Inverse Deductive or Historical method. Societies perpetually change—though Mill is quick to point out that change does not necessarily mean progress. (Nevertheless, he asserts his agreement, in general, with the idea that humanity is progressing.) But how to decipher the laws of such change? History itself provides valuable clues that may even attain to the status of empirical laws. Linked up by deduction with the laws of human nature, such historical laws will make significant contributions to the science of human growth. Not only the "dynamics" of society must be studied, but the "statics" as well, and so Coleridge is cited on the requirements for a stable society. In later editions of the *Logic* Mill brought the whole controversy of historical science up to date with an additional chapter containing some fascinating speculations on the role of great men in history. It was a courageous affirmation, because by this time (1862) he knew what repellent conclusions Carlyle's hero worship had come to. Still, he was unwilling to withhold praise from famous men, especially men like Newton, Plato, and Jesus.

The *Logic*'s final pages move from social science to the logic of practice or Art, laying the foundation for a bridge to Mill's later works, *Utilitarianism* in particular. Science and Art become personified in this closing chapter, each playing a separate role in the drama of social progress. Art proposes a worthy end to be achieved, Science clarifies the means to achieve it, and then Art judges whether the means are practical and, if so, desirable.

Art and Science, Poetry and Logic—did these grand distinctions spring from Mill's regard for Coleridge and Bentham as completing counterparts? Did they grow in turn from Coleridge's distinction between Reason and Understanding, from Bentham's portraits of Censor and Expositor? For Coleridge, Reason soared above the sense world, while Understanding loitered below examining phenomena; Reason sought out ultimate aims, while Understanding studied means. In Bentham's *Fragment on Government* the Censor tells what the law ought to be, the Expositor tells what it is. Taking the Expositor's science of law, the Censor converts it into an art to guide the legislator in the future.

Whatever the origins of the contrasts, Mill came to see his relationship with Harriet Taylor as that of Scientist with Artist. In his autobiography he assigned to her "the region of ultimate aims" as well as "that of the immediately useful and practically attainable." In the same passage he depicts his own role as lying "wholly in the uncertain and slippery intermediate region, that of theory, or moral and political science." On one level, then, the *Logic*'s final chapter dramatizes the philosophic union of John Mill and Harriet Taylor.

Every Art, Mill concludes in the *Logic*, must have its ultimate ends.

For the Art of Life, there are three departments in which such ends may be found—the moral (concerned with what is right and wrong), the prudential (concerned with what is expedient), and the aesthetic (concerned with what is beautiful and noble). Without attempting to justify his choice, Mill pronounces the final moral end to be the greatest happiness principle. But it is not exactly what Bentham had in mind by the phrase. Instead of utilitarian hedonism, Mill hymns each individual's "cultivation of an ideal nobleness of will and conduct." Though adhering to such nobility of character may in the short run bring pain, in the last analysis it is the surest way of promoting humanity's greatest happiness-through-growth.

As the prose rises ever higher to match its lofty matter, Mill's voice can be heard speaking in the accents of a thinker who unites the logic of science with the moral vision of art. The transformation from logician to philosopher is at last complete.

With the *Logic* finally in print, the next item on Mill's intellectual agenda was his new science of ethology. Though Owenite fatalism was anathema to him, equally abhorrent was the blindness of those who failed to recognize how extensively human character was shaped by environment. Particularly irksome were people who assumed the "natural" theory of character—thus, women were "naturally" less intelligent than men, Negroes were "naturally" childish, Irishmen were "naturally" lazy and dirty. On occasion intuitionists pandered to these beliefs by talking of them as intuitive truths. As a result, almost nobody thought it necessary to reform the conditions that produced such "natural" characteristics.

If Mill, however, could demonstrate how environment helped to mold these traits, then a great blow would be struck for social reform. With this end in mind he set about the task vigorously. But he made no headway at all—perhaps because the needed scientific background was not there, perhaps because his associationist psychology was too simplified, or perhaps because he was distracted.

In the early 1840s the "condition of England question" had again become critical. An 1837 crash, followed by a run of bad harvests, had reduced workers to a level of poverty never again reached in later English history. Despite reform, government was still controlled by land-owning interests who kept their Corn Laws on the books. Meanwhile, fewer and fewer workers could afford bread. So bad were matters that Carlyle interrupted his reverential researches into Oliver

Cromwell's life to issue a fiery call to compassion in *Past and Present* (1843). Up in the slums of Manchester, Friedrich Engels had only to look around to gather the grim details that would make *The Condition of the Working Class in England* (1845) so potent a social tract.

And then, just as the English economy began to make a feeble recovery in 1844, there came a terrifying report that the Irish potato crop—the mainstay of that country's food supply—was ruinously blighted. For Mill pondering the principles of ethology was now entirely out of the question.

CHAPTER SEVEN

ECONOMIC REALITIES AND SOCIAL VISIONS:

The Principles of Political Economy

When wealth is centralized the people are dispersed.
When wealth is distributed the people are brought together.
—CONFUCIUS, *Analects*, Book 14

 THE next six years were among the most catastrophic in Ireland's long history of catastrophes. Between 1845 and 1851, more than a million Irish perished amid famine and disease; another million fled abroad.

Throughout the havoc, British government coped uncertainly. The hated Corn Laws were at last repealed in 1846, but free-trade advocates permitted food to be shipped out of starving Ireland, while landowning interests blocked needed land reform. In 1847, to relieve the already strained British Treasury, Parliament extended the Irish Poor Law, thereby throwing the cost of Irish poverty back upon Irish property. The relief was heartbreakingly inadequate.

Mill was appalled. Opposed to the Poor Law extension, he was indefatigably advocating another plan in the columns of the *Morning Chronicle* during 1846–47. The long-term problem in Ireland, he felt, was the land rental system. The Irish cottier, leasing his meager plot by the year, had no incentive to improve it, for his landlord could readily wipe out his gains by raising the rent or evicting him on short notice. Accordingly, Mill wanted the British government to seize and parcel out uncultivated Irish waste lands, thereby converting the new occupants into peasant proprietors with long-term tenure at fixed rents. That way the Irish farmer would be rescued from the insecurities of eviction and rack-rent. He would have land of his own to improve and thrive on. Above all, he would have reason to limit the number of his children.

But the government rejected the plan. Disgusted, Mill went back to his writing, more convinced than ever that he had made the right decision to abandon ethology and instead produce a practical, popular treatise on political economy.

Once he got started on the book in 1845, the writing sped along, despite time off for the *Morning Chronicle* articles. Indeed, the whole book of some 450,000 words took only eighteen months to complete. But no wonder: ever since childhood he had been breathing an atmosphere charged with political economy. At Queen Square Place Turgot and Adam Smith were household names; Ricardo and Malthus were likely to be household guests.

In fact Mill had grown up just as Classical Economy was being transformed—partly through the exertions of his father—from the rambling, observational approach of Adam Smith to Ricardo's more rationally austere procedures. But for all their high and dry ratiocinations, neither James Mill nor Ricardo ignored down-to-earth problems. In their day, the word "economy" seldom strayed far from the word "political."

As evidence, there was the view of history they shared with their brother Classical Economists.

Looking back on the bad old days, they saw what they called the "Mercantilist" tradition as the grand rotten prop of past tyrannies. According to Mercantilists, the nation was a merchant in fierce competition with other nation-merchants. Consequently, the ultimate economic objective was to stock the national coffers with gold and silver. In those days of unredeemed despotism, the nation meant the court and the nobility, with practically everybody else—farmer, worker, colonist—sacrificed to the main business of amassing the royal hoard. To this end, vast armadas were built to ransack the world for precious metals, and to carry on a "favorable balance of trade," meaning more exports than imports. Thus, more money would pour into the imperial treasury. It was a cut-throat situation: one nation could grow rich only at another's expense. At home, government subsidized manufacturing, reduced agriculture to a subordinate role, and awarded monopolistic

Starving Irish children foraging for potatoes. "Boy and Girl at Cahera," drawing by James Mahony published in *Illustrated London News*, 20 February 1847.

trading privileges to companies willing to exploit new markets for even greater national wealth. But there was a fatal flaw in the scheme, as Queen Elizabeth I had discovered during a triumphal progress across England. Despite all the "national" wealth, paupers were everywhere. The Mercantilist scheme had a way of enriching only the upper classes.

The whole Mercantilist tradition was turned inside out by the Physiocrats, a group of prerevolutionary French economists who insisted that wealth—food, wood, fibers, minerals, stone—came from the land. Hence, the Mercantilist "favorable balance of trade" merely meant that more national wealth was leaving the country than was entering it. Not only did Physiocrats exalt agriculturalists as "productive" and denigrate industrialists as "sterile," they also denied the wisdom of the government's running the economy. "Laissez faire et laissez passer, le monde va de lui-même," they said; let things alone, the world will take care of itself. Strangely, they combined their revolutionary free marketplace with loyalty to absolute monarchy.

Of all the Physiocrat sympathizers, none was more inspiring to Mill than Turgot, a man too many-sided to classify with any group. Put in charge of the distressed province of Limoges in 1761, Turgot made such economic headway that Louis XVI eventually summoned him to Paris to straighten out the stricken national finances. To accomplish this feat, Turgot proposed some disturbing remedies, like taxing the nobility and clergy along with the people. Naturally, he had to go. With a show of reluctance, Louis dismissed him—and reaped the whirlwind of revolution several years after his death. Turgot's life story, as told by Condorcet, was ever inspirational reading for Mill.

Across the channel from Turgot's France, economic thought was taking a decisive turn with the work of Adam Smith, another of those puckish geniuses that eighteenth-century Scotland seemed to specialize in. Appearing in the revolutionary year of 1776, his *Wealth of Nations* presented a vast panorama of life and lore, bound together untidily with a new theory of wealth. Not to be identified with money or agricultural produce, wealth really consisted of all goods and services with exchangeable value. And now the great economic question was: how could this wealth be increased to support an expanding population? In short, the patriarch of Classical Economy was working out a theory of economic growth.

There were a number of ways to keep the economy burgeoning, Smith noted. One was division of labor or specialization of workers: in that way goods could be produced faster, as on an assembly line. Another was labor-saving machinery, which also increased productiveness. The kind of work people did also counted: "productive employments," like making a plow, helped the economy's growth, because the plow could be used to produce more goods. But "unproductive employments," like acting in a play, did not help economic expansion. However enjoyable the performance, once it was over, it was "consumed" and could not be used for creating other goods. Savings, however, helped the cause of economic growth. Transformed into capital, savings fostered more production. But spending on unproductive employments didn't. Not that Adam Smith meant to pass value judgments on plow makers and actors, savers and spenders; he intended only to assess them in terms of advancing the economy.

Of course, all this expansion required free trade and competition. On this point, Classical Economists and Physiocrats saw eye to eye. The less government intervention, the better. Left to itself, the free marketplace would find its "natural" price levels, its "natural" distribution of wages, rents, and profits. Everyone would benefit, including those hand-to-mouth workers multiplying their numbers with rabbit-like abandon. As the economy expanded, the fund of wages would expand, thereby permitting the nation to maintain more and more people—at least at the level of subsistence. But such goals required a competitive economy, completely devoid of power and privilege.

Early-nineteenth-century England was far from Smith's competitive ideal. As if in fulfillment of his warnings, depressions and financial crises were reducing the lower classes to a rock-bottom existence with no relief in sight. Aside from the economic strain of the Napoleonic wars, the Industrial Revolution was contributing its own legacy of unemployed and displaced workers. Amid the general food shortage, England began importing more grain. Swiftly protecting themselves, British landowners in 1815 had enacted Corn Laws to prevent cheap foreign grain from underselling theirs. This move, of course, left the poor less able than ever to buy a loaf of bread. Small wonder if some observers began to entertain the notion that England had too many mouths to feed.

The notion found its spokesman. "The view has a melancholy hue," groaned Thomas Malthus, as he matched population growth against the means of subsistence, and found the latter sadly lacking. While subsistence growth crawled along in arithmetical ratio (1, 2, 3, 4, 5 ...), population zipped ahead in geometrical ratio (2, 4, 8, 16 ...). What kept the two in some sort of balance were the various "checks." War, famine, plague, and other catastrophes that periodically thinned humanity's ranks—these Malthus named, somewhat incongruously, the "positive" checks. But there were "preventive" ones, too. Not contraceptives, heaven forbid—for Malthus was a parson. But late marriages were an acceptable preventive check. Still, given the notorious lack of sexual restraint among the lower orders, the prospects for economic improvement were anything but rosy.

Initially published in 1798, Malthus's *Essay on the Principle of Population* went through six stormy editions, the last in 1826. "For thirty years," notes a biographer, "it rained refutations." But the Malthusian specter refused to be exorcised; it continued to haunt the English mind —and none more than John Stuart Mill's.

There was worse news in store for anyone brave enough to enter the rarefied atmosphere of David Ricardo's *Principles of Political Economy and Taxation.*

The author, basically a kindly man, occasionally left off amassing a fortune to dabble in economic controversy. In this way he caught the attention of James Mill, who in 1815 decided that his new friend had made enough money and ought to devote his genius to the cause of liberal reform. With his usual cast-iron resolve, James soon had Ricardo in harness and was trotting him out for long walking lectures. The economist's protests and pleas were unavailing; James exacted his required assignment from the new pupil, and the *Principles of Political Economy and Taxation* duly appeared in 1817. Later, when Ricardo went into Parliament, there were some who professed to hear in his high-pitched voice the transmitter of James Mill's political opinions.

Ricardo's *Principles* constructed, almost in thin air, an intriguing model of the economy in operation. The oft-repeated word "suppose" is a clue to the book's method: the reader must continually suppose that such-and-such a situation exists, that such-and-such a variation occurs in it. While Smith's *Wealth of Nations* came laden with a rich freightage of earthly details, Ricardo's *Principles* soared above everyday events to more universal truths.

The truths weren't exactly reassuring. As the Ricardian model went into motion describing distribution, the poorer classes indulged themselves frightfully in sexual license, thereby creating more mouths to feed. Consequently, more land had to be cultivated for food. As the really good land had already been taken for cultivation, less desirable land had to be pressed into service. Cultivating this land was more costly, so the cost of food rose. As it did, workers needed higher wages to subsist. The capitalist had to trim his profits to meet the demand for higher wages. The only one gaining from the worsening situation was the landowner, whose rents were swelling obscenely.

Here was gloomy news indeed. Adam Smith's competitive harmony was turning into class warfare, a theme to be given Beethovian orchestrations by Karl Marx later in the century. The landowner, who usually did not contribute anything to greater production, was raking in higher and higher rents. The capitalist, who sparked economic growth, was steadily losing interest in further investment because of falling profits. And meanwhile the workers were still multiplying recklessly. Worse, as there was only so much capital in the wage fund, no amount of agitation could really raise wages. The whole economy was undercutting itself and sinking into the dreaded stationary state where further expansion would cease.

This ghastly consummation might be held at bay, however—if not avoided in the end. And here Ricardo turned liberal propagandist. Employing those Malthusian preventive checks was essential. Poor Law relief had to be curtailed, as it only encouraged additional procreation among the poor. Free trade ought to be the rule. Certainly the Corn Laws ought to go. Taxes on profits were hurtful; those on rents and unproductive spending would probably help.

Such was the bitter brew of early-nineteenth-century Classical Economy, and young John Mill imbibed it all.

In 1819 at the age of thirteen he had been put through a course of Ricardian economics, his father lecturing him on the subject during their walks and he submitting written summaries the following day. These summaries served James as the basis for his own *Elements of Political Economy* (1821), a "schoolbook" exposition for anyone too daunted to attempt Ricardo's *Principles* itself. There were, of course, some innovations, including James's veiled but still daring hint that contraception was the most appropriate Malthusian check.

In the following year when *The Traveller* ventured to dispute James's notions of measuring value, sixteen-year-old John made his debut in print with two learned letters defending his father's doctrine. A year later he was still at it, this time taking issue with Malthus himself in the pages of the *Morning Chronicle*. Having tasted economic controversy early, John composed during the next twenty-five years a string of articles, reviews, and even a book (*Essays on Some Unsettled Questions of Political Economy*, 1844) sufficient to establish him as one of England's most promising economic thinkers. During those years, of course, his entire outlook was being rocked by seismic intellectual shocks, the repercussions of which carried over into his economic thought.

Following the 1826 mental crisis, Mill's search for many-sidedness soon brought him face to face with some of political economy's most outspoken opponents. The Romantic poets, for example, never wearied of reviling it as inhuman; even the Saint-Simonians had their doubts about it. To Carlyle it was the "dismal science," to Comte it wasn't a science at all. Then came Macaulay's withering assault upon his father's deductive procedures, forcing Mill to question their appropriateness for political economy.

But he was not about to jettison the idea of political economy as a viable scientific discipline. Instead, he drew up a new program of procedure in "On the Definition of Political Economy; and on the Method of Investigation Proper to It" (*London and Westminster Review*, October 1836)—a splendid preview of the insights that would later light up the *Logic*'s final book. Science deals in facts or truths, he argued; art in rules or directions for conduct. Political economy, then, is a body of truths—though practical rules may be derived from it. As in the other social sciences, the proper methodology must be one that combines induction and deduction. Induction is needed to construct general premises and to verify conclusions arrived at deductively. In the complicated world of political economy, "disturbing causes" can easily falsify the deductive process; hence, the political economist must keep induction handy to prevent serious slippage between reasoning and reality. And when applying scientific theory to actual situations, he must keep a close inductive eye on the world.

Having thus cleared the methodological ground with this essay, Mill commenced a revision of Ricardian economics parallel to the one he was performing on Benthamite utilitarianism. While reaffirming the basic Ricardian foundation, he was busy expanding it with all sorts of intriguing turrets and towers drawn from his own many-sided insights. Though some commentators question whether the old foundation can support the soaring new superstructure, others marvel at the ingenious new additions. The grand edifice itself was unveiled in *The Principles of Political Economy* of 1848, a two-volume masterwork reconciling the dismal science with social consciousness and visions of human progress.

It was a huge best-seller, even at a moment in British history when publishing hefty tomes on political economy had developed into a national failing. But Mill's book immediately distinguished itself as a classic. Its lucidity and logic, its vision and scope clearly displayed the master's hand. It was read by everyone—students, serious-minded businessmen, aspiring workers, even young ladies at school. It had its share of hostile readers, to be sure; none more so than John Ruskin, art critic turned social prophet, who lashed out at it vehemently. Notwithstanding, the *Principles* went through eight editions in Mill's lifetime, and for almost half a century dominated English economic thinking. The inevitable late-Victorian reaction has by now melted into warm respect for the book's enormous role in the history of economic thought.

The *Principles* is no mere fossil, however. To the modern reader it offers the fascination of a supremely sensitive mind probing an industrial, capitalist world that is recognizably his own in embryo. In the course of his comprehensive survey Mill explores the future of working people, the problems of overpopulation, the ambiguities of abundance, the question of government role in the economy, the choices offered by socialism and capitalism, and a host of other timely matters.

And finally: despite its starchy title, the *Principles* is a superbly written book. Even for the nonspecialist, much of it is a marvelously good read.

Right from the start, the *Principles* shows Mill to advantage as expositor and popularizer, combining Ricardo's analytical acumen with Adam Smith's sharp eye for fascinating detail.

The opening chapter of Preliminary Remarks sweeps from principles to particulars, from a definition of wealth to a splendid survey of wealth in all its concrete variety. Wealth is the subject of political economy, Mill begins, quickly linking it with liberty: "A people has sometimes become free, because it had first grown wealthy; or wealthy, because it had first become free." The point will be taken up at length in the *Principles'* final book. Meanwhile, the alleged Mercantilist confusion of wealth with money is exploded, and wealth is defined (with a nod to Adam Smith) as "all useful or agreeable things which possess exchangeable value." Having thus fixed his subject theoretically, Mill displays its fascinating multiformity—in primitive hunting tribes, in pastoral and agricultural societies, in Oriental palaces and feudal castles.

This abundance of detail is the first clue to the work's enduring popular interest. Amid what the nonspecialist would regard as barren stretches of economic theory, the *Principles* sprouts frequent oases of intriguing illustrations. The reader can never be certain as he turns the page just where he will be imaginatively whisked off to next—to the West Indies where slaves drudge despairingly, to the Rochdale Cooperative Store with its bustling prosperity and serene craftsmen, to ancient Mediterranean seas where Grecian vessels ply their trade, to the Irish cottier's desolate farm, to thriving independent homesteads on American prairies, to India or Exeter, Paraguay or Pennsylvania. When Mill exhausts his own supply of illustrations, he readily appropriates someone else's. So we get Adam Smith describing the manufacture of pins, Sismondi picturing snug peasant properties in Switzerland, and a veritable army of other authorities each lending a tile or two to Mill's vast economic mosaic.

A second clue to the book's readableness can be found in its full title: *The Principles of Political Economy, with Some of Their Applications to Social Philosophy.* Those applications lead Mill into lively polemics on the Irish question, population control, and a swarm of other controversial concerns. To be sure, he notes the difficulties of moving from theory to practice, but—luckily—he is seldom deterred from doing so. As a result, the *Principles* boasts some of Mill's most energetic commentaries on social matters.

And finally, since the *Principles* had the benefit of Harriet's artistic insights, it contains striking speculations on the future of industrial society.

Viewed as a whole, Mill's grand compendium exhibits God's plenty —economic theory and lore, social commentaries and political polemics, glimpses of the future. Yet all is subordinated to an overriding vision of human progress. Given the kind of intelligent concern that the *Principles* attempts to foster in its reader, the gradual improvement of the human lot can become a radiant reality. At one stunning stroke, Mill transforms the dismal science into an instrument of hope.

In the first three books of the *Principles*, Mill surveys the "statics" of political economy—production, distribution, and exchange. Book Four explores the "dynamics" of a progressive society, while the fifth book provides an extended commentary on government and human improvement.

In discussing production, Mill arrives at what might be called the economics of abstinence—financial and sexual. Like other Classical Economists, he rejects the eighteenth-century notion that aristocratic extravagances produce wealth for all, an idea irreverently allegorized in Bernard Mandeville's *Fable of the Bees: Or, Private Vices, Public Benefits,* first published in 1705. In the fable, Mandeville's metaphoric bees wax prosperous because:

> *The root of evil, avarice,*
> *That damned, ill-natured baneful vice,*
> *Was slave to prodigality,*
> *That noble sin; whilst luxury*
> *Employed a million of the poor,*
> *And odious pride a million more:*
> *Envy itself, and vanity,*
> *Were ministers of industry.*
>
> . . .
>
> *Thus vice nursed ingenuity,*
> *Which, joined with time and industry,*
> *Had carried life's conveniencies,*
> *Its real pleasures, comforts, ease,*
> *To such a height, the very poor*
> *Lived better than the rich before,*
> *And nothing could be added more.*

Suddenly, Jove makes everyone honest and virtuous.

> *Those that remained, grown temperate, strive,*
> *Not how to spend, but how to live,*
> *And, when they paid their tavern score,*
> *Resolved to enter it no more.*

The result, of course, is total economic collapse.

The Classical Economists weren't entirely convinced. As they saw it, an expanding population can be supported only by an expanding economy, which in turn requires the old-fashioned virtue of abstinence. Savings are necessary for the capital investment that makes increased production possible. In Mill especially, savings are called "abstinence," the capitalist being one who abstains from spending his income unproductively in order to invest it productively.

Likewise, to keep down population growth requires sexual abstinence, especially among the poorer classes. (Perhaps for fear of irremediably alienating his audience, Mill in the *Principles* does not openly cite contraception as a means of population control.) On the other hand, "spending"—in either its financial or sexual sense—does not help prosperity. Intemperate financial spending diminishes the amount of capital available; intemperate sexual spending increases the number of mouths to feed. Accordingly, Book One of the *Principles* notes the capitalist's crucial role in economic expansion, while vigorously advocating population control as the only way for humanity to clinch the gains of increased production.

But the book is not hopelessly puritanical by any means. Its praise of abstinence is merely provisional; in itself, spending is desirable. Mill's line of reasoning, though convoluted to a fault, is basically a follow-up of Adam Smith's ideas. Like Smith, he distinguishes between "productive" and "unproductive" employments and consumption, the distinction being whether they increase production. To keep the economy expanding, productive work and consumption had to be encouraged. Capital abstinence was necessary. Yet in the end unproductive spending is desirable: "It would be a great error," Mill remarks, "to regret the large proportion of the annual produce, which in an opulent country goes to supply unproductive consumption."

What is regrettable is the "prodigious inequality" of distribution that prevents more people from spending unproductively. At this point, the argument begins to resemble a running *double entendre*. With better social arrangements, Mill insists, the wealth for unproductive spending will go to the many, not just the few. As it does, the many will employ the plutocrats' family-planning techniques. Wealth and birth control go together, he hints: the rich get richer, and the poor get children. By advocating unproductive spending for the masses, Mill may have sneaked in his plea for contraception after all.

In any event, it is on a note of determined reform that the memorable second book begins. "The laws and conditions of the production of wealth partake of the character of physical truths," Mill proclaims; but "it is not so with the Distribution of Wealth." As Robert L. Heilbroner has remarked: "This is perhaps the biggest *but* in economics."

Production depends on three things—natural resources, labor, capital. To increase production, society must improve its natural resources, restrict population growth, and increase capital investment. If people want their economy to expand, they must follow the laws governing the expansion of productiveness. Not so, when it comes to distributing the produce. There are no laws here that require a society to stick with its present methods of distribution.

As early as 1834 Mill had been irked by political economists who seemed to enshrine the status quo as an unalterable scientific fact. "They revolve in their eternal circle of landlords, capitalists, and labourers," he complained in a review of Harriet Martineau's contribution to *Illustrations of Political Economy*, "until they seem to think of the distinction of society into those three classes, as if it were one of God's ordinances, not man's, and as little under human control as the division of day and night." What they lacked was the artist's vision of how society might be altered in the interests of people as progressive beings. Far from offering incense to present modes of distribution, Book Two conducts a lively inquiry into how they might be improved.

Mill starts off the book considering communist and socialist schemes of distribution—and immediately lands the reader in the middle of a controversy that has kept scholars second-guessing each other for the past hundred years. The big question is: Was Mill a socialist? In the *Autobiography* he states that he and Harriet had reached a position that "would class us decidedly under the general designation of Socialists." Clear enough, were it not for some vexing considerations. Terms like "socialist" and "communist" are notoriously slippery in meaning, and what exactly did Mill have in mind? Also, some critics have argued that Mill's about-face approval of socialism, written into later editions of the *Principles*, occurred only at Harriet's insistence and against his own better judgment. Was he returning, they wonder darkly, to an antisocialist position after her death? Alas, his *Chapters on Socialism*—which presumably would have settled the matter—remained uncompleted at his death, leaving his commentators in roughly the same situation as those Dickens critics trying to solve the unfinished *Mystery of Edwin Drood*.

To complicate Mill's socialist mystery, the *Principles'* key chapter on the question ("Of Property") is really weighing the merits of two nonexistent systems—private property as it might be versus untried socialist schemes. Surely, Mill argues, it would be folly to discard private enterprise when it never had a fair trial, perhaps least of all in England. On the other hand, Utopian Socialists like Saint-Simon and Charles Fourier might be on to something, especially if their communities of farmers and workers could guarantee subsistence living, while relying upon the old work incentive for private gains above that minimum. More dubious were the communist schemes—by which Mill means extreme socialist associations distributing goods with absolute equality. With the old incentive of working for gain removed, the whole community would have to keep its eye on each individual to be certain that he performed his share of work. Predictably, this thought makes Mill uneasy. To him, liberty would be the final weight to tip the scales in favor of perfected private property or future socialism. Tomorrow belongs to whichever system will allow greater room for self-development. In the meantime a dual policy of reform and experiment is in order—reform of the present system of private property, and experiment by Utopian Socialists.

Anyone lusting for certainties can at least be sure that Mill proclaimed no violent revolution, gave no blessing to totalitarian socialism where the state runs the economy and everything else. The socialists and communists considered in the *Principles* generally envisioned something nearer to hippie communes than national politburos. Though Mill apparently never knew of his down-and-out fellow Londoner Karl Marx, his antipathy for tyranny of the majority guarantees his taking a dim view of proletariat rule.

Whatever the vagaries of Mill's own socialism, succeeding editions of the *Principles* depicted vividly his warming up to the socialist idea. At each rewriting, the book frowned less and less on such systems and began proclaiming their potential. Ultimately, the book gave its seal of approval to voluntary socialist experiments, thereby paving the way for Fabianism and a range of other socialist variants. Surely Harriet deserves something better than the backhanded acknowledgments she usually receives for thus bolstering Mill's tolerance level.

Creating utopian experiments was not in Mill's line, however. Offering ideas for reforming the present system was.

Especially when it comes to land reform, Mill is in his element, being a hardened veteran of the Radical wars on landed privilege. With obvious relish, he suggests inheritance laws to break up huge family fortunes. Proclaiming that the land belongs to all the people, he argues that British landlords hold it only on trust, and may be removed for violating that trust. Some of the best chapters in Book Two are devoted to demonstrating the virtues of small private land ownership (not, interestingly, to socialist associations). Mill generally works through contrasted images. A grim glimpse of the slave's lot in one chapter is followed in the next by Arcadian visions of peasant proprietors growing prosperously self-reliant, while a later chapter depicts the Irish cottier sinking into a bog of rack-rent and eviction. So dark is this last picture that Mill digresses at length to suggest remedies—and in later editions to inveigh against British failure to apply them.

Having promulgated the absolute laws of production and argued the

The Ejectment. Illustrated London News, 16 December 1848. Despite tenant pleas, the landlord's eviction orders are being carried out. Under the eye of troops, the cottage is being destroyed. During the Irish famine, such evictions were numerous, leaving thousands of Irish peasants with little choice but to emigrate or starve.

relativist means of distribution, Mill in Book Three of the *Principles* turns to exchange, raising questions of value, money, and commerce. Though these items might well have been considered earlier in the *Principles*, their more technical interest is wisely sandwiched in between matters of broader interest contained in Books One and Two, Four and Five. Besides, Mill is apparently intent on continuing the old Classical Economist feud with the Mercantilists, and thus minimizes the role of money in the economy. Rather than the end-all of economic activity (as Mercantilists supposedly maintained), money is merely a means of facilitating exchange. It doesn't even affect the laws of value.

Value—it was the old reliable of Classical debates. A standing dish at Political Economy Club dinners, the value question occasioned Mill's first foray into print; Ricardo's last illness in 1823 found him hard at work on it. How was a commodity's exchangeable value (not to be confused with its price) determined? Clearly, *both* usefulness and difficulty of attainment were the conditions of any value at all, plentiful water and air (for example) having no exchangeable value for all their usefulness. But what determines how much of one item will exchange for another? This time around, Mill settles for cost of production as the main ingredient of value—and then constructs on this base some important theorizing on international values. (The paradox of value was finally "solved" by Jevons—and independently by Karl Menger and Léon Walras—with the insight that value is proportional to marginal utility, not to total utility.)

Getting around to world trade, Mill praises it for the most un-Mercantilist of reasons: besides lowering production costs around the world, commerce stimulates stagnant societies and fosters world peace. So carried away is Mill on this latter point that he predicts international trade will soon render war obsolete.

Despite its reputation for containing some of Mill's best theoretical work, Book Three has its share of such infelicities. "Happily, there is nothing in the laws of Value," he beams in the opening chapter, "which remains for the present or any future writer to clear up"—a remark which later economists have not let pass gracefully.

On the same page, he observes: "Political economy has nothing to do with the comparative estimation of different uses in the judgment of a philosopher or a moralist"—an unfortunate comment suggesting that he has thrown philosophic and moral considerations to the economic wolves. Of course he hasn't. He is merely pointing out that the political economist, when operating in his discipline, must isolate exchangeable value from all other kinds. The point had been made more judiciously, however, in his earlier essay "On the Definition of Political Economy," where he signaled his awareness that no one can really survive in a remote palace of economic abstractions. And his performance in the *Principles* demonstrates his own readiness to vacate those esoteric premises on short notice. But if the passage does not merit Ruskin's wrath in "Ad Valorem," it hardly represents Mill at his rhetorical best.

After the lapses and longueurs of Book Three, the *Principles* picks up momentum again in Book Four, building to an extraordinary climax in two of the most astonishing chapters Mill ever wrote—"Of the Stationary State" and "Of the Probable Futurity of the Labouring Classes."

The "statics" of the economy—production, distribution, exchange

—have been spelled out; Book Four sets them in motion, adding the "dynamics" of change. As the progressive economy advances, new inventions provide greater control over nature, industry and saving both thrive in an atmosphere of increasing security from war and governmental pilfering, and cooperation begins to replace competition. Population begins to fall off, production increases. Still, rising food costs mean rising labor costs and falling profits. Likewise, with more capital competing, profits begin hitting minimal levels. All the signs are there: the economy is approaching the stationary state so dreaded by earlier economists. And with good reason: with the economy halted and population surging onward, the Malthusian nightmare will at last become horrifying reality.

In a breathtaking reversal of these baleful predictions, Mill envisions the stationary state as a veritable utopia. Of course, population growth must cease. But once that is achieved, the stationary state has much to recommend it.

> I confess I am not charmed with the ideal of life held out by those who think that the normal state of human beings is that of struggling to get on; that the trampling, crushing, elbowing, and treading on each other's heels, which form the existing type of social life, are the most desirable lot of human kind, or anything but the disagreeable symptoms of one of the phases of industrial society.

Clearly, it is a blessing that people are devoting to financial gain those energies once expended in military conquest. Still, the struggle to get ahead—useful as it may be for stirring up otherwise stagnant characters—is itself but prelude to more finely motivated human activity aimed at nobler goals. "While minds are coarse they require coarse stimuli," Mill observes realistically, "and let them have them."

But the ultimate aim of economic endeavor is not a perpetual keeping up with the Joneses to the end of time. Eventually, with financial security, people can and will devote their energies not to the Art of Getting On, but to the Art of Living (a point, incidentally, that Ruskin of all people should have caught). "It is scarcely necessary to remark," Mill makes a point of remarking emphatically, "that a stationary condition of capital and production implies no stationary state of human improvement." Freed from the compulsion to better themselves financially, people will at last turn to bettering themselves morally, culturally, and intellectually. In a dramatic alteration of the human condition, expansion will have leaped from the economic to the spiritual plane.

There are other surprises in this splendid chapter. Mill enters a final argument for population control, an argument so extraordinary that it deserves quotation at length. "A population may be too crowded, though all be amply supplied with food and raiment," he begins, following up with a subtle inversion of the Biblical observation "It is not good that the man should be alone":

> It is not good for man to be kept perforce at all times in the presence of his species. A world from which solitude is extirpated, is a very poor ideal. Solitude, in the sense of being often alone, is essential to any depth of meditation or of character; and solitude in the presence of natural beauty and grandeur, is the cradle of thoughts and aspirations which are not only good for the individual, but which society could ill do without. Nor is there much satisfaction in contemplating the world with nothing left to the spontaneous activity of nature; with every rood of land brought into cultivation, which is capable of growing food for human beings; every flowery waste or natural pasture ploughed up, all quadrupeds or birds which are not domesticated for man's use exterminated as his rivals for food, every hedgerow or superfluous tree rooted out, and scarcely a place left where a wild shrub or flower could grow without being eradicated as a weed in the name of improved agriculture. If the earth must lose that great portion of its pleasantness which it owes to things that the unlimited increase of wealth and population would extirpate from it, for the mere purpose of enabling it to support a larger, but not a better or a happier population, I sincerely hope, for the sake of posterity, that they will be content to be stationary, long before necessity compels them to it.

Seldom has the case for preserving wilderness been stated more precisely or the argument for responsible population control been presented more coherently. Seldom have the virtues of solitude and meditation been formulated more sanely. And to find such a passage in the midst of a treatise on political economy is to be reminded anew of Mill's superlative many-sidedness.

After a chapter like this, what can one do for an encore? Mill's answer is "Of the Probable Futurity of the Labouring Classes," a dilation upon some of Harriet's richest speculations.

Actually, two futures for the laboring classes are contrasted—the paternalistic versus the self-dependent. In the first (so dear to the hearts of Carlyle, Ruskin, Disraeli, and other conservatives, though Mill names no names) the wealthy would function *in loco parentis* to the poor, directing their lives as the old-time nobility should have but seldom managed to do. Alas, it is too late for such feudal dreams, Mill insists; awakened workers will (and should) demand greater self-determination. In time, when working for fixed wages has grown distasteful, they will organize their own corporate associations, competing with the capitalist on his own grounds and possibly taking over his functions altogether.

What he didn't foresee in the workers' future was rising trade unionism. On this score, his vision was blocked by the old wage-fund theory which insisted that workers already shared among themselves the entire fund of wages available. So no amount of agitation or striking could increase the fund, but would only redistribute it to the benefit of some, the detriment of others. At last in 1869 his India House colleague W. T. Thornton dented the theory, pointing out that no economic law determined precisely how much of the capitalist's profits had to be devoted to wages. With enough pressure from workers, the capitalist might cut back on private spending and pay out more for salaries. Mill was sufficiently convinced to recant the old iron law of wages and give his blessing to responsible unionism. But rather than incorporate the ongoing discussion into the *Principles*, he merely referred readers of the 1871 edition to his two *Fortnightly Review* articles on the question and to Thornton's reply.

If Book Four is the *Principles'* climax, Book Five is both denouement and prelude, a fitting conclusion to Mill's economic humanism and a prologue to his classic work on liberty.

As Book Five opens, the tangy topic of government and the economy is served up. In the quarrel between government supremacists and laissez-faire liberals, Mill takes a flexible middle position. Questions of governmental control must be decided with one eye on the ultimate goal of people's development. Thus, the state ought to provide education of a quality higher than the uneducated masses would insist upon. But in most cases people need to be left alone, economically and otherwise. They need to be left free to learn from their experience and experiments, so long as they violate no one else's rights. Thus, among its many other riches, the *Principles'* final book offers spirited defenses of freedom of the press, equality for women, and workers' rights of association.

In this way, the *Principles* closes with a grand preview of Mill's humane liberalism. The proper study of the political economist, as stated in the work's opening chapter, is wealth—both private and social. But as the book ends, wealth is viewed from a perspective beyond the political economist's. To the moralist, wealth is to be used as means, not worshiped as end; it must be directed toward human improvement. And only insofar as wealth fosters this goal is Mill at all its advocate.

Thus, the two voices in the *Principles*. Mill slips from one to the other, as easily as he moves from deductive reasoning to inductive verification. The first voice is that of the economist popularizer, enriching his theory from a lode of vivid illustrations. The second is that of the moralist, informed and concerned, whose language glows with prophecy and polemic. While one voice asserts that people seek wealth, the other raises the question of whether they always ought to. Once again Scientist and Artist engage in fruitful dialogue.

In the final chapter Mill writes, "There is a circle around every individual human being, which no government, be it that of one, of a few, or of the many, ought to be permitted to overstep." Already we can catch the accents of that heroic individualist who will speak so memorably in *On Liberty*.

But eleven eventful years were to intervene before the world would hear that voice.

No sooner was *Political Economy* safely launched in print than Europe erupted in the revolutions of 1848. The French "bourgeois king" Louis Philippe escaped to England disguised as "Mr. Smith," while old Prince Metternich fled the Viennese mob in a washerwoman's cart. But after a year the upheavals petered out, and the old reactionism crept back into power. By 1851 Louis Napoleon had set himself up as emperor of the French, and once again it was business as usual on the continent.

England was able to carry off the crisis with a bit more aplomb than most countries. When labor unrest attempted to show its muscle in a Chartist monster rally, the demonstration somehow failed, mercifully absolving the government from doing anything about the situation. Even Ireland, seething with armed rebellion after famine and mismanagement, soon abandoned the struggle—for a time anyway. And so England settled down to a well-deserved snooze through the fifties. It was a time of peace and prosperity, Queen and country, Crystal Palace and Crimea. In short, the age of mid-Victorian equipoise.

Mill's life seemed to be following a similar pattern of crisis followed by comparative quiet. But in his case, there was to be a final catastrophe.

The rupture with Carlyle, threatening since the late thirties, broke into open hostilities in 1849–50. In perhaps the most heartbreaking creative decline of the Victorian age, Carlyle's genius had been undergoing a sinister transformation. Impatience with an audience that heard but did not heed him, inability to maintain the faith of his youth, increasing ill health, sexual problems (if there be any truth to rumors of his impotence or sexual dysfunctioning)—any or all may have contributed to the ominous change. He had never been a democrat, but compassion for the poor and downtrodden had regularly pulsed through his earlier social writings. Now, however, he began to look for a hero-ruler who would—literally—whip the population into shape. Virtue meant manliness, and manliness meant strong-arm tactics. Predictably, he also began envisioning Britain as the world's imperialistic savior. And all the while the splendid orchestrations of his earlier prose declined into mere sound and fury.

It was no surprise, then, when Carlyle's "Repeal of the Union" in the *Examiner* of 29 April 1848 proclaimed that "the stern Destinies" had decreed England should rule Ireland, and grimly reminded the Irish of the cruel fates to be suffered by those defying providence. Mill dashed off an abrupt reply, "England and Ireland" (signed "M" and printed two weeks later), pointing out that "the Ezekiel of England" had lately altered the letter and spirit of his earlier prophesying:

> Instead of telling of the sins and errors of England, and warning her of "wrath to come," as he has been wont to do, he preaches the divine Messiahship of England, proclaims her the prime minister of Omnipotence on this earth, commissioned to reduce it all (or as much of it as is convenient to herself) into order and harmony, or at all events, under that pretext, into submission, even into "Slavery," under her own power —will it or will it not.

Separation would probably do neither England nor Ireland any good, but it was preferable to continued bad governance—a most unpopular theme in Victorian England, as may be imagined, but one which Mill

Scene on a West Indian plantation: slaves receiving the news of their emancipation, 1834

courageously took up again some twenty years later in *England and Ireland*.

Meanwhile, Carlyle was not to be daunted, and in *Fraser's Magazine* of December 1849 appeared his spectacularly offensive "Occasional Discourse on the Negro Question," which he later expanded and republished as *The Nigger Question*.

The fictitious discourse is delivered to a crowd of Exeter Hall do-gooders by a leather-lunged prophet, who supposedly enlightens a minority of them with his home truths. Taking up the economic problems of the West Indies, Carlyle's speaker puts them all down to lax white rule over lazy blacks. Consequently, "Quashee" (Carlyle's stereotyped black man) merely lolls about, picking "pumpkins" off the trees and refusing to work the white man's plantations. Clearly, this was an intolerable state of affairs, especially since the destinies had decreed the gospel of work for all men. And so the speaker is soon recommending the "beneficent whip" for all recalcitrant blacks, despite the fact that slavery had been abolished throughout the British empire in 1833. Heaven forbid that anyone mistake our speaker for a reactionary bigot, however:

> Do I, then, hate the Negro? No; except when the soul is killed out of him, I decidedly like poor Quashee; and find him a pretty kind of man. With a pennyworth of oil, you can make a handsome glossy thing of Quashee, when the soul is not killed in him! A swift, supple fellow; a merry-hearted, grinning, dancing, singing, affectionate kind of creature, with a great deal of melody and amenability in his composition.

This dubious tribute notwithstanding, the speaker ends up classifying blacks in a sort of evolutionary limbo, somewhere above the domes-ticated animals and below the human (meaning "white") pinnacle. Nothing if not prolix, Carlyle's speaker concludes with a sputtering denunciation of palaver.

This time, Mill's rejoinder was pure acid. "The Negro Question," published in *Fraser's*, January 1850, wrote a sizzling finale to his friend-ship with Carlyle.

In the opening paragraph, Mill strings together snippets from Car-lyle's discourse, judiciously exposing the prophetic voice as that of an authoritarian ranter. In contrast, Mill speaks with the voice of impas-sioned reason, his carefully constructed parallelisms holding his sense of outrage in check. Throughout the essay, considerable infighting goes on between the lines. Denouncing the gospel of work, for exam-ple, this sentence jabs at Carlyle from several angles:

> I do not include under the name labour such work, if work it be called, as is done by writers and afforders of 'guidance,' an occupation which, let alone the vanity of the thing, cannot be called by the same name with the real labour, the exhausting, stiffening, stupefying toil of so many kinds of agricultural and manufacturing labourers.

Besides being a barbed reminder that Carlyle has nothing to do all day but write (while other people engage in exhausting physical labor), the sentence abruptly reduces Carlyle from the status of prophet to that of mere "afforder of guidance," from (so to speak) Jeremiah to Ann Landers. Also, it accomplishes intentionally what Ford Madox Brown accomplished unintentionally in his famous painting *Work*. In the center of Brown's canvas a group of navvies is busily tearing up the

Ford Madox Brown, *Work*, 1852–65. Carlyle is the figure with hat and cane, standing at the right.

main street of Hampstead, while off to the right Carlyle and F. D. Maurice smile their approval of this sweaty labor. Unfortunately, the two sages of work look like smirking idlers. Mill creates a similar effect: amid "the exhausting, stiffening, stupefying toil" of "real labour," he places Carlyle dispensing his "guidance" and having the vanity to call this dilettantism work.

One of Mill's first concerns in the essay is to discredit Carlyle's proslavery sentiments. Grandly invoking the memory of the British antislavery activists, he depicts Carlyle as one who would undo their great work, only to reinstate the barbarities of West Indian slavery—barbarities which Mill recalls for the reader with grim vividness.

Carlyle's racism receives an especially severe manhandling. Laying siege to the idea of inherent Negro inferiority, Mill suggests that the white man's treatment of blacks goes far toward explaining their supposed natural deficiency. As usual, Mill flails those who chalk up racial or sexual differences of character to "nature," while disregarding entirely what environment has done to shape those "natural" characteristics. Such a view, he realizes, was the sure prelude to do-nothingism. Worse, by dealing in grotesque caricatures like "Black Quashee," Carlyle was pandering to white smugness about white superiority. Like all oppressed groups, blacks needed education, guidance, and gradually increasing liberty to develop into self-dependent, liberated human beings. But beneficent whips and demeaning portraits of Quashee would only insure that blacks would never develop at all.

Even the gospel of work comes in for some hard knocks. Yes, work done for noble goals is laudable, but Carlyle's peevish preoccupation with keeping the lower orders busy is something else again. "On the contrary, the multiplication of work, for purposes not worth caring about, is one of the evils of our present condition," Mill asserts, neatly skewering the Carlylean work ethic.

After a vision of humanity laboring to rid the world of removable suffering and pain, Mill turns for a final fling at Carlyle's attempt to block these efforts. Britain, he insists, will never again regress to the barbarity of slaveholding, but because *The Nigger Question* will give aid and comfort to American slaveowners, Mill denounces it in closing as "a true work of the devil."

Thus, Carlyle's self-appointed spokesman for the gods is reduced in the end to the devil's worker. In "Bentham" Mill had presented the old utilitarian as annoying and disappointing; in the *Autobiography* he would depict his father as cold and arrogant. But in "The Negro Question" he portrays Carlyle as actually evil.

Shortly after "The Negro Question" appeared in print, Carlyle discovered its author's identity. "Nigger article has aroused the ire of all philanthropists to quite unexpected pitch," he confided to his journal on 7 February 1850. "Among other very poor attacks on it was one in 'Fraser;' most shrill, thin, poor and insignificant, which I was surprised to learn proceeded from John Mill." In future the two men would eye each other with hostility in private, and with guarded civility on the rare occasions when they met or exchanged a letter.

But the break with Carlyle was not the major upheaval in Mill's life by any means.

On 14 May 1849 Harriet Taylor had returned from a visit to France, only to find her husband dying of cancer. For two harrowing months, she watched him "die by inches" (as he put it), her grief and guilt flaring into occasional outbursts to Mill. At last on July 18 the ordeal was over. Harriet held herself in check until after the funeral and then indulged in a breakdown.

During the next two years, John and Harriet visited discreetly, consoling each other and tearing off indignant letters to the newspapers on matters of social injustice. But would they marry? Since neither was enchanted with the Victorian institution of marriage, there was room for doubt on the question. Further, as John Taylor had left his wealth to Harriet, would Mill be open to the humiliating charge of fortune hunting? Considering his well-known Malthusian views, would he be open to ridicule? With her distaste for sex and his repeated denunciations of "brute instinct," what sort of marriage would it be? As their newspaper letters show, their minds were running much on the nasty topic of brutality to wives and children. Both were appalled at the moral deterioration which seemed to afflict married people. No; if John and Harriet were to wed, theirs would be a different kind of marriage.

A clue as to what was in the wind came on 6 March 1851, when John wrote out a formal protest against the legal rights conferred on men by Victorian marriage laws. A month later, the couple (both in their mid-forties) slipped off to the seaside town of Melcombe Regis and were quietly married there on Easter Monday, April 21, at the Register Office. Harriet's two younger children, Algernon and Helen, acted as witnesses. Part of the honeymoon was devoted to touching up "The Enfranchisement of Women" for the press.

The marriage proved to be a parting sword between Mill and his family. At Kensington Square, where his mother and two unmarried sisters Harriet and Clara now lived, news of the impending nuptials was apparently received with insufficient enthusiasm. Worse, their failure to call upon Harriet immediately afterward was taken as an insult, and Mill cut them mercilessly. Stunned, the women fumbled to make amends, but all to no avail. Meanwhile, younger brother George Mill, having learned of the marriage at second hand, dashed off some ill-advised lines to Algernon Taylor and thus brought John's wrath thundering down upon his head. Mary Colman Mill joined the fray, remonstrating with her older brother about his hardheartedness. Her efforts were greeted with similar savagery. Even his mother's death in 1854 failed to create a thaw. "There are some of us," complained the hapless Clara, still reeling under her brother's affronts, "myself among the rest, whom you hold in the same estimation as my father did." Alas, in these dealings with his family, Mill proved all too clearly to be his father's son. Perhaps no other episode in his life shows his character to less advantage.

But his love for Harriet had reached religious proportions, and he brooked irreverence from no one.

He had never had a God to believe in, really. And then faith in his godlike father had soured, trust in Bentham had eroded. Yet his personality, so severely dominated from childhood, cried out for some authority figure to obey, for some ideal vision to worship. Then into his life had come Harriet—strong-willed, intelligent, difficult to please. It was almost as if he had willed her into existence; indeed to some extent he had. She became the saint in his Religion of Humanity, the ideal person whom he would strive to emulate and please.

The fear of disappointing her haunted his dreams, as this 1855 letter to her reveals all too pathetically:

> She will not have to wait very long for me at or near Paris and I shall see her in a fortnight at farthest. I look forward to it with delight—but ah darling I had a horrible dream lately—I had come back to her and she was sweet and loving like herself at first, but presently she took a complete dislike to me saying that I was changed much for the worse—I am terribly afraid sometimes lest she should think so, not that I see any cause for it, but because I know how deficient I am in self consciousness and self observation, and how often when she sees me again after I have been even a short time absent she is disappointed—but she shall not be, she will not be so I think this time—bless my own darling, she has been all the while without intermission present to my thoughts and I have been all the while mentally talking with her when I have not been doing so on paper.

Eventually, he endowed her with almost magical powers, taking her as a sort of talisman that kept away his dangerous illnesses.

She was, then, his substitute for father and God. And so their marriage was to be a union of mind and soul, rather than of brute instinct. Indeed, so devoid of the latter does the marriage appear, that commentators have repeatedly wondered whether it was consummated at all.

Outwardly Mill was blissful with this kind of union; inwardly he knew its deficiency. Perhaps nowhere is the awareness more compellingly revealed than in an 1857 letter to Harriet recounting two other dreams, one alluding to that familiar Victorian sex symbol, Mary Magdalen:

On Saturday night at York I slept little and dreamt much—among the
rest a long dream of some speculation on animal nature, ending with my
either reading or writing, just before I awoke, this Richterish sentence:
"With what prospect then, until a cow is fed on broth, we can expect
the truth, the whole truth and nothing but the truth to be unfolded
concerning this part of nature, I leave to" etc. etc. I had a still droller
dream the same night. I was seated at a table like a table d'hôte, with a
woman at my left hand and a young man opposite—the young man said,
quoting somebody for the saying, "there are two excellent and rare
things to find in a woman, a sincere friend and a sincere Magdalen." I
answered "the best would be to find both in one"—on which the woman
said "no, that would be *too* vain"—whereupon I broke out "do you
suppose when one speaks of what is good in itself, one must be thinking
of one's own paltry self interest? no, I spoke of what is abstractedly good
and admirable." How queer to dream stupid mock mots, and of a kind
totally unlike one's own ways or character. According to the usual
oddity of dreams—when the man made the quotation I recognised it and
thought he had quoted it wrong and the *right* words were "an *innocent*
magdalen" not perceiving the contradiction. I wonder if reading that
Frenchman's book suggested the dream. These are ridiculous things to
put in a letter, but perhaps they may amuse my darling.

A Freudian gold mine, to be sure. But the basic pattern seems to be
this: initial puzzlement about "animal nature" leads to a wish that
humaneness and "animal" sexuality might coexist in "a sincere friend
and a sincere Magdalen." This in turn yields to a vision of the two
opposites fused in "an *innocent* magdalen."

All of which suggests that, to Mill's mind, his spiritualized marriage
was a temporary and conditional good—not an ultimate one, not "abstractedly good and admirable." It was a necessary antidote to prevailing conditions. Indeed, he seems to have viewed marriage much as he
viewed the economy, where imperfect conditions required imperfect
virtues. So long as an expanding population required an expanding
economy, abstinence—both capitalistic and sexual—was a virtue. But
when at last humanity was freed from the cares of expansion, then
unproductive spending would be seen as the greater good. So also with
imperfect marriage. So long as Victorian marriage merely enshrined
sexual inequality and exploitation, so long as most marriages were
barren of intellectual and moral growth, so long as husbands cared
only for moneymaking, and wives for childbearing and social-

climbing—so long as this was the stultifying thesis of the day, then Mill's own marriage—free, equal, sexless, uplifting—would be the needed antithesis. But his mind retained, if only in its deepest recesses, the vision of a fuller synthesis, a marriage of equals in which sexuality and true humanity were perfectly fused.

Whatever their psychological intricacies, the happy couple set up housekeeping at Blackheath Park, seven or eight miles southeast of London. Helen and, for a time, Algernon completed the household. Near enough for John to catch the morning train to work, far enough to shut out the chatter of London society, Blackheath was an ideal location. Their square brick house, though a trifle gloomy and unsteady of foundation, boasted ivy-covered walls atwitter with sparrows, as well as a fine view of rolling meadows and distant blue hills. In the evenings John would extemporize upon the piano, conjuring up musical impressions of sunshine and storm, passion and peace, letting his mind wander back no doubt to the old days at Ford Abbey when Bentham would fill the rooms with organ music. In fine weather the couple would stroll out to admire the view. But their more serious hours were reserved for the pemican.

Haunted by life's brevity, John had reminded Harriet that much of their best thought remained unexpressed. In about two years' time, he estimated, it could all be compressed into "a sort of mental pemican, which thinkers, when there are any after us, may nourish themselves with and then dilute for other people"—a pemican being a kind of food concentrate prepared by North American Indians to tide themselves over during long journeys or winters. Setting to work with a will, the two thinkers completed *On Liberty,* most of the *Autobiography, Thoughts on Parliamentary Reform, Utilitarianism,* "Nature," and "The Utility of Religion," besides laying plans that would later take shape as *Considerations on Representative Government, Auguste Comte and Positivism,* and *The Subjection of Women.* Just how they went about composing their impressive roster of "joint productions" is anything but clear. That the writings originated in husband-and-wife discussions seems likely. Apparently, John would do the first drafts, Harriet the revisions. In any event, after the triumphs of the *Logic* and the *Principles,* John's creative energies underwent an astonishing renewal during the collaboration with Harriet. No longer was it *his* genius; it was *their* genius.

But they had reason for urgency. John had already contracted the family disease of consumption, and now Harriet began exhibiting the dread symptoms. Indeed, much of their married life was marred by ill health. Often enough, the doctors ordered off one or the other to sunnier climes, and they went, separately or together, dragging their consumptive lungs across Europe. During one such enforced leave from India House in winter 1854–55, John took occasion for a six-month visit to Italy and Greece. Despite—or perhaps because of—his strenuous activities (he was ever an inveterate walker and mountain scaler), the invalid recovered remarkably. Harriet was not so fortunate. In 1853 she had nearly died at Nice, rescued only by the prompt arrival of Dr. Cecil Gurney, a resident English physician. During the same year came distressing news of George Mill's suicide during the final stages of consumption. Little wonder, then, if the two thinkers worked with a sense of doom upon them.

And now India House affairs came to another boil. Barely had Mill settled in as Chief Examiner (his father's old post) than the so-called Indian Mutiny of 1857 made chaos of his administrative life. Indian disaffection with English rule had crystallized in the Bengal army when rumor spread that cartridges for a new rifle were greased with animal fat. Worse, the cartridges had to be bitten before insertion into the rifle, thereby defiling Hindu soldiers if the fat came from cattle, Muslim soldiers if it came from pigs. Before long a small-scale revolution was raging in the north, during which Indian atrocities provoked fierce British retaliation. It was the death knell for Mill's dream of a gradually liberated India. At home, resentment against Indians mounted. Clearly, a more aggressive rule was needed to subdue natives "half-devil and half-child." Control of India could no longer be left to the company; the British government itself would take over the job, with Queen Victoria to be crowned Empress of India many years later.

Mill fought the proposed takeover with all his logical and rhetorical skill, his petition to Parliament being praised by Lord Grey as the ablest state paper he had ever read. Cold comfort. The East India Company was abolished, though Mill's arguments probably had something to do with the new India Council's similarity to the old Board of Control. Predictably, he was offered a flattering position on the council, but declined, seeing nothing but trouble in the new arrangements. Instead, he retired with a handsome pension and went home to Blackheath, where he and Harriet promptly packed their bags for the Continent.

It was October 1858. Helen was away in Scotland, a fledgling actress with the stage name of "Miss Trevor." The couple had no further family or business cares to delay the long-awaited holiday.

At first, all went well. Paris was a delight. But at Lyon Harriet developed a cough. Then came congestion and fever. Desperately the two travelers pushed on to Avignon, where Harriet arrived in a state of collapse. At the Hôtel de l'Europe, her condition grew better—then worse. Terrified, John wrote to Dr. Gurney at Nice, begging him to come at once. On November 1 Helen was alerted by telegram and set out from Aberdeen in a fright.

Mill returned to the hotel room and the awful bedside vigil. For nearly two days, his taut nerves were attuned only to the sound of his wife's labored breathings. Then, sometime on November 3, he heard them stop forever.

CHAPTER EIGHT

HEROIC INDIVIDUALISM:
On Liberty

Man has distinguished himself from the animal world by
thought and speech. And these, naturally, should be free. If they
are put in chains, we shall return to the state of animals.
—ALEKSANDR SOLZHENITSYN

 HARRIET was dead.

For twenty-four hours, Mill was alone in Avignon,
bowed by the storm raging over him. In the past, simply separating from her had terrified him. Starting his
1854 continental travels, he had all but panicked in the
French railway, all but turned around and sped home to her. Now she
was gone forever. And just as they were free to enjoy life together! As
he stared at the lifeless body, his own life seemed to die with her. "It
is doubtful if I shall ever be fit for anything public or private, again,"
he wrote shortly afterward; "The spring of my life is broken."

Then Helen arrived. Things began to get done. A gravesite was
selected in the cemetery at nearby St. Véran. As a memorial, Mill sent
off a thousand francs for the Avignon poor. Dr. Gurney arrived, unluckily too late. The burial took place. At last it was all over.

Or was it? Now Mill began those rituals to Harriet's memory that
he would dutifully reenact until his own death. Purchasing a small
house overlooking the cemetery, he installed the furniture from the
fatal room at Hôtel de l'Europe. Later, with meticulous care, he would
erect a sumptuous white marble monument over her grave, composing
for it an epitaph of elaborate hyperbole. Here at St. Véran he would

(139)

The avenue of trees leading to Mill's house at St. Véran

spend six months of every year, daily walking the short distance from house to shrine, pausing there for an hour's meditation.

And Helen? "I must go with him," she had cried in a grief-stricken note to her brother just before the funeral. And so she did. Gradually, she was metamorphosed into her mother's image, becoming Mill's comforter and guide, model and inspiration. "Miss Trevor" was never to be heard from again.

Together the two mourners limped back to Blackheath Park. For Mill the only thing left in life was to do what *she* would have wished. At least he could publish what they had written together. Within a month of her death, he wrote to John Parker: "You can have my little book 'On Liberty' for publication this season."

It was their special book, liberty being a theme to which their hearts had ever beat in time. Mill had already devoted an 1854 essay to the topic, but in the following year while mounting the steps of the Roman Capitol—precisely where almost a century earlier Gibbon had envisaged *The Decline and Fall of the Roman Empire*—he determined to do the subject proud in a full-length volume. (Or so says the *Autobiography;* his letters suggest a less fortuitous story.) Harriet had given consent to this plan, and in 1856–58 the book was written twice through, the two of them fussing over it like an adored child. Still unsatisfied, they planned to revise the whole thing during the winter of 1858–59, when Harriet's death intervened. After that, Mill solemnly refused to alter a line.

Its appearance in February 1859 caused something of a sensation, sending the book into a second printing the following August. "I do not know whether then or at any time," John Morley recalled in 1917, "so short a book ever instantly produced so wide and so important an effect on contemporary thought as did Mill's *On Liberty.* " It also produced a considerable controversy, one that has not ceased raging to this day.

The most sustained (or at least prolonged) assaults were James Fitz-james Stephen's 1872 *Pall Mall Gazette* articles, collected the following year into a volume entitled *Liberty, Equality, Fraternity.* Once hailed as "the finest exposition of conservative thought in the latter half of the nineteenth century," the book nowadays seems a bravura performance that somehow leaves Mill largely untouched. To be sure, Sir James has his legitimate quarrels with Mill, but failure to keep his eye on what Mill actually says all but buries them in a glut of irrelevancies. And then Sir James has a way of spoiling his best effects. A rousing procla-

mation that free discussion produces only general skepticism concludes with the brisk advice: "If you want zealous belief, set people to
fight"—which rings less of conservatism than of fascism. Indeed, the
book waxes ominously reverential on the subject of force. Much might
be said for Mill's own response to it: "He does not know what he is
arguing against; and is more likely to repel than to attract people."

Following the all too smooth path of Sir James's steamroller, some
later critics have zipped past the letter of *On Liberty* to challenge what
they take to be its spirit. In these high-speed critiques Mill is apt to be
portrayed as anything from a raving anarchist to a totalitarian in
disguise. Happily, many of these open-throttle assessments have since
been flagged down by later critics. Some other attacks, however, have
been high-pitched as well as high-speed. "Hardly less than Ma-
chiavelli, again," inveighs one critic, "he is a teacher of *evil.*" Still
another characterizes him as "a man of sneers and smears and pervading certainty."

To be sure, *On Liberty* has drawn its fair share of level-headed criticism, too. Yet when all is said, the book remains a major contribution
to liberal thought. De Tocqueville had earlier perceived the approaching tyranny of the majority, but Mill was the first to suggest a way of
dealing with it. Soon after *On Liberty* appeared, liberals and radicals
had taken it to heart, its influence being traceable in controversies,
party programs, and statutes from Victorian times to the present.
Indeed, Mill can still be heard between the lines of much current
debate on matters as far-ranging as information gathering and surveil-
lance, sexual relations between consenting adults, censorship of books
and media, draft resistance and conscientious objection, dissemination
of birth-control information, legalization of abortion and marijuana,
the legitimacy of protest actions, enforced population control, and just
about any other topic in which the claims of individual freedom clash
with those of public well-being.

Far from being a frozen classic, *On Liberty* has thus grown ever more
pertinent with the passage of time, as Mill predicted it would. In 1859
Macaulay could huff that Mill was crying "Fire!" amidst Noah's flood
—and be partly justified. Because of intellectual and social ferment, the
mid-nineteenth century permitted by default a surprising leeway of
thought and behavior. But Mill knew it would not last. Once the
majority began to flex its political and social muscles, once governments began envisioning themselves as instruments of majority will,
then intolerance of diversity would rapidly infect public attitudes.

And few would now argue that his prognosis was seriously in error, the twentieth century having repeatedly witnessed the tyranny of the majority in democratic countries, the tyranny of party bosses in totalitarian ones. That the fate of individual freedom has been less catastrophic than it might have been is due to the persistence of a hardy spirit of independence, a spirit owing much to *On Liberty*'s enduring power.

For the book is, and was designed to be, a powerful experience. Charles Kingsley's reaction is by no means atypical. Discovering *On Liberty* at the publisher's shop, he read it then and there, declaring it had made him "a clearer-headed, braver-minded man on the spot." Precisely what Mill had aimed at.

Today, perhaps more than ever, the inspiriting power of *On Liberty* is its most precious component. As representative government threatens to become tyranny of officialdom, as wholesale conformity to middle-class blandness blights the national soul like some unsightly sprawling suburb, as socialist republics proscribe individuality and free speech as crimes against "the people," and as behaviorist brave new worlds beyond freedom and dignity take ominous shape—we may discover even greater need for this bracing defense of human liberty.

For what Mill champions here is a liberty that lies deep in the heritage of the Western world. It is a liberty that was born in the fierce independence of Greek city-states, that was nurtured by medieval faith affirming the infinite worth of every human soul. It is a liberty that came to maturity proclaiming as self-evident truth that all men are created equal.

This liberty, even as mass societies and collectivist governments were taking shape around it, is the sacred fire that Mill sought to snatch from their potential tyranny by igniting it in as many minds and hearts as his book could reach.

"The object of this Essay," Mill announces forthrightly in chapter one of *On Liberty*, "is to assert one very simple principle," a principle to regulate the conflicting claims of public authority and private freedom. So far we are on familiar ground: once again Mill is the balanced philosopher adjusting opposing yet legitimate truths against each other.

Then, in chapters two and three, Mill surprises all expectations, throwing balance to the winds with a dazzling defense of free discussion and a soaring celebration of individuality. No wonder most readers find these the book's most soul-stirring sections. Only in chapter four does Mill return to his simple principle, again weighing the rival claims of authority and freedom. And the final chapter shows his principle at work in specific instances.

But where, asks the bewildered reader, are the corresponding chapters extolling the claims of government and society over the individual? For quite clearly Mill acknowledges these claims as legitimate and extensive. At first glance, then, *On Liberty* seems radically off-balance, an impression which has propelled some critics to the conclusion that Mill spurns public authority altogether.

No such thing. A clue to *On Liberty*'s actual strategy and structure occurs at the end of chapter three, in one of Mill's most thought-provoking passages. People, he is saying, are rapidly becoming more and more like each other, his prose echoing the dismal sameness of it all: "Comparatively speaking, they now read the same things, listen to the same things, see the same things, go to the same places, have their hopes and fears directed to the same objects, have the same rights and liberties, and the same means of asserting them." In short, people soon will be vapid photocopies of each other. And why? As Mill lists the various causes, we note with mounting dismay that these are the very things that have made modern civilization possible—greater equality among classes, more widespread education, more sophisticated means of communication, the increase of industry and commerce, the spread of social aspirations to all classes, and the greater voice of the majority in government. By a perverse fate, some of humanity's chief blessings threaten to destroy human individuality.

Is there no escape from universal Tweedledee and Tweedledum? There is, if people will accept Mill's principle of roping off an area for individuality, safe from social and political encroachments. But does humanity at large really prize singularity of thought and life-style? Wouldn't the modern world just as soon dispense with such diversity as an obstacle in the path of more efficient social organizations? Quite clearly so. If individualism is to survive, people must "be made to feel its value—to see that it is good there should be differences." In brief, Mill must make a powerful pitch for freedom and originality. Government and society, on the other hand, have their claims so widely acknowledged, so sturdily supported, that Mill would be wasting his ink to defend them. No; in the world of the future, it is the individual who will need help. Big Brother and Mrs. Grundy can fend for themselves quite nicely.

Now it is clear why, after introducing his one very simple principle, Mill then digresses so glowingly on liberty and originality, why he offers no corresponding eulogy to authority. Liberty's claims not only must be adjusted with authority's, but must be recognized as rightful claims in the first place. Unless people value freedom, it is pointless to argue a formula designed to protect it. So, besides quietly propounding its principle, *On Liberty* lifts grand choruses to independence, and trumpets alarms to preserve it from imminent danger.

Strictly speaking, *On Liberty* "begins" with its title, but an epigram and a dedication (neither of which mentions liberty) should not be overlooked. "The grand, leading principle, towards which every argument unfolded in these pages directly converges," intones the epigram (quoted from Wilhelm von Humboldt), "is the absolute and essential importance of human development in its richest diversity." Not liberty, but human improvement, is the keynote—repeated in a *cri de coeur* dedication to the dead Harriet. She is "the inspirer, and in part the author, of all that is best" in Mill's work, he being the worshipful mediator of her excellence. Whether his portrait of her is justified is almost beside the point: she is *On Liberty*'s first and loftiest image of human development in its richest diversity.

What all this indicates, moreover, is that Mill will argue for liberty, not as an end in itself, but as a means to improvement. The cry for freedom and the cry for progress are half-truths to be reconciled by philosophy. Despite their occasional spats, "the only unfailing and permanent source of improvement is liberty."

Keeping Mill's priorities straight is crucial, especially considering the number of commentators who insist he assigned absolute value to liberty. On the contrary, he is careful to stress liberty's utility, that is, "utility in the largest sense, grounded on the permanent interests of man as a progressive being." Freedom and originality, it seems, have a way of opening up diverse lines of future development for that progressive being.

But, to the work itself. *On Liberty*'s opening sentence is a model of Millian clarity and directness:

> The subject of this Essay is not the so-called Liberty of the Will, so unfortunately opposed to the misnamed doctrine of Philosophical Necessity; but Civil, or Social Liberty: the nature and limits of the power which can be legitimately exercised by society over the individual.

Immediately, the air is tense with antagonism of opposites; "the individual" faces off against "society," "liberty" against "power." These adversaries will continue their opposition throughout the entire chapter. Meanwhile, another touch of drama is introduced, with dark hints that an impending crisis will soon make liberty's claims "the vital question of the future."

Having thus commandeered our attention, Mill rapidly throws the whole problem into historical perspective. "The struggle between Liberty and Authority is the most conspicuous feature in the portions of history with which we are earliest familiar, particularly that of Greece, Rome, and England." At the word "struggle" the chapter erupts in open battle, with the slings and arrows of military metaphors filling the air. In the fray, rulers and subjects are the principal combatants, with Mill piling on references to harpies and vultures to underscore the primitive bestiality of their warfare. In time, however, subjects manage to wrest power from despots; the great victory of popular government (so yearned for by Bentham and James Mill, among others) has now been won. But a new struggle is beginning, this time between the conquering governments and the individual (Mill's comments offering shrewd insight into modern democracy):

> The "people" who exercise the power, are not always the same people with those over whom it is exercised; and the "self-government" spoken of, is not the government of each by himself, but of each by all the rest. The will of the people, moreover, practically means, the will of the most numerous or the most active *part* of the people; the majority, or those who succeed in making themselves accepted as the majority: the people, consequently, *may* desire to oppress a part of their number; and precautions are as much needed against this, as against any other abuse of power.

Worse, tyranny of the majority has mustered formidable forces, with government controls and social pressures simultaneously on the march.

With the individual thus embattled on two fronts, Mill sounds a call (one of several in *On Liberty*) to man the barricades: "There is a limit to the legitimate interference of collective opinion with individual independence: and to find that limit, and maintain it against encroachment, is as indispensable to a good condition of human affairs, as protection against political despotism." The crisis, alas, is further confused by uncertainty as to where the barricade should be. Thus, one of the crucial needs of the day is to erect a recognized principle between the skirmishing forces of liberty and authority.

On this cue, Mill formulates his principle. It is the book's single most important passage:

> The object of this Essay is to assert one very simple principle, as entitled to govern absolutely the dealings of society with the individual in the way of compulsion and control, whether the means used be physical force in the form of legal penalties, or the moral coercion of public opinion. That principle is, that the sole end for which mankind are warranted, individually or collectively, in interfering with the liberty of action of any of their number, is self-protection. That the only purpose for which power can be rightfully exercised over any member of a civilized community, against his will, is to prevent harm to others. His own good, either physical or moral, is not a sufficient warrant.

People need not abandon arguing with or persuading or even begging the individual to change his ways. But they must not force him, so long as he is hurting no one but himself. The paragraph ends by crowning the individual as monarch of his own realm: "Over himself, over his own body and mind, the individual is sovereign."

Needless to say, this principle raises a swarm of problems, though some are fairly easy to flap. Take, for example, the idea that the principle is belied by history, where force, not freedom, has dominated the scene. Trust Fitzjames Stephen to wax eloquent on this theme, though some more recent critics have eagerly advanced it. But the point requires not so much refutation, as attention to the text of *On Liberty*. Mill is all too aware of force's role in past history: witness the violent battle imagery. Also, he positions his principle in the chapter *after* the historical survey. Clearly, the principle is not a description of past events, but a formula to guide civilized nations in the present and the future.

Never one to leave a main point to rhetorical subtleties, however, Mill announces it outright. Immediately after formulating his principle, he says it is not meant to apply to minors or to "backward stages of society in which the race itself may be considered as in its nonage." Under such conditions, despotism is in order, provided the despot aims at improving his subjects. "Liberty, as a principle, has no application to any state of things anterior to the time when mankind have become capable of being improved by free and equal discussion."

A related disagreement is more to the point. Mill feels that Western nations are now sufficiently advanced to benefit from liberty, and here Stephen, who emphatically demurs, is on arguable ground. Not that Mill himself has any grand illusions on the score. "On any matter not self-evident, there are ninety-nine persons totally incapable of judging it, for one who is capable," he observes—and elsewhere defines the public as "that miscellaneous collection of a few wise and many foolish individuals." Still, those individuals can rectify their foolishness through experience and discussion. Once people (and nations) have grown up, Mill contends, they should be treated as grown-ups, allowed to make their own mistakes, explore their own visions of truth, pursue their own ideas of good—so long as they harm no one else. Stephen's view of things is quite different:

> Estimate the proportion of men and women who are selfish, sensual, frivolous, idle, absolutely commonplace and wrapped up in the smallest of petty routines, and consider how far the freest of free discussion is likely to improve them. The only way by which it is practically possible to act upon them at all is by compulsion or restraint.

Stephen's solution, of course, lies with those Carlylean strong men he is so partial to. All things considered, one may be pardoned for regarding the cure as worse than the disease.

Still another question raised by Mill's principle has occasioned considerable spilling of critical and explanatory ink. Are there really "self-regarding" acts, that is, are there any acts which do not affect in some way somebody other than the doer? Since no act occurs in a vacuum, is not all behavior "other-regarding" and therefore subject to government or social authority? In less extreme form, the question resolves itself into the difficulty, or impossibility, of deciding which acts really do harm others. And of course the word "harm" is slippery in the extreme.

Suffice it to say here that Mill's own clarifications in *On Liberty* go far toward explaining his position. In general, whenever someone knowingly injures another's interests or person, violates another's rights, or denies another's legitimate expectations, then "harm" has been done, then government and society may step in. Beyond that,

Mill's position has been ably interpreted and defended on a number of occasions, though nobody (least of all Mill himself) has ever contended that drawing the line between harmful and harmless acts is always easy. Still, as A. W. Levi notes, " 'the drawing of the line'— difficult as it may be in practice—is an absolute necessity."

To be sure, Mill foresaw many of these problems with his principle. Having once propounded it, he spends the remainder of the chapter clarifying and qualifying it. But he also restates it in ringing tones. Once more, the dangers to liberty are vividly depicted (with Comte cited as a modern menace), and in the penultimate paragraph we are summoned to the barricades again. In all, it is a stirring introduction to one of the crucial problems of modern times.

Chapter two finds Mill himself on the barricades, defending liberty of thought and discussion with dazzling swordplay.

Before examining his tactics, however, it is important to ascertain his exact line of defense—the more so, as it has been occasionally misdrawn by critics. Mill does not champion absolute freedom of thought and speech; he makes a distinction. Freedom of thought (opinion, conscience, feeling) ought to be absolute, that is, completely free from coercion. Not so, freedom to express those thoughts:

> No one pretends that actions should be as free as opinions. On the contrary, even opinions lose their immunity, when the circumstances in which they are expressed are such as to constitute their expression a positive instigation to some mischievous act.

Ordinarily, opinions about corn-dealers ought to be tolerated, but anybody inflaming "an excited mob assembled before the house of a corn-dealer" is legitimately liable to a little constabulary coercion. In short, Mill is not defending freedom to express opinions that cause direct, serious, unjustifiable harm to someone else.

Mill's actual views in chapter two ("Of the Liberty of Thought and Discussion") suggest that his purpose is to cultivate a vigorous respect for innocent minorities and individuals in order to offset the appeal of power-hungry demagogues. He admits that considerable freedom of expression already exists in the Western world, that governments usually do not try to suppress an opinion unless they have the backing of majority sentiment. And that is precisely the danger: conspiracies between government and "the people" to silence opinions that are essentially harmless but unpopular. "If all mankind minus one, were of one opinion," Mill pronounces memorably, "and only one person were of the contrary opinion, mankind would be no more justified in silencing that one person, than he, if he had the power, would be justified in silencing mankind."

His case for such tolerance is simple enough. First, the opinion suppressed may be true. Of course, the suppressors don't think so, but they are not infallible. And to prevent others from judging an opinion for themselves is to claim infallibility. History, alas, abounds with examples of truth quashed by all too fallible authorities. Second, the opinion suppressed may be false. But false opinions serve a useful purpose: their pertinacious presence keeps truth from ossifying into dead dogma. To be reasonably certain of our opinion, nothing excels hearing the worst that can be said against it (from dissenters themselves, if possible) and formulating our own position accordingly. When our beliefs have survived this ordeal, we can then be more assured about our allegiance to them, our acting upon them. So salutary is the challenge of dissent, we would do well to invent nay-sayers when we cannot find any. Third, the suppressed opinion may be partly true. In fact, this is apt to be the case, there usually being some element of truth in even the most inane opinions. Leaving the nonsense in circulation at least leaves its element of truth available for more comprehensive minds, who will often piece together their philosophies from the most diverse and unlikely materials, achieving thereby a many-sidedness impossible in a more hidebound society.

But such an outline does no justice whatever to the chapter's riches of insight and argument. And clearly Mill is in top form artistically, his prose rising or hushing in eloquent accompaniment to his thought as in this passage exalting the dauntless thinker:

> In the case of any person whose judgment is really deserving of confidence, how has it become so?

A pointed question in this context. How *does* fallible man achieve reasonable certitude? By testing his judgment doggedly. And the repeated grammatical patterns subtly imitate the required resoluteness:

> Because he has kept his mind open to criticism of his opinions and conduct. Because it has been his practice to listen to all that could be said against him; to profit by as much of it as was just, and expound to himself, and upon occasion to others, the fallacy of what was fallacious.

Because he has felt, that the only way in which a human being can make some approach to knowing the whole of a subject, is by hearing what can be said about it by persons of every variety of opinion, and studying all modes in which it can be looked at by every character of mind.

The passage climaxes in a sentence of almost Biblical dignity, indeed one modeled on Biblical parallelism:

No wise man ever acquired his wisdom in any mode but this; nor is it in the nature of human intellect to become wise in any other manner.

Winding down to an expressive finale, the passage is an individualist's eloquent version of "let us now praise famous men."

A similar effect of doggedness, but significantly brusquer, occurs a few pages later:

The Reformation broke out at least twenty times before Luther, and was put down. Arnold of Brescia was put down. Fra Dolcino was put down. Savonarola was put down. The Albigeois were put down. The Vaudois were put down. The Lollards were put down. The Hussites were put down.

Trust entrenched intolerance to be violently resolute where the lone truth-seeker is subtly so.

For all his subtlety, though, this solitary truth-seeker is the hero of *On Liberty*, appearing again and again, standing alone against the crowd. He is the Individual pitted against Society. He is the one person capable of forming judgments as opposed to the ninety-nine who are not. He is the wise man who has a right to trust his judgment against that of any unreflecting multitude. Amid widespread religious intolerance, he is one of the few preaching otherwise. Sometimes he is put to death for his ideas. Socrates and Jesus are historical versions of him.

And Mill's persona is still another version. In reading *On Liberty* we hear the voice of a heroic individual, braving the multitude when it is acting foolishly or criminally: "But I deny the right of the people to exercise such coercion, either by themselves or by their government." Not that Mill's "I" is hopelessly alienated from "the people," but he is sufficiently independent to take a Lutherlike stand against popular wrongdoing.

Other voices are also heard in *On Liberty*. Time and again, Mill gives speech to his opponents, stating their case against him in a dramatization of free expression. In this way Mill frequently takes his own advice about inventing dissenters. And if he reaches his own conclusions in these debates, that is just what the reasonable man should do —after he has demonstrated that he knows his opponents' position.

And here we encounter still another oft-repeated charge against *On Liberty*'s second chapter. Mill denies, in one critic's words, "the existence . . . not only of a public truth, but of any truth whatever unless it be the truth of the denial itself." On the contrary, Mill affirms that "as mankind improve, the number of doctrines which are no longer disputed or doubted will be constantly on the increase: and the well-being of mankind may almost be measured by the number and gravity of the truths which have reached the point of being uncontested." That, of course, is no reason for muzzling someone who chooses to contest one of those truths. And, again, in stressing our fallibility Mill is not condemning us to eternal skepticism. "It is not the feeling sure of a doctrine (be it what it may) which I call an assumption of infallibility. It is the undertaking to decide that question *for others*, without allowing them to hear what can be said on the contrary side." He has no objection to individuals or societies reaching reasonable conclusions and acting on them; he often does so himself. His quarrel is with the silencing of differing views.

Besides its dialectical voices, *On Liberty* sports a large cast of characters, most of them seen in brief generalized portraits, like the "absolute prince" who has never had the advantage of having his opinions roundly contradicted. But the larger historical figures of chapter two are the most memorable—Socrates, Jesus, and above all Marcus Aurelius.

Socrates is Mill's image of the heroic truth-seeker whose truths continue to thrive despite persecution. Jesus is the saintly individualist whose truths are allowed to petrify when his later followers insist upon holding them as dead dogmas, imperiously suppressing all deviant belief. These ideas are encapsulated in superbly skillful imagery:

> Socrates was put to death, but the Socratic philosophy rose like the sun in heaven, and spread its illumination over the whole intellectual firmament. Christians were cast to the lions, but the Christian church grew up a stately and spreading tree, overtopping the older and less vigorous growths, and stifling them by its shade.

While Socrates' philosophy shines out to humanity, the Christian church, at first a healthy growth, becomes a source of darkness by stifling other growths.

Though sad, the fates of Socrates and Jesus are not tragic. That of Marcus Aurelius is. Indeed, as Mill portrays the great Roman emperor, *On Liberty* rises to the stature of ancient tragedy. A man of brilliant attainments, great learning, and moral enlightenment, he yet persecuted the early Christians. And why? To preserve the great god Society. In his blindness he mistook Christian teaching for a threat rather than a blessing. That assumption of joint infallibility between himself and society was an act of hubris, an error constituting a tragic downfall. Here is the heroic individual as tragic figure, here is intolerance as tragic flaw.

Like some horrible nemesis, intolerance begets further intolerance. Officially recognized by the despotic Constantine, Christianity soon developed its own intolerance of other creeds. And now Mill, steeling himself for the onslaught, mounts one of his few open raids on Christendom. The crusade is directed against neither Christ's teachings nor Christianity as it might be, or as it sometimes is. Indeed, one of Mill's chief complaints is that Christians are not Christian enough. "Whenever conduct is concerned, they look round for Mr. A and B to direct them how far to go in obeying Christ." But he does assail Christianity which has compromised itself to make friends with the Mammon of Society. This sellout, of course, required diluting Christian morality to acquiescence-inducing virtues, like other-worldliness and obedience. So much so that now "pagan" self-assertion needs to be reconciled with "christian" self-denial. "There is a Greek ideal of self-development, which the Platonic and Christian ideal of self-government blends with, but does not supersede," Mill argues (in chapter three), fusing Hebrew and Hellene. "It may be better to be a John Knox than an Alcibiades, but it is better to be a Pericles than either; nor would Pericles, if we had one in these days, be without anything good which belonged to John Knox."

While discussion of these matters is proceeding, *On Liberty*'s battle metaphors are still raging, with the struggle between individual and society in chapter one being replaced by the collision of conflicting viewpoints in chapter two. On the whole, this latter is a bracing, beneficial warfare. "Not the violent conflict between parts of the truth, but the quiet suppression of half of it, is the formidable evil." Indeed, during dishonorable truces, "both teachers and learners go to sleep at their post." Everybody, in fact, snores away in "the deep slumber of a decided opinion." Lest that happen here, *On Liberty* is soon trumpeting further alarms and excursions, the melee swelling furiously till chapter's end.

Chapter three champions the individual as endangered species.

Technically, the stress is upon the utility of individuality, but it is hard to miss the feeling that Mill (like G. M. Hopkins) rejoices in "all things counter, original, spare, strange"—and active. Delightedly, Mill savors the tang of sharply differentiated personalities, pines nostalgically for the vital individuality of people like Jeremy Bentham. Unless something can be done, all this marvelous human diversity is scheduled for dilution into the homogenized mediocrity of mass society. Polishing up logic and rhetoric, Mill sets out to do something.

Once again, the argument from utility is simplicity itself. Since people are naturally different, they need to develop themselves differently. Leaving them free to do so makes for personal happiness and, sometimes, social progress. (A few of them may come up with improvements beneficial to others.) At least this way, lines of possible future development are left open. But if people are compelled into conformity, or if they bovinely submit to it, they will atrophy into automatons. It is only by making choices—even if one chooses the traditional—that people develop their character at all. For Mill, the test of any civilization is the quality of its people, an idea that here finds noble expression:

> It really is of importance, not only what men do, but also what manner of men they are that do it. Among the works of man, which human life is rightly employed in perfecting and beautifying, the first in importance surely is man himself. Supposing it were possible to get houses built, corn grown, battles fought, causes tried, and even churches erected and prayers said, by machinery—by automatons in human form —it would be a considerable loss to exchange for these automatons even the men and women who at present inhabit the more civilized parts of the world, and who assuredly are but starved specimens of what nature can and will produce. Human nature is not a machine to be built after a model, and set to do exactly the work prescribed for it, but a tree, which requires to grow and develope itself on all sides, according to the tendency of the inward forces which make of it a living thing.

All too clearly Mill foresaw that modern mediocrity, fearful of autonomous man, would aim at producing anonymous man—and eventually automatic man.

Painfully aware of the almost universal indifference toward individuality, Mill musters such superb rhetorical powers that his chapter reads like an anthology of great quotations on the topic. He does achieve chapter unity, however, partly through a network of interacting metaphors and allusions. Gone are the battle figures of earlier chapters, replaced by organic ones: the human being is a living creature who needs to grow and develop, like a tree or plant. The evils of repression are abundantly evident in references to painful confinement of one sort or another, in allusions to yokes, chains, molds, patterns, clothes that don't fit, shoes that pinch, Chinese ladies with bound feet, pollarded trees, and clipped hedges. Mill's love of energetic character finds expression in references to exercise, movement; and in ominous allusions to chaining up, fettering, inertia. Throughout the chapter, joyous movement and growth alternate with painful restriction and atrophy. The wildness of Niagara is set against the sluggishness of a Dutch canal; the dynamism of the Western world contrasts with Oriental stagnation. (Once again, the East is an image of political rigor mortis.) The unfavorable animal and machine references are readily explained: how better to depict the dignity of the individual, who is neither a sheep nor a steam engine, but a unique human being?

Once again, however, it is essential to pin down what Mill is *not* saying. Liberty of life-style does not apply to minors, to the mentally undeveloped or disturbed, to criminals. For them, benevolent despotism is in order. Nor does it sanction acts harmful to others, Mill being fully aware that freedom for the pikes is death for the minnows.

Also, Mill does not exalt eccentricity into an absolute good, though the accusation is all too frequently made. "This is simply to substitute one error for another," snaps one critic, "bohemian nonsense for bourgeois nonsense." Usually, the criticism has an ancillary twist: Mill ignores or despises traditional wisdom, fomenting "a deliberate determination to revolt against custom."

But surely the very chapter title ("Of Individuality, as *One* of the Elements of Well-Being") forestalls much of this criticism. Also, Mill carefully picks his way past extremism:

(155)

It would be absurd to pretend that people ought to live as if nothing whatever had been known in the world before they came into it; as if experience had as yet done nothing towards showing that one mode of existence, or of conduct, is preferable to another. Nobody denies that people should be so taught and trained in youth, as to know and benefit by the ascertained results of human experience.

What, then, is he recommending? Simply that the responsible adult be allowed "to use and interpret experience in his own way. It is for him to find out what part of recorded experience is properly applicable to his own circumstances and character." It is perfectly valid to choose the customary, so long as it is *chosen*. That is the point: one must not be strong-armed by government or society, one must not passively accept. The choice is all. If Mill occasionally yearns for widespread eccentricity, it is only because the tyranny of conformity could use the shock. Mill is no mere apologist for hippies.

But then there is the claim that he is "an apologist for intellectual snobs," trying to foist upon us an aristocracy of eggheads. To be sure, Mill does prize thinking people, would love to see their ascendancy. But he firmly rejects any scheme to give them power to coerce others. All they can legitimately do is point the way. When they do, it is "the honour and glory of the average man . . . that he is capable of following that initiative . . . with his eyes open." In short, Mill wasn't buying Carlyle's brand of muscular hero worship. Nor was he particularly enchanted with the idea of a learned elite, isolated in country-club exclusiveness from the masses. When Bain misread him on the point, Mill swiftly informed him otherwise: "The notion of an intellectual aristocracy of *lumières* while the rest of the world remains in darkness fulfils none of my aspirations." John Morley saw the point clearer. *On Liberty*, he said, is "one of the most aristocratic books ever written." But, he added, not "British aristocratic."

In the final two chapters, *On Liberty*'s orchestrations are mostly muted—and suitably so. Having outlined his principle and extolled the claims of free expression and individuality, Mill is now ready to examine the principle more quietly.

What does he find? Many of the matters already mentioned: public and private acts can and must be distinguished; law and society have legitimate jurisdiction over public or other-regarding acts; society can rightfully inculcate its values and customs during juvenility; the mature person should be free of coercion in self-regarding matters. But there are some additional twists.

For example, the claims of one person's freedom need not restrict others to sitting by silently while he makes a fool of himself or behaves like a depraved animal. They can argue, cajole, tell off, or avoid him. But they must not coerce him. An unfavorable reaction is one thing; persecution and prosecution something else—a distinction missed by a number of Mill critics. We need not suffer fools gladly, though we should not loose law and society upon them unless they are harming others.

To illustrate, Mill spends nearly half of chapter four giving carefully selected examples of self-regarding acts being suppressed. The list starts with cases that Mill's readers will regard as unwarranted interference, then quietly modulates into examples of equally offensive interference that the audience itself probably countenances. The law against eating pork in Mohammedan countries heads the list, clearly a case of peculiar religious preferences erected into national law binding everyone. Then comes Spanish outlawing of all forms of Christianity except Roman Catholicism. Then (we are getting closer to home here) Puritan prohibition of music, dancing, theater, and other harmless diversions. Then the distaste that average Americans exhibit toward displays of wealth greater than theirs. Then the efforts of bad workmen to prevent good workmen from earning more than they do. So far Mill and his audience are probably at one in denouncing such interference. But now he turns the tables. Ah yes, those laws prohibiting the sale of liquor to everybody. And those Sunday-closing laws. And those sentiments to suppress Mormonism, sentiments so widely applauded in England. By chapter's end, intolerance is exhibited, not as an exotic foreign bloom, but as a hardy homegrown variety.

In chapter five, "Applications," Mill gets down to practical matters. His principle, up to now floating in ethereal abstractness, appears concretely in specific cases, each a little drama of conflict in which liberty and authority are the chief antagonists. Now at last the claims of authority are given their due. Indeed, the state in this chapter emerges as such a major character that Mill feels obliged to close *On Liberty* with a stirring indictment of its potentially excessive power. He could hardly have chosen a more resoundingly relevant finale for the book.

At first, however, he sets out "to assist the judgment in holding the balance" between freedom and authority. So concerned about balance is he, that his one simple principle is here subdivided into two matching maxims which are then set teetering in seesaw fashion. First, the individual is not accountable to society for self-regarding behavior; second, he is accountable for other-regarding acts. Not that society and government ought to leap in with regulations at every other-regarding opportunity. Trade, for example, is other-regarding activity that might well be left to free enterprise. In fact, whenever matters can justifiably be left to individuals, Mill strongly feels they ought to be.

Now appear the dramatic vignettes of the maxims at work. While clarifying matters, they also provide occasion for some choice Millean observations on a variety of topics from the preventive function of government to the sale of weapons to individuals. Sailing into yet choppier waters, Mill argues that divorce ought to be easily obtainable, though he refuses to go the whole length with von Humboldt on a unilateral demand for divorce being sufficient. After all, one partner has staked much on the other's promises, and children may be involved —though it is foolish to pretend that theirs are the only important interests.

On the topic of public education, he offers some especially brisk home truths. For decades Victorian England had been dithering about state-financed education. The hang-up, of course, was which religion would be taught to the poor. Meanwhile, the poor were taught nothing. At his scathing best, Mill assails this self-defeating impasse, insisting that different religions can be studied as easily as different philosophies and that the state should require a certain level of education but not monopolize the educational system. "A general State education is a mere contrivance for moulding people to be exactly like one another; and . . . the mould in which it casts them is that which pleases the predominant power in the government." Rather than hold exclusive rights to education, state schools should be one of many competing systems.

While on the subject of children, Mill begins handling again the explosive topic of overpopulation. Remembering his Malthus, he argues that "in a country either over-peopled, or threatened with being so, to produce children, beyond a very small number, with the effect of reducing the reward of labour by their competition, is a serious offense against all who live by the remuneration of their labour." When thus faced with overpopulation, the state may legitimately hinder people from having children they cannot support.

His applications ended, Mill retunes argument and art for a grand finale on the dangers of government bureaucracy. Though government interference in social matters is sometimes desirable, three objections to much of it can be made. First, individuals can sometimes do the job better. Second, even when government can outperform individuals, fending for themselves can be valuable training for people. Third—and this is the major concern—government powers may swell to such proportions as to overwhelm individual effort. Invoking the Poor Law Board as illustration, Mill argues for "the greatest dissemination of power consistent with efficiency; but the greatest possible centralization of information, and diffusion of it from the centre." In this way, centralized government and local autonomy may then achieve a balance of power.

On Liberty ends with neither a bang nor a whimper, but with a sustained reiteration of its principal themes and images. Once again, individual and society are poised against each other in a series of dramatic contrasts—activity versus fetters, expansion versus dwarfing, the vital versus the mechanical, "everything" versus "nothing." Throughout this splendid coda of contrasts, Mill's love of human individuality sings out in grand affirmation, keens in ominous warning:

A government cannot have too much of the kind of activity which does not impede, but aids and stimulates, individual exertion and development. The mischief begins when, instead of calling forth the activity and powers of individuals and bodies, it substitutes its own activity for theirs; when, instead of informing, advising, and, upon occasion, denouncing, it makes them work in fetters, or bids them stand aside and does their work instead of them. The worth of a State, in the long run, is the worth of the individuals composing it; and a State which postpones the interests of *their* mental expansion and elevation, to a little more of administrative skill, or of that semblance of it which practice gives, in the details of business; a State which dwarfs its men, in order that they may be more docile instruments in its hands even for beneficial purposes, will find that with small men no great thing can really be accomplished; and that the perfection of machinery to which it has sacrificed everything, will in the end avail it nothing, for want of the vital power which, in order that the machine might work more smoothly, it has preferred to banish.

On Liberty had been published, but what next?

Would Mill be unfit for anything public or private again? Was the spring of his life really broken? Hardly. If anything, his obsession with Harriet's memory spurred him on to greater philosophic and social activity. Between the brokenhearted notes to friends and the protracted correspondence over the St. Véran mausoleum, Mill was firing off scrappy epistles on political matters—without the slightest sense of inconsistency. It was what *she* would have wanted. Besides, Helen was already standing at his side as instructor and *femme inspiratrice*, and there was nothing like an upcoming political tussle to perk up Mill's interest in life. Such a tussle was indeed upcoming: reform was in the air once again.

It was just like the old days. Mill had, of course, been weaned on reform politics which stressed the unique value of representative government for getting the interests of the community acted upon by officials. True, his conservative reaction of the twenties and thirties had given him political second thoughts. And then those two volumes of de Tocqueville's *Democracy in America* (1835, 1840), with their misgivings about tyranny of the majority, were enough to give pause to any old-time Benthamite radical. Still, Mill's loyalty to representative government survived fairly intact. It was still the wave of the future, and the grand problem now was how to avoid its possible abuses. In particular: how to prevent the educated minority (or indeed any minority) from being totally overwhelmed by the mediocre majority's voting clout.

By the 1860s his scruples about democracy had suddenly become timely again. What with workers excluded from the 1832 voting reforms, labor unrest had gathered slowly for a major cloudburst of protest, but the great Chartist rally of 1848 had proved all eye and no hurricane. After that, stillness reigned. In the high noon of mid-Victorian equipoise, reform breezes barely stirred at all, and it was not until decade's end that a few faint gusts could be felt. Shrewd political animal that he was, Mill immediately sniffed out the change in atmosphere.

Rapidly dipping into the pemican, he came up with a batch of political odds and ends, added a suggestion about giving plural votes to the educated, entitled the resulting pamphlet *Thoughts on Parliamentary Reform*, and hurried it into print so fast that it jostled *On Liberty* on its way to the booksellers. But he soon repented his haste. Immediately after, he discovered in Thomas Hare's *Treatise on the Election of*

John Stuart Mill and Helen Taylor (ca. 1865)

Representatives (1859) an even better suggestion for curbing tyranny of the majority. Through a bewildering tangle of proportional representation and multiple voting, Hare had ingeniously secured minority votes for prominent representatives outside the range of majority opinion. Fired with enthusiasm for this plan, Mill was soon writing fan mail to Hare, recommending the book to correspondents, and puffing it energetically in the reviews. Still not satisfied, he wrote out a full-length study of representative government in which Hare's plan bulks large in the practical suggestions department.

The fullest statement of Mill's mature political thought, *Considerations on Representative Government* (1861) finds him happily back in argumentative harness. Immediately, Mill encounters two opposing views of government—the mechanical view that almost any kind of government can be tinkered into existence at any time or place, and the organic view that governments grow naturally into shape as the nation develops. In brief, a variant of Bentham versus Coleridge on politics.

In a trice, Mill is extracting partial truths from each view and merrily synthesizing away. Yes, the organicists are correct to see the broad connection between level of civilization and type of government, but their view is too deterministic. The mechanists are correct to see that a nation can reshape—within limits—its form of government for greater utility, to help boost its people up to the next rung on the ladder of progression. For this purpose, representative government now serves best, because of its wider demands for intelligent citizen involvement. But it has its dangers. Instead of appointing and supervising capable administrators, amateur politicians may attempt the job themselves. Also, representative government can overgovern, thereby stunting its people's development. Likewise, it can knuckle under to sinister interests which are opposed to the community's. But the overriding danger is omnipotence of the majority. And here, of course, Mill provides a peppery defense of Hare's voting scheme. Nowadays, the plan's feasibility may be debatable; less so is the evil it attempts to remedy.

Mill then explores the mechanics of representative government, splendidly supporting widespread suffrage and restricted campaign spending. Other arguments seem less happy: the demand for voting literacy tests, the preference for open rather than secret balloting. And his continued allegiance to plural voting, on top of Hare's proportional representation, is apt to daunt even today's headiest computer enthusiast. The book closes with considerations on governing colonies and dependencies, considerations that rapidly turn into a spirited vindication of the East India Company. Better a corps of trained administrators supervised by elected officials, than the officials themselves with their primary allegiance to mother-country party politics.

The East India experience had helped widen Mill's political horizons, and in an 1859 *Fraser's* article, "A Few Words on Non-Intervention," he grappled with one of the thorniest issues of modern foreign policy. Prompted by Lord Palmerston's chauvinist objections to a French canal across the Suez, Mill devotes the first half of the article to skewering the British diplomatic penchant for acting, or appearing to act, from Machiavellian motives. Similarly, he deplores the idea that England, acting on narrow motives of self-interest, should retard the advance of any backward country. But in the article's final half, he settles down to probe "the whole doctrine of non-interference with foreign nations." That is, when (if ever) is a nation justified in intervening in another's internal affairs?

Careful treading is in order here, for a slight distortion will caricature Mill's ideas. A quick review of his historical perspective also helps. Humanity, as he saw it, began scratching out its existence in barbarism, where the rule of force necessarily dominated individuals. But as humankind developed, the protracted struggle between liberty and authority waxed ever more intense, with people increasingly capable of governing themselves and casting off the restrictions of despotism. The peoples of nineteenth-century Europe, Mill felt, were engaged in various stages of this war of liberation, with future happiness and progress hanging on their success. This vision of struggling, evolving humanity forms the context for his few words on nonintervention.

He first distinguishes between barbarian and civilized nations, the capacity for popular government being the major means of discrimination. Barbarians are as yet unripe for the freedoms and responsibilities of representative government. (Mill saw it as folly to assume that all nations can handle democracy as easily as those with a long tradition of liberty to draw upon.) As a people, barbarians are unprepared for governing the nation by themselves; consequently, it must be done for them—by a despot or a ruling class or a foreign power. This rule of force is justified, however, only—and the "only" is important—if rulers aim at their subjects' development and eventual liberation. So concerned is Mill with the value of self-sufficient liberty that despotism itself can be justified when it helps develop free people from savages.

Predictably, this point leads him onto the subject of British rule in India, and we get an ever-so-brief glimpse of his views on that vexed question. Like his father, Mill sees pre-British India as a country groaning under political and social despotisms that would effectively lock the mass of people into long-term subjugation, ignorance, and poverty. Once England had entangled itself in Indian affairs, it could justify the intervention only by going the whole distance and establishing a benevolent despotism aimed at raising the Indian people to a level of prosperity and civilization where independent popular government became possible. This eventual liberation of India was, of course, the leading idea behind Mill's thirty-five years of service to the East India Company. In all his thinking on India, there is no hint of white-man's-burden racism, no trace of messianic imperialism.

When Mill turns to intervention among civilized nations, the discussion nowadays rings with added meaning, recent history having provided some painfully concrete examples of the cases he discusses abstractly.

Among civilized nations—that is, those whose peoples are ripe for representative government—nonintervention is Mill's rule. People capable of liberty deserve to have their liberty respected. In particular (and here Mill hits a nerve), "assistance to the government of a country in keeping down the people, unhappily by far the most frequent case of foreign intervention, no one writing in a free country needs take the trouble of stigmatizing." Little did he know. Perhaps surprising is his argument that intervention on the side of freedom is also unwarranted, because struggling for liberty is the only sure test that a people are fit for freedom. Different is the case of a people battling a foreign power or a local tyranny upheld by such a power: then intervention is justified as redressing an unfairly disturbed balance.

Finally, intervention to enforce nonintervention is always worthy, if not wise. Mill closes his article with a resounding call to England to stand against the practice of despotisms aiding each other against rebellion. Let England, he cries, be "the first nation . . . to say that not a gun shall be fired in Europe by the soldiers of one Power against the revolted subjects of another."

In all these political tracts, Mill seemed to be enjoying himself immensely. Most likely, it was an especial delight to see his name boldly appended to the *Fraser's* article, for that minor detail represented a most significant fact: he was now free from India House restrictions on political controversy. And for the first time in his life he was free to run for public office.

CHAPTER NINE

THE ETHICS
OF HUMANISM:
Utilitarianism

All the religion we have is the ethics of one or another
holy person.
—RALPH WALDO EMERSON, *Journals*, 1861–65

 "THIS short work has many volumes to answer for,"
wrote Alexander Bain in 1882, grimly surveying the
mounting tide of commentary upon Mill's *Utilitarianism* (1861). And that was before the floodgates had burst
altogether. After Bain, the deluge. Nor has the inundation yet receded. To this day *Utilitarianism* remains one of the most
widely read and quarreled over expositions of modern ethical thought.

The search for new moral underpinnings had been going on ever
since some eighteenth-century thinkers had begun to fear the imminent collapse of Christian belief. Like Bentham before him, Mill felt
it essential to get ethics out of the damps and fogs of intuition and
revelation, and into the sunlight of reason. But the old Benthamite
ethic, admirable as it was, achieved its dazzling clarity only by working with an oversimplified picture of people as selfish children, calculating their greedy little pleasures and pains. Such a picture would
not do for Mill. Where in it were people's nobler impulses, their
sympathy for each other, their love of beauty, their sense of dignity?
And how could such a static ethic serve a people evolving toward

greater humaneness? So Mill as moralist had his problems. His new vision of humanity had to be grafted successfully onto the old utilitarian stock. And in public arguments he would have to disentangle his new utilitarianism from the older Benthamite version.

It was bound to be a troublesome business. So multifarious were the misconceptions surrounding utilitarianism that anyone even whispering the word was immediately open to ambush from almost any critical direction. Back in Bentham's day, those who talked of the pleasure-pain principle were charged with "sensualism," utility being seen as a sort of philosophical Circe's wand that changed men into swine. Carlyle, for one, had never ceased decrying it as "pig philosophy." From a somewhat different direction came an almost opposite complaint: utilitarians were cold, hard, inhuman; always overlooking the beautiful and the good; always obsessed with the moral and the practical. Dickens and Ruskin would play creative variations on this theme, as indeed Mill himself did during his anti-Benthamite salad days. Conversely, still others saw utilitarians as wildly impractical visionaries who believed people would behave morally out of respect for the greatest happiness of their fellow creatures.

But perhaps the most frequent objection was to utility's unworkableness. To figure out the morality of an act by toting up the pleasures and pains it would produce! Really, even if such an arithmetic were possible, the consequences of an act were never perfectly predictable anyway, so what was the use of all that felicific calculation? Surely— so these opponents were apt to argue—the rightness or wrongness of an act is determined by people's intuitive moral sense, the more pious controversialists taking the existence of this convenient organ as further proof of providential design. Predictably, voices raised in behalf of this view could be heard amidst the dreaming spires of Oxford and Cambridge, both universities being locked into an Anglican orthodoxy currently giving its blessing to intuitionism.

To complicate matters, Mill was already identified as a defender of old-line Benthamism, having on two occasions crossed swords with intuitionist professors. In the April 1835 *London Review* he had carved up Cambridge's Adam Sedgwick for taking a high moral line with utility for "denying the existence of moral feelings." Nobody denies moral feelings exist, Mill retorted. The real questions are: what are their origin and nature? and can they be guided by rational principles? For Mill, moral feelings did not emanate from any intuitive sense of right and wrong; they grew from ordinary human nature and were shaped through pleasure and pain by education and experience. Of course, they could be misshaped, and so the grand task for society was to cultivate them according to a principle fostering the general happiness of all sensitive creatures—in this world, not the next. Countering another of the professor's assaults, Mill insisted that one need not predict perfectly the results of one's actions. Ordinary foresight, aided by the accumulated wisdom of past ages, would suffice for calculating consequences. Even in 1835 Mill's utility plotted no violent overthrow of traditional wisdom, only a gradual perfecting of it.

If Mill's pro-utilitarianism in "Sedgwick's Discourse" seems way out of line with his anti-Benthamite remarks in Bulwer's *England and the English* (1833)—to say nothing of the forthcoming strictures in "Bentham" of 1838—it should be noted that "Sedgwick" originally contained a few pages on the errors of past utilitarian moralists. But the heresy had caught James Mill's watchful eye, and John had to excise it before publication.

Spirited as "Sedgwick" had been, an even snappier riposte from Mill's pen peppered the *Westminster*'s pages in October 1852, when he tangled with his old enemy from the *Logic*, Whewell of Cambridge. For Mill the professor personified everything infuriating about intuitionism, especially its habit of passing off prejudices as intuitively known truths requiring no rational justification. So when Whewell's *Lectures on the History of Moral Philosophy in England* (1852) slung some mud at Bentham, Mill lost no time girding himself for battle. It was perfectly permissible for Mill himself to point out Bentham's faults to fellow radicals, but let anybody else berate the old philosopher to score points for intuitionism, and Mill was there sword in hand to defend him. On this occasion he made such short work of Whewell's attacks on utility that he had room left in the review for a few incursions of his own upon the professor's moral intuitions. While Whewell's reasoning spun around in vicious circles, Mill noted that his intuitions sped straight to the mark of reactionism.

Victories for utility these reviews no doubt were. Still, they fell short of what Mill knew was needed. For one thing, their partisanship left the impression that utilitarians were wranglers instead of serious moralists. For all his success in cutting up the Cambridge dons, Mill could report in 1861 to a French correspondent who imagined utility the dominant English philosophy: "Most English writers not only deny it, they insult it; and the Benthamite school has always been regarded (I say it with regret) as an insignificant minority." Besides, defending utility meant defending Bentham, and Mill had definite reservations on that score. Indeed, Sedgwick and Whewell at times had come perilously close to some of his own objections to old-line utility. No; what was needed was a positive statement of the case for utility in its highest terms, by a writer of unimpeachable moral earnestness. More, this apologia ought to shun the cloisters of academia for the marketplace of ideas where politics and society were vigorously discussed at first hand.

But where was such a treatise to be found? Certainly not in Bentham's *Introduction to the Principles of Morals and Legislation* with all its gaping philosophical holes. Not in James Mill's *Fragment on Mackintosh* (1835). True, it dealt with ethics, but old-style ethics. Besides, its tone of nonstop asperity would hardly dress up the utilitarian image. And so, when a correspondent asked him to recommend a book or a set of books on moral philosophy, Mill had nothing to offer. "In my opinion," he concluded, "ethics as a branch of philosophy is still to be created."

Clearly it was up to him to create it. He had set about the task in 1854, working away at an essay on justice during the downpours in his European sojourn. Around the same time he seems to have worked up a second paper on utility. Grafting the two essays together in 1859, he revised the hybrid during the following year and published it in *Fraser's Magazine* of October, November, and December 1861. Calmly Mill awaited the response.

Surprisingly, almost none came. Yes, there were a couple of stray counterblasts (apparently from distraught clergymen), but the major reviews and magazines remained almost alarmingly silent. Even when *Utilitarianism* appeared in book form in 1863, the precarious quiet continued. Miraculously, Mill had managed to avert the expected howls of sensualism and materialism. It was only in 1869, when moral philosophy became a burning issue in the press, that Mill as moralist began to be discussed—and then the tone was mostly respectful. Though critics aplenty were ready to dispute his arguments, nearly all were agreed on his integrity. English writers might still be denying utilitarianism, but they were no longer insulting it. Mill's little book had turned the tide.

With the increasing acceptance of utility as an ethical standard, *Utilitarianism* has become a landmark volume, its five short chapters managing to touch upon nearly all the major concerns of modern moralists. True, the book went through a period of profound eclipse around the turn of the century, but the criticisms of F. H. Bradley and G. E. Moore, once thought so damaging to Mill's case, have in their turn drawn fire from some more recent commentators. Not that there is now anything resembling chapter-and-verse assent to Mill's book, but modern reassessments have left no doubt about its importance in ethical history. "More than any other thinker," observes D. P. Dryer, "Mill is responsible for laying down the principal directions ethics has taken since his day."

With the publication of *Utilitarianism*, Mill had taken a giant step toward his goal of creating ethics as a branch of philosophy.

Anybody writing about ethics faced special problems, as Mill knew only too well.

For one thing, the ultimate end of morality was not amenable to proof. At least not the kind of proof Mill had spelled out so painstakingly in the *System of Logic*. There, proof verified *what is*. But ethics raised questions about *what ought to be*, and how could one "prove" that?

Besides, for a practical moralist like Mill, proof was no good without persuasion. What was the point of "proving" the greatest happiness principle if nobody was moved to adopt it? Of course proof helped to persuade, but complete convictional success hinged on the person offering the proof. Mill's earliest moral associations, as he knew to his sorrow, had been shaped not so much by his father's lofty teachings as by his less-than-lofty character. The love of virtue, he had concluded back in 1834–35, is "caught by inspiration or sympathy from those who already have it." On the written page, such emotional transfer required a poet capable of embodying those ideals in powerful images. Even when Plato's moral arguments failed to convince the head, his noble portrait of Socrates seldom failed to win the heart. Christian morality was impressive, not because Jesus offered impressive arguments for it, but because he lived it so impressively in the Gospel accounts. In ethical writing, argument was helpful but art was essential.

Of course, nearly everything Mill wrote had an ethical dimension, but *Utilitarianism* being about morality itself stood in special need of the moralist's art—and Mill rose to the occasion splendidly. Perhaps in no other work is his persona so pacifically rational, so temperately earnest. The polemical tidal waves that had lashed Sedgwick and Whewell are mere undercurrents here, barely disturbing *Utilitarianism*'s serene surface. Speaking softly to intuitionists, Mill is usually content to emphasize utility's value to everyone—regardless of epistemological persuasion. True, an indignant thunderbolt or two is unleashed against low controversialists, but Mill amiably exempts opposition "thinkers" from these strictures. And when he does disagree, his delicacy of touch would leave an opponent hard put to take offense.

Mill's mixture of earnestness and charm radiates from every corner of the book, even the footnotes. One such note, for example, declares that the author, having made the word "utilitarian" current coin, eschewed it entirely when it became a party slogan; now he uses it solely as a convenient philosophic term. No party zealot, he. Besides loyally puffing one of Bain's works, other notes contain friendly disagreements with dissidents, one of whom is described as "an opponent, whose intellectual and moral fairness it is a pleasure to acknowledge." Mill of course goes on to disagree at length, but in *Utilitarianism* he seldom forgets sweetness when dispensing light.

Further enhancing this image of sunny rationality, Mill mediates between extremes whenever possible. With status-quo traditionalists to the right of him and ethical revolutionaries to the left, he gracefully advocates an ethic which retains the best of older morality while providing for its gradual improvement. But when it comes to a choice between human and swinish pleasures, Mill's opting for the former brooks no compromise with the latter. Tolerating different opinions is one thing, condoning sensualism quite another. So much for pig-philosophy detractors. With his voice of sweet-tempered earnestness, Mill in *Utilitarianism* becomes the spokesman for a new and nobler utilitarianism.

As things have turned out, the book's brevity has been as important as its persona. Whatever the reasons for it, Mill's decision not to produce a shelf-long ethical *summa* has proved momentous. By leaving others to elaborate upon and puzzle out the intricacies of his cryptic argument, he ensured its endurance. Like a child's coloring book, *Utilitarianism* has shaped the very participation it invited.

More conventionally, Mill put metaphors to work to convey his ethical vision. Trees and plants crop up fairly frequently in the book, illustrating the argument that moral feelings are a natural growth, not a supernatural special creation. The animal world comes off less well. Pigs especially represent appetite divorced from rational benevolence, while Socrates, Jesus, and Mill's persona portray the higher end of the ethical scale.

John Stuart Mill (ca. 1865)

For all its sweetness and light, *Utilitarianism* is still a polemical work. Right from the start, argument and art are operating together. Even as Mill begins constructing his rationale for utility, he is busy refurbishing its image. Take, for example, the opening paragraph in which he maps out the main area to be discussed—"the criterion of right and wrong." It is a question on which agreement is no nearer now "than when the youth Socrates listened to the old Protagoras, and asserted . . . the theory of utilitarianism against the popular morality of the so-called sophist." Obviously no fad, utility is as venerable as Socrates himself, whose name here and elsewhere in the book lends it a glow of secular sanctity. (In the next chapter Jesus is enlisted in the cause, his golden rule being cited as "the complete spirit of the ethics of utility.") Meanwhile, Mill has quietly linked anti-utilitarians with the sophists and their slightly shady reputation. Yes, Mill has come out fighting again, though the gloves are velvet.

Having won the opening round with fancy footwork, Mill settles down to a more sustained contest, arguing the need for first principles in ethics and tracing the sources of confusion over them. Before long, he has located the problem in the differences between intuitionist and experiential epistemology. But this time around, Mill declines to quibble with controversialists, suggesting instead that intuitionist "thinkers," in their disagreements over morality, might cast a sympathetic eye upon utility for solutions. Indeed, "to all those *a priori* moralists who deem it necessary to argue at all, utilitarian arguments are indispensable," he asserts, borrowing Kant by way of illustration.

But before utility can be acceptable to intuitionists it must first be made presentable, vulgar controversy having beclouded its pristine glory. And some sort of proof must be offered in its behalf. So Mill has his work laid out for him.

Launching into the first part of his program, he provides in chapter two a brisk run-through of the principal misconceptions concerning utility—including, incidentally, those of its friends as well as its enemies. Now at last Mill has his chance to differ with both Bentham and Whewell.

Leading off with the notion that utilitarians advocate the starkly useful rather than the enjoyable, Mill swiftly dismisses the charge with a definition that links "pleasure" and "happiness"—an association that makes pleasure instantly more respectable:

> The creed which accepts as the foundation of morals, Utility, or the Greatest Happiness Principle, holds that actions are right in proportion as they tend to promote happiness, wrong as they tend to produce the reverse of happiness. By happiness is intended pleasure, and the absence of pain; by unhappiness, pain, and the privation of pleasure.

A succinct definition, to be sure. And if it takes Mill the rest of the chapter to elucidate it, that is partly because he is using the opportunity to advance his own brand of utility.

Immediately he answers the formidable charge of pig philosophy. Is utility a siren call to sensual pleasure? Not at all: there are the pleasures of a Socrates and the pleasures of a pig—and Mill is firmly on the side of Socrates. So firmly in fact that he insists it is compatible with utility to hold that some pleasures are qualitatively better than others. Further, those who have tasted both higher and lower pleasures markedly prefer the former. This moral elite can judge which pleasures are higher. Knowing the difference between human happiness and bestial pleasures, they can serve as moral guides to average humanity. "It is better to be a human being dissatisfied," Mill concludes dramatically, "than a pig satisfied; better to be Socrates dissatisfied than a fool satisfied. And if the fool, or the pig, is of a different opinion, it is because they only know their own side of the question." A dazzling display of rhetorical fireworks, the passage no doubt helped rescue utilitarians from the pigsties to which most Victorians had mentally consigned them.

But of course it raises problems, and later critics have been nothing loath to tussle with them. The major question is whether Mill has burst the Benthamite framework altogether. How, ask many critics, can an ethic based on calculating the *quantity* of pleasure and pain accommodate a notion which distinguishes their *quality?* If pleasure-happiness is the highest good, how can Mill distinguish between "higher" and "lower" pleasures without dragging in something else as the highest good by which to differentiate them? For other critics, this is no insuperable problem. Both Bentham and James Mill, they insist, talked of higher pleasures, though they envisioned ways of quantifying those qualities. Similarly, Mill's higher pleasures can also be translated into quantifiable terms, if need be. A mental pleasure of rational benevolence, as compared with a physical one of hedonistic indulgence, produces a happiness more lasting, less mixed with pain, and more productive of general happiness.

Still others, taking Mill at his word on the quality of pleasures, argue that happiness must be keyed to the being who experiences it. The pleasures of Socrates, not those of the fool or the pig, are the real pleasures of a developing human being. It is not that Mill has introduced a good greater than pleasure so much as a new concept of the person experiencing pleasure. For a developed person, virtue is pleasure, despite the discomforts it may occasion. Thus, for this person, a seemingly smaller quantity of a higher pleasure may be said to outweigh a larger quantity of a lower one. And since individual development is the best way to achieve the greatest happiness of the greatest number (virtuous people being notable for their benevolence to others), Mill's new vision of people dovetails neatly with the old Benthamite criterion of morality.

Whatever Mill's success in getting his new wine into the old utilitarian wineskins (and the point is still hotly disputed), the psychological effect of the effort is enormous. To nerves rattled by Bentham's seeming flippancy toward human values ("Quantity of pleasure being equal, push-pin is as good as poetry"), Mill's high-minded distinction between Socrates and the pig brings reassuring balm.

Mill next tackles the question of whether happiness is really man's highest good. Since Carlyle had been advancing the point as an objection to utilitarianism, Mill throws in a few lines of *Sartor Resartus*'s pulpit oratory: "What right hast thou to be happy? . . . What right, a short time ago, hadst thou even *to be?*" In less dramatic terms, the objection is: since happiness in this life is impossible, people should cultivate renunciation and heroic dedication to duty. But, Mill insists, this exaggerates the case. Clearly, a life of ceaseless rapture is out of the question, but a moderately happy existence is within the grasp of many—and with some social reforms it might be within the grasp of most. Renunciation and heroism are virtues—but only if they contribute to the greater happiness of humanity. Otherwise they are empty asceticism. Swept on by this challenge of the future, Mill out-Carlyles Carlyle with a stirring portrait of utilitarians amid the battle for human betterment. By the time he has finished, he has stolen much of Carlyle's thunder—moral as well as rhetorical.

Gaining momentum, Mill weeds out a variety of other objections. Can we expect people always to act for the greatest happiness of humanity? We don't have to: acts not harmful to others can be performed for any reason, and in most cases one need think only of those affected by his act—not of the whole world. Though, Mill adds, if the act belongs to a class which, if practiced generally, would be harmful, then it must be avoided. Doesn't utility chill people's sympathies, making them rigidly obsessed with morality? Not if they cultivate their feelings and artistic perceptions along with their moral sentiments. Isn't utility a godless doctrine? Not if we believe in a God who wills the greatest happiness of his creatures. And, finally, how can utility work when there often isn't time to calculate consequences? Casting scorn on this hoary remonstrance, Mill offers a crucial modification of old-style utility:

There is no difficulty in proving any ethical standard whatever to work ill, if we suppose universal idiocy to be conjoined with it; but on any hypothesis short of that, mankind must by this time have acquired positive beliefs as to the effects of some actions on their happiness; and the beliefs which have thus come down are the rules of morality for the multitude, and for the philosopher until he has succeeded in finding better.

At one stroke Mill has made utility more conservative. Though not infallible, the axioms of traditional morality are accepted as useful moral guidelines—at least until moralists have succeeded in bringing them closer into line with the primary goal of promoting the general happiness. It is a *tour de force* reconciliation of Coleridgean traditionalism and Benthamite progressivism.

Finally Mill answers those references to human weakness that are frequently entered as evidence against utility. Yes, utilitarians are liable to talk themselves into self-serving acts that harm others. But intuitionists can as easily talk themselves into self-serving intuitions. Indeed, a person adhering to any moral code whatever can perform similar ethical gymnastics. Mill is not throwing dust in our eyes, as F. H. Bradley charged. He is merely pointing out that an objection raised against utility is one that can be brought against any other moral code.

After all the negativism, Mill rounds off the chapter positively with a reference to the well-tempered utilitarian, solving commonplace moral questions with commonsense morality and, in stickier situations, appealing to the first principle of general happiness. The tangle of arguments has at last resolved itself in moral confidence.

Now that Mill has cleared away the misconceptions that distorted utility, the next question is: can it work? Is it strong enough to motivate people as effectively as old-time religious beliefs? If belief in God and the afterlife fail (and such belief seemed to be failing fast in Mill's day), what can replace it as a source of ethical motivation?

Any self-respecting Victorian knew the answer to that one—Duty. Of the "inspiring trumpet-calls of men,—the words *God, Immortality, Duty*—," said Mary Ann Evans ("George Eliot"), "how inconceivable was the *first*, how unbelievable was the *second*, and yet how peremptory and absolute the *third*." Nor is Victorian duty by any means an absurd fossil; transformed into "love of humanity," "commitment," "getting involved," or whatever the going phrase is, it remains a powerful moral force in the modern world.

Mill orchestrates this "ultimate sanction" of utility in chapter three, conducting a stately largo on the theme of "the internal sanction of duty"—that feeling in the mind which, when highly cultivated, becomes the strongest of all moral forces. If Mill's logic cannot exactly prove duty's emotive power, his prose can suggest it—as it does eloquently, building to a finale of sober grandeur.

Of course it would ruin the solemnity of the occasion for Mill to start a row with intuitionists, so he is willing to let them believe that moral feelings are innate, so long as they will concede that the aim of such feelings is the greatest happiness of our fellow creatures. But if moral feelings are acquired, as Mill believes, then it makes sense (he argues) to reform society and education lest those feelings be distorted or eroded. "There is hardly anything so absurd or so mischievous," he warns, "that it may not . . . be made to act on the human mind with all the authority of conscience." Nor must the sentiment of fellow feeling be analyzed away, but nourished continually. (As might be expected, this passage in *Utilitarianism* reads like a theoretical replay of the mental crisis.) Luckily, the rise of greater social equality tends to cement the association between personal and general happiness. Presenting the other side of the coin explored in *On Liberty*, *Utilitarianism* hymns the harmony of individual and society. Though even here Mill staunchly insists upon equality of individuals within the society, and the mere mention of Comte is enough to start him off on a sermonette against social oppression.

Turning from the reasons of the heart to those of the head, Mill in chapter four sets out to demonstrate "Of What Sort of Proof the Principle of Utility is Susceptible." A worthy aim, and in his simplicity he could hardly have foreseen that responses to this modest little chapter would swell to gargantuan proportions in the subsequent history of moral philosophy. "So obvious does this appear to me," he remarks of one of his arguments in the chapter, "that I expect it will hardly be disputed." Unsuspecting soul. Almost nothing in this chapter has escaped being disputed, defended, explained, and reinterpreted *ad infinitum*.

In considering what sort of proof he can offer for utility, Mill is picking up where he had left off in the last chapter of *A System of Logic*. There, he had pictured Art as defining ultimate aims, aims not amenable to scientific proof. The Good, the Wise, and the Beautiful cannot be verified by the Scientist, however helpful he may be in providing means to achieve those exalted ends once the Artist has defined them. Still, the Artist's choices would be disturbingly arbitrary were it not that they conform to general premises sorting out what things are "worthy and desirable" and fitting them into "the scale of desirable things." These general premises are to make up the Art of Life which, alas, is largely uncreated at present. So any "proof" of ultimate aims right now is a chancy business at best.

Mill had said as much early in *Utilitarianism:* "Questions of ultimate ends are not amenable to direct proof." Still, their selection need not be left to the haphazard mercies of "blind impulse" or "arbitrary choice." There are "considerations" which may be presented, "capable of determining the intellect either to give or withhold its assent to the doctrine; and this is equivalent to proof." Anyone complaining that Mill's proof is logically unsatisfactory can hardly say he wasn't warned beforehand.

Three paragraphs into chapter four Mill begins his momentous proof:

> The only proof capable of being given that an object is visible, is that people actually see it. The only proof that a sound is audible, is that people hear it: and so of the other sources of our experience. In like manner, I apprehend, the sole evidence it is possible to produce that anything is desirable, is that people do actually desire it.

Long exhibited as a trophy of Mill's muddled thinking, the passage supposedly confuses the desirable (the good, what is worthy of being desired) with the desired (what is actually desired). Thus, anything anyone desires is a good. "Is it merely a tautology when the Prayer Book talks of *good* desires?" G. E. Moore asks. "Are not *bad* desires also possible?" But recent defenders have argued that Mill is not *defining* the desirable or the good in this passage; rather he is offering a proof or a test for determining that something is a good. And certainly one test of a good is that it is desired. Not that everything desired is good, but that a good can be known by at least somebody's desiring it. Who ever heard of a good that nobody desired?

But is Mill's analogy a disanalogy? Can he legitimately leap from the visible and the audible to the desirable? "But *visible, audible* mean what *can* be seen or heard," according to one famous critique of the passage, "whereas Mill is trying to prove that happiness *ought to be* desired, or is the thing *worth* desiring." Well, perhaps not. Mill's point may be that a proof or test of the desirable (the good) *is* that somebody desires it. If so, he has not made a forbidden leap from *is* to *ought*.

But this, alas, is only the beginning of the paragraph, and if possible matters get more tangled toward the end:

> No reason can be given why the general happiness is desirable, except that each person, so far as he believes it to be attainable, desires his own happiness. This, however, being a fact, we have not only all the proof which the case admits of, but all which it is possible to require, that happiness is a good: that each person's happiness is a good to that person, and the general happiness, therefore, a good to the aggregate of all persons.

Here's a how-de-do. How can Mill get from our personal happiness (which we know is desirable from consulting our consciousness) to the general happiness? Doesn't individual happiness frequently conflict with general happiness? And hasn't Mill leaped (again?) from *what is* (we do desire our own happiness) to *what ought to be* (we ought to desire the general happiness)?

Perhaps nothing short of a small volume could hope to sort through this mare's nest, but a few observations may tidy up things a bit. First, it takes little reflection, Mill indicates, for each person to recognize that his own happiness is a good. Next, as he commented in 1868, "since A's happiness is a good, B's a good, C's a good, etc., the sum of all these goods must be a good." Whatever problems lie ensnarled within this argument, Mill apparently has not leaped from *is* to *ought*. His point seems to be that, if we reflect a little, we will recognize that our own happiness *is* a good, and if we consider the matter sanely we will conclude that the general happiness *is* a good. Though hardly formal proof, this is a "consideration" to move the intellect toward assent.

The worst is over, but all is not smooth sailing yet. Mill has indicated that happiness is a good; he now has to demonstrate, as the chapter proceeds, that it is the only good. And immediately he faces a palpable contradiction: people desire money, power, and even virtue, as well as happiness. But, Mill counters, these other things are originally desired as means to happiness, and eventually—through the magic of association—they become *part* of happiness. "Happiness is not an abstract idea, but a concrete whole; and these are some of its parts." But virtue, because it so directly fosters the general happiness, is especially to be cultivated by utilitarians until it becomes an integral part of their individual happiness. Thus Mill can say that virtue is desirable for itself. And if these considerations leave strict logicians blinking, they are likely to score points with strict moralists.

A final demur is quickly quashed. Yes, people can form habits and go on willing something they no longer desire—or desire only because they will it. But this merely proves what Mill admits: will and desire are not the same thing. All the more reason, then, to train the will aright, lest the person be left habitually willing what he no longer desires for itself. The will to virtue may begin in desire but is confirmed in habit. "Will is the child of desire, and passes out of the dominion of its parent only to come under that of habit"—a sentence that, translated into personal terms, traces the outline of Mill's *Autobiography*.

Though confident that "the doctrine of utility is proved," Mill concludes the chapter with: "Whether it is so or not, must now be left to the consideration of the thoughtful reader." The word "consideration" brings us back to where we started, back to those "considerations capable of determining the intellect." And if the intellect is given adequate considerations, the will (so Mill believes) will be directed toward the greatest happiness principle. And that is the only reason why he ventured into this thicket of proof at all.

If chapter five ("On the Connexion Between Justice and Utility") now reads like an epilogue to the rest of *Utilitarianism*, it apparently was at one time a separate essay and was first published as an individual installment in *Fraser's*. The problem Mill takes up here (somehow justice seems to be something more solemn than the idea of merely promoting the general happiness) is treated as yet another objection to utility. Predictably, he argues that the concept of justice does not originate in intuitions, revelations, or innate moral senses; rather it is a natural outgrowth of human nature and experience. But the trick here is to point out the natural origins of justice without diminishing its grandeur and importance. And, in the process, to demonstrate that the utilitarian can take justice as seriously as any intuitionist.

The bulk of the chapter consists of an almost painfully thorough inquiry into the nature of justice. After much sifting of ideas, Mill finds justice linked with a cluster of notions—legal rights, moral rights, giving a person his due, not breaking faith, being impartial to others. Even the word's etymology is scrutinized and found to link the idea of justice with conformity to law. Injustice, then, involves a wrong done to some assignable person or persons. Justice is concerned with acts we ought to perform because someone else's rights are involved. Other acts (like giving money to the poor) may be admirable, but failure to perform them does not involve the violation of anyone's rights. Further, acts of injustice, we feel, ought to be punished—a feeling that Mill explains as the "spontaneous outgrowth" of our impulse of self-defense and our sense of sympathy with others. However powerful, this "natural feeling of retaliation or vengeance" must be moralized through intellect and emotion. When it is, it will be directed toward injuries that hurt us through or in common with society at large. In short, matters of justice require the individual to turn his attention from merely personal concerns to more universalized ones. And since the very security of individual and society are at stake in these matters, the emotions attaching to justice will be—understandably and properly—strong ones.

Though justice has been accounted for in natural (even utilitarian) terms, the powerful emotions surrounding it are thus fully justified. So, retuning his rhetorical orchestra, Mill closes *Utilitarianism* with a grand symphony of prose hymning the stern demands of justice.

Though it looks tacked on, *Utilitarianism*'s final chapter shows its kinship with the earlier ones by pulling off effects similar to theirs. Here again is that sense of returning to where one started—but the journey has made significant changes. A reference to Bentham late in chapter five, for example, gracefully recalls the origins of Mill's ethical thought, while underlining how significantly it has branched from its Benthamite roots. As in earlier chapters, there is here a sense of puzzling questions yielding to credible answers, of cacophony yielding to harmony.

Above all, in *Utilitarianism* the originally implausible idea of an effective humanist ethic gradually grows credible. As Mill's voice, alternately stern and gracious, takes its effect, the humanism for which he speaks seems increasingly capable of providing a morality as exalted as any the world has known before.

Even before *Utilitarianism* appeared, Mill's life had been turning into second spring.

As his old amiability reblossomed, he dropped in on George and

Harriet Grote for the first time in sixteen years and reopened correspondence with Gustave d'Eichthal after a twenty-one-year hiatus. The house at Blackheath Park, after almost a decade of musty seclusion, now took on a convivial glow. With Harriet gone, it was safe to throw open the sanctuary to friendly eyes.

CHAPTER TEN

MEMBER FOR WESTMINSTER:
Works of the Middle Sixties

A politician thinks of the next election and a statesman thinks of the next generation.
—JAMES FREEMAN CLARKE

 BEING invited to one of Mill's five o'clock dinners became the new badge of intellectual status. The knot of favored guests set out from Charing Cross and, after a speedy ride by rail, found Mill awaiting them on the Blackheath platform. During the ten-minute walk to the house, Mill played the perfect host, graciously priming his guests for the exhilarating table talk to follow. Presiding airily over the feast of reason was Helen Taylor, now exuding all the cool graciousness of an established household goddess. If some visitors were taken aback by the weight Mill attached to her words, none was foolhardy enough to betray suspicions in his presence.

Besides old friends like the Grotes and the Bains, guests were apt to include Victorian giants like T. H. Huxley and Herbert Spencer, as well as Mill's new following of younger men whose names were to become renowned in afteryears—John Elliott Cairnes, as kindly an economist as Ricardo had been; Henry Fawcett, sublimely undeterred by being blinded in a hunting accident; Theodor Gomperz, Mill's German translator, whose affection for Helen Taylor went unrequited; John Morley, soon to be editor of the *Fortnightly Review* and Mill's heir-designate in the cause of liberal reform. Unquestionably, the most scintillating new disciples were young Lord and Lady Amberley, brilliant and short-lived. Their third child—precocious little Bertrand Russell—began life with the distinction of having John and Helen as his godparents.

If Mill's character was mellowing with age, his enthusiasm in a noble cause had lost none of its youthful verve. Given his abhorrence of slavery, it is easy to guess where his sympathies lay when the American Civil War broke out in 1861. But to his horror the *Trent* affair pushed Britain and the North to the brink of open warfare with each other, while English upper-class sentiment veered dangerously pro-Southern. In a furious effort to reverse the trend, Mill pulled out all the rhetorical stops for "The Contest in America" (*Fraser's*, February 1862). After smoothing feathers ruffled by the *Trent* episode, the article went on the offensive with eloquent appeals to British antislavery feeling. In a situation so fraught with peril, Mill dispensed with the niceties. "It will be desirable to take thought beforehand," he remarked of the Confederacy, "what are to be our own future relations with a New Power, professing the principles of Attila and Genghis Khan." Proving himself no pacifist, he closed the article with ringing support for just wars. "War is an ugly thing, but not the ugliest of things: the decayed and degraded state of moral and patriotic feeling which thinks nothing *worth* a war, is worse."

Having redeemed the moment, Mill felt it safe for Helen and himself to leave for a holiday in Greece. But no sooner was he back than he sprang into action again, this time in the *Westminster* with a strongly supportive review of Cairnes's *The Slave Power*, which blamed the American war on the slave states. Mill was always gratified to think his articles had helped prevent English intervention in the war. And when it was all over, not even the catastrophe of Lincoln's assassination could diminish his sense of triumph. "Lincoln is a glorious martyr if ever there was one," he wrote to a friend. "He is not to be pitied—to be envied rather. One's feeling is all personal—it is as if a ruffianly assassin had deprived one of a dear personal friend. I do not believe the cause will suffer."

Mill's intellectual life was also astir. In 1865 two new major works appeared—*Auguste Comte and Positivism* and *An Examination of Sir William Hamilton's Philosophy*. They were his "Bentham" and "Coleridge" of the sixties.

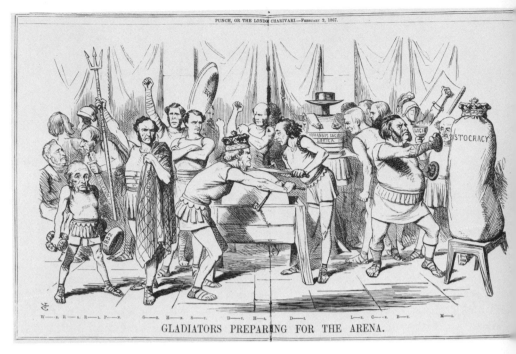

GLADIATORS PREPARING FOR THE ARENA.

Gladiators Preparing for the Arena. Punch, 2 February 1867. *Punch* takes a look at the 1867 parliamentary factions. In the left foreground, liberal Lord John Russell lifts weights, while Gladstone holds aloft his trident. In the center, conservative Lord Derby turns the grindstone for Benjamin Disraeli who sharpens his sword edge. To the right, radical John Bright takes another jab at the aristocratic punching bag, while (behind) Mill fortifies himself with the cup of logic.

He had been introduced to Comte's work in 1829, when d'Eichthal was trying to win his soul for Saint-Simonism. But Mill was wary—much in Comte was brilliant, much absurd. He was to return to this verdict in later years, but meanwhile in 1837 the first two volumes of Comte's monumental *Cours de Philosophie Positive* filled him with almost unbounded enthusiasm. Hailing it as "one of the most profound books ever written on the philosophy of the sciences," he eagerly incorporated many of its insights into the *Logic*.

So carried away was he that in 1841 he threw out the bait of an adulatory letter to the author. It hooked a queer fish indeed. Rancorous, brilliant, messianic—Comte had early quarreled with Saint-Simon, then gone on to expound his dazzling philosophy of positivism. Soon he would dream dreams of reigning as Grand Pontiff in the new Religion of Humanity he intended to found. Initially convinced that

(184)

Mill was profferring his services as disciple, Comte was soon vexed by his worshiper's obstinate independence of thought. For his part, Mill discovered that his hero's views of psychology, education, economics, the family, and women were as reactionary as those of any purblind Tory intuitionist. Still, he kept on doggedly with the correspondence, patiently explaining his ideas, gently commiserating with Comte's mounting misfortunes—unhappy marriage, loss of teaching position, and the death of Clotilde de Vaux, with whom Comte had known a year of platonic passion. Though his own finances had suffered a reversal, Mill set about raising funds for the distressed philosopher. But in 1847 their correspondence trickled out. And not a moment too soon. As Comte's later works appeared in the early fifties, Mill discovered that the errors and arrogance had grown perfectly baroque. When the Pontiff himself was gathered to Humanity's bosom in 1857, his reputation flourished sufficiently thereafter to prompt Mill's public assessment of him—as yet another seminal thinker whose promise had been greater than his performance.

Divided into two sections, *Auguste Comte and Positivism* sweeps from the extraordinary to the extravagant. The book's general direction can be plotted from the word "great," repeated often during the early part, to the word "ridiculous," which ends the essay. In short, anticlimax is again the order of the day.

Early on, Comte is placed among the elect for espousing phenomenalism of the kind Mill regards as the scientific way of viewing things. All we can discern of reality are its various phenomena; intuition gives us no glimpses into the essences of external reality. Other philosophers had seen as much, but Comte's glory was to fit this mode of thought into a stunning historical survey. Humanity, he taught, passed through three stages—the Theological, in which the universe was seen as governed by spirits, gods, and finally a God; the Metaphysical, in which these supernatural beings were replaced by semiliving abstractions, such as Nature, essences, and vital principles; and the Positive, in which phenomena are scientifically observed and used to predict future occurrences. These three stages have always existed simultaneously, though at any given time in the past, one had dominated. Thus, ancient times and the Middle Ages were Theological. Since then, the times had been Metaphysical. Now the Positive age was dawning.

But Comte topped even this splendid insight with his classification of the sciences. Not content with merely distinguishing one science from another, he placed them in a sequence which showed how one

Auguste Comte

science developed from previous ones, how in the course of time one area of thought after another became truly positive, that is, truly scientific. Thus, once the truths of number (arithmetic and algebra) were established, geometry was possible, then mechanics. In turn came astronomy, physics, chemistry, biology, and—in the fullness of time—sociology, the science of human phenomena.

Mill enthusiastically champions these perceptions, sparring vigorously in footnote and text with Herbert Spencer's demurs. How damaging, then, when Comte's defender begins entering demurs of his own. Comte supplies no test of proof for the sciences, Mill complains. He ignores syllogistic deduction. Dismissing psychology as a science, he offers instead phrenology! Nor does he rate political economy as a science. He is politically short-sighted, passing off democratic views as a mere bubble of the Metaphysical brain. He fears diversity of opinion. Worse, he believes in the indissolubility of marriage. After years of patronizing women as grown children, he has latterly taken to revering them as goddesses. As Part I ends, the way has been prepared for the withering revelations of Part II.

In this section, "The Later Speculations of M. Comte," one has the feeling of sinking under an accumulation of absurdities and outrages. In Comte's later works, positive philosophy has been metamorphosed into the Religion of Humanity—to which Mill has no objection, being a regular worshiper at the same shrine. But Comte's mania for "unity" and "systemization" has transformed the religion into an extravaganza of thought control and despotism. As Mill portrays it, Comtean sociology becomes a nightmare of sociolatry, with Comte as Pontiff resembling a fearful cross between Big Brother and the Grand Inquisitor. "Others may laugh," Mill concludes, "but we could far rather weep at this melancholy decadence of a great intellect."

Like "Bentham," *Comte* studies a half-thinker, while Mill's persona exemplifies the whole thinker. Once again, the most absurd aspects of the half-truths are left till last. Even some of the specific criticisms sound familiar: Comte failed to learn from others, he tried to formulate a philosophy for the whole man from his own too-slender resources, he was concerned only with the morality of acts while ignoring their other qualities.

The few passages concerning Clotilde de Vaux merit special attention. Comte's idealizing her intellect and virtue, his worship of her memory—both are perfectly acceptable to Mill, who had been engaged in much the same pursuits in his affair with Harriet. He regrets only that Clotilde lacked the intellect Comte attributed to her. Were she really so perceptive (he seems to suggest), she would have curbed her lover's rage for authoritarian order, as Harriet had done for him during the thirties and forties. Though worshiping Clotilde's memory is a legitimate private ritual, Mill feels that imposing similar practices upon the rest of humanity smacks of religious coercion. A mismatch of thinker and poet, Comte and Clotilde stand in contrast to the shining example of John and Harriet in the *Autobiography*.

An Examination of Sir William Hamilton's Philosophy treats still another disappointing half-thinker. Unfortunately, a rather lackluster one too. Not that Mill had always seen him that way. Initially he had been beguiled by Sir William's reputation into believing him another Coleridge, an enlightened member of the opposition from whom valuable insights could be culled. But further reading was a jolt. "I was not prepared," he wrote Bain, "for the degree in which this complete acquaintance lowers my estimate of the man and of his speculations. I did not expect to find them a mass of contradictions." Still, having got so far, Mill decided to go the whole distance with a full-fledged study that would expound some matters left deficient in the *Logic*, while providing occasion for another polemic on behalf of experientialism. Of course such a plan required more spacious dimensions. And so Mill's study of Hamilton grew from an article into a two-volume colossus, swelling to even greater proportions in later editions as Mill answered its numerous critics.

Throughout the book's protracted examination, Mill generally avoids the sort of acid commentary that had made his father's *Fragment on Mackintosh* a model of corrosive vehemence. Patiently he sifts through Hamilton's contradictions, and methodically expounds his own view of the truth. If he often seems to be chewing more than he bit off, the effect at least reinforces his persona's thoroughness of thought. Having accused Sir William of intellectual carelessness, Mill attempts to prove to the point of exhaustion his own innocence of the same charge.

To be sure, *Hamilton* gets off to a promising start. Discussing Sir William's theory of "the relativity of human knowledge," Mill quotes him as apparently on the side of the phenomenalists. The mind knows only the phenomena of external objects, Hamilton pronounces; of things in themselves, it knows nothing. So far so good. Then, in a sudden reversal, he throws all overboard, insisting that we have intuitive knowledge of both self and nonself. Intuitive knowledge of the ego Mill would buy, but not of the non-ego. This was the sort of intuitionism he had been battling since youth. And how can Hamilton reconcile his phenomenalism with his intuitionism? He can't, Mill concludes after a lengthy investigation.

From this point matters get progressively worse. There is Sir William's "Philosophy of the Conditioned." Human knowledge is relative or "conditioned," he argues; yet the mind knows that certain things, though inconceivable, are true. Space, for example, is either limited or unlimited. Both propositions are inconceivable, yet one must be true. Thus, faced with two equally inconceivable alternatives, one of which must be true, the mind must fall back on faith to decide.

As applied to religious thought, this line of reasoning produced results that exasperated Mill. According to Henry Mansel, one of Hamilton's disciples, God's goodness is one of those inconceivables, having little or no resemblance to what we understand by human

Sir William Hamilton

goodness. In fact, many things that strike us as evil deeds, if performed by God, would be good. Mill was furious. Summoning up a Lutherlike defiance ("Here, then, I take my stand . . ."), he concludes with a thundering declamation that would have done his father proud: "I will call no being good, who is not what I mean when I apply that epithet to my fellow-creatures; and if such a being can sentence me to hell for not so calling him, to hell I will go."

No doubt this blaze of indignation owed something to the fact that his old friend F. D. Maurice had lately crossed swords with Mansel. In any event, it gives *Hamilton* its liveliest moments and demonstrates anew that, for all his intellectual tolerance, Mill can still muster outrage for "the most morally pernicious doctrine now current."

After dissecting to death the "introspective" or intuitive view of matter, Mill rehearses once again the "psychological" or associationist view. Again he insists that the laws of mental association can account for our belief in external reality. Experience of phenomena coheres in a mental pattern that suggests a world outside us, operating on its own. Still, we have no intuitive knowledge of things in themselves; all we have to go on are the sensations that phenomena excite in us. On this view of things, matter becomes "a Permanent Possibility of Sensation." And mind is "the Permanent Possibility of feeling, which forms my notion of Myself." This view, he is quick to argue, need not rule out belief in fellow creatures, in God, and even in immortality. But there are peculiarities about mind that puzzle Mill. Memory and expectation are especially mysterious. Yet they are crucial, for the mind not only receives sensations but "is aware of itself as past and future." And how to account for this quirk of inner reality Mill abandons as inexplicable.

By the time he reaches volume two, Mill's patience is fraying a bit, but he plods on as equitably as possible, moving from psychology to logic, explicating Hamilton's lapses, fixing his own views as carefully as he can. Toward the end, the question of free will and determinism gets another go-round, Mansel having misunderstood his position in the *Logic*. In the concluding remarks, Hamilton's reputation is left dismally diminished. As charitably as he can, Mill tries to puzzle out what went wrong in his thought. Perhaps Hamilton was too dedicated to the free will doctrine to think about it clearly. Certainly his imagination failed him: while he often knew other thinkers' positions in great detail, he had trouble looking at the world through their eyes. As a result, he was forever missing the forest for the trees.

Though hardly pulse-stirring fare, *Hamilton* is a must for Mill specialists, providing a sort of stereoptic view of his position on a number of crucial issues discussed elsewhere in his work. If most other readers find it slow going, the problem is partly that Hamilton (at least as Mill portrays him) is no Coleridge—nor Bentham nor Comte. Lacking a first-rate mind to react to, Mill spends much of the book elaborately breaking a butterfly upon a wheel.

Shortly before *Hamilton* appeared in print, Mill received a head-spinning inquiry from one James Beal, Radical electioneering reformist. With a general election upcoming, Westminster Liberals had decided during February 1865 to solicit an eminent man as candidate for one of Westminster's two available seats. Would Mill be willing to stand as a candidate should there be sufficient support among electors to nominate him?

It was almost too good to be true. How Mill had wished he and his father were in Parliament back in the thirties. But their positions at India House had precluded that. Now here was his chance. But then second thoughts crept in. Did he really want to upset the comfortable routine of his life? And weren't his writings more important for future improvement than anything he could do in Parliament? Still, it was an opportunity to assert the claims of the future in the national forum. All in all, Mill thought he would be willing to be a candidate—but only on certain conditions.

The conditions were spelled out in a letter to Beal. If elected, Mill would not undertake to push any local interests in Parliament. His opinions were in his writings for all to see; those opinions he would support, but other than that he would make no promises to electors. Since he didn't approve of personal campaign spending, he wouldn't spend anything on his campaign. Indeed, he wouldn't campaign at all, though he would answer questions about his views. It was, as Mill described it, "one of the frankest explanations ever tendered, I should think, to an electoral body by a candidate." Quipped one incredulous wag: Not even the Almighty could get elected on such a program!

But the letter was printed in the *Daily News* of March 23, and its candor caused a sensation. Not only was Mill's nomination assured, but a run on his books began, with even the elephantine *Hamilton* doing a brisk business. A subscription was started to defray campaign costs, and a committee undertook to drum up support. True to his word, however, Mill refused to campaign. To his backers' horror, he slipped off to southern France, and not even their most urgent appeals could drag him home. Enemies leaped at the opportunity. The whispers started—he was devoted to population control, his defiance of Mansel's God reeked of atheism, he was chief of the Satanic School. Though surprisingly few citizens were stampeded by these charges, Mill's supporters were thrown into panic. At last he yielded to their entreaties and landed back in England—with less than two weeks to go before election day.

With the candidate at last on the scene, the curious noncampaign came to a zany finale. Mill allowed himself to be hauled off to several meetings, and all went well until the evening he appeared before an assemblage of workingmen. (Though not voters, workers were allowed to look over the candidates.) During the program, someone passed Mill a placard with embarrassing words from his *Thoughts on Parliamentary Reform*: "The higher classes do not lie, and the lower, though mostly habitual liars, are ashamed of lying." The candidate was asked: Did you write that?

Mill replied, "I did."

For a second the audience was thunderstruck. Not because the speaker had written the offending words, but because he had openly admitted it to them—without equivocation, without excuse. A moment later and cheers were resounding everywhere. One workingman rose to declare stoutly that his people wanted no flatterers, but friends who would tell them their faults. The crisis had passed off in triumph.

On July 12 Mill and the other Liberal candidate were elected with comfortable margins over the Tory candidate.

After all the bustle of election, Parliament delayed until February 1866 before convening. By then two events of the previous October had determined its principal preoccupations. "The two great topics of the year," Mill declared, "will be Jamaica and Reform." And in that order too, as far as he was concerned. "There is no part of it all, not even the Reform Bill, more important than the duty of dealing justly with the abominations committed in Jamaica."

What abominations? On the island colony of Jamaica, Carlyle's Quashee, instead of lolling up to his muzzle in pumpkins, often found himself in straitened circumstances due to social and political disabilities. Antagonism between blacks and the ruling white minority erupted into violence at the little town of Morant Bay early in October 1865 when about 400 Negroes clashed with the local volunteer guards. Twenty-one men, mostly whites, were killed. The island's governor, a former Australian explorer and administrator Edward John Eyre, sailed to Morant Bay, where his forces promptly quelled the disturbance with hangings and floggings. All dangers of a full-scale uprising (if any had existed) were now past, but Eyre apparently decided to quench any lingering revolutionary embers. Keeping martial law in force, he turned his men loose in an orgy of hanging, shooting, flogging, and house burning that raged for a month. The governor himself saw a rare opportunity to rid himself of a virulent critic, the mulatto George William Gordon. He arrested Gordon in Kingston (which was not under martial law), shipped him to Morant Bay (which was), had him improperly tried, sentenced, and hanged. By early November Eyre's vengeance had claimed over 400 lives.

As word of the atrocities filtered back to England, Victorian teacups began to rattle. Before long, the nation was divided into two hostile camps, one defending Eyre's law-and-order, the other denouncing it as brutal overreaction. Mill was prominent among the latter group. Besides the all too obvious racism motivating Eyre and his supporters, he was appalled at the idea of a British official's suspending civil law on a trumped-up threat of insurrection. If this were allowed to pass, no British citizen's rights were secure. Determined to punish Eyre judicially, Mill took command of a newly formed Jamaica Committee whose aims included removing the governor from office and prosecuting him for murder. Naturally, an Eyre Defense Committee sprang up, and naturally its first meetings were chaired by Carlyle, whose hero worship had been growing progressively senile since the mid-forties. But the burdens of age soon led him to turn over the reins to John Ruskin, whose brilliant mind (be it noted in extenuation) had lately become none too steady. Throughout his parliamentary career, Mill strove implacably to bring Eyre to justice. In time, the governor was removed from office, but the murder charge was dismissed. Mill went after his underlings, but with no success. In afteryears a Liberal government paid Eyre's court fees and voted him a pension, leaving Mill disgustedly wishing for a return of the Tories. Still, something had been salvaged from the debacle. "Colonial Governors and other persons in authority," he assured himself in the *Autobiography*, "will have a considerable motive to stop short of such extremities in future."

The question of parliamentary reform had also been transformed by an event of the previous October: Lord Palmerston's death had removed the last great roadblock to a new reform bill.

Gathering unsteady momentum since 1832, the drive to enfranchise the working classes had lurched to another of its climaxes in the mid-sixties. Under the Liberal leadership of Lord John Russell and William Ewart Gladstone, a mild reform bill was introduced in March 1866. Mill spoke in its behalf, but a band of disgruntled Liberals joined with Conservatives to torpedo it. When Russell and Gladstone resigned, a Tory government under Lord Derby and Benjamin Disraeli was formed. The national reform mood grew noticeably nastier.

As the demonstrations multiplied, the Reform League scheduled a monster rally for July 23 in Hyde Park at 7 P.M. The government decided to close the park at five. On the fateful day, 69,000 demonstrators converged on Hyde Park, only to find it ringed with railings and police. Before the crowd could be nudged on to Trafalgar Square, some of its less orderly elements tore up a mile of railings, capered across the grass, and completed the outrage by trampling some flowerbeds. Next day, when an angry League deputation protested the park's closing to the Home Secretary, the distraught official burst into tears—a display of emotion so disconcerting that it somehow convinced the reformists they had obtained permission to hold another

"FOR THE DEFENCE."

SHADE OF PALMERSTON. "BENJAMIN! BENJAMIN! *I* WOULDN'T HAVE LEFT HIM IN THE LURCH."

For the Defence. Punch, 6 June 1868. The ghost of Lord Palmerston, the late conservative prime minister, upbraids the new conservative leader, Benjamin Disraeli, for not defending Governor Eyre more vigorously.

rally in the park. When the government informed them of their error, it seemed as if defiant workingmen and government troops were set on a perilous collision course.

Positively frantic now, the Home Secretary prevailed upon Mill to head off the impending explosion, a diplomatic feat that Mill carried off with unusual aplomb by talking sense to League leaders and offering himself as crowd bait for another League assembly. "And I do not believe it could have been done," he observed with justifiable pride, "at that particular juncture, by any one else." Some time later when the government tried to legalize its power to close the park against unwelcome public gatherings, Mill and other liberals successfully filibustered it. Since then, of course, Hyde Park has become England's most famous haven of free speech.

Meanwhile, with reform fever still running high, Disraeli decided to pull off another of his dazzling coups. Insisting that Conservatives had a better claim to reform than Liberals did, he introduced in March 1867 a reform bill more sweeping than Gladstone's. In the melee of political maneuverings that followed, the bill underwent such drastic alteration that, as the current witticism went, the only thing left intact was the word "whereas." What emerged was a bill far more radical yet. Even Mill was dazed by it all: "I never supposed that I should see such a Reform as this adopted in my life." It was nothing less than an epoch-making "leap in the dark." The entire middle class was now enfranchised, along with virtually all city workers. Nearly a million men were added to the electoral rolls. Overnight, England had become a democracy.

Of course Mill voted for the bill, though he had his reservations. He wanted women enfranchised as well as men. And he wanted safeguards against tyranny of the majority. "If 50,000 electors have to elect five members, it is not fair and equal representation that 30,000 of them should be able, by outvoting the others, to elect all five," he argued. "The 30,000 are only entitled to three members and the remaining 20,000 to two." But victory on these measures was hardly to be expected. "I look upon the House of Commons," he consoled himself, "... as an elevated Tribune or Chair from which to preach larger ideas than can at present be realised."

If '67 was the year of Reform, '68 was the year of the Irish question. Once again, Parliament had decided that something must be done about Ireland, and once again balked at doing it. Meanwhile, John Bull's other island was growing increasingly restive. Acts of violence

The riot in Hyde Park. "The Mob Pulling Down the Railings in Park Lane," *Illustrated London News*, Supplement, 4 August 1866.

and even a small revolt in 1867 had been touched off by the Fenian Brotherhood, a band of Irish-American émigrés. When two of the captured Fenians were condemned to death, Mill moved swiftly and successfully to have the sentence commuted. But that was a minor victory; more permanent reforms were needed to head off further trouble. Mill decided to meet the crisis head on. In February 1868 he published a fiery tract entitled *England and Ireland*, certainly one of the livelier contributions to the debate on Irish matters during the late sixties.

Written in his best popular style, the pamphlet bluntly accused England of past spoliation in Ireland and warned that, unless Parliament took drastic steps soon, nothing could save or justify the continued union of the two countries. Once again, Mill went to the heart of the problem, as he had been doing for more than forty years, since at least 1826, when his article "Ireland" appeared in the short-lived *Parliamentary History and Review*. British worship of landlordism had created intolerable problems for the impoverished Irish tenant farmer, whose rent could jump upward with every improvement he made on the land—land, incidentally, owned by someone most likely residing in England and doing nothing but collecting the fruits of his tenant's labor. Should the farmer grumble, his landlord could rapidly evict him and choose a ready replacement from Ireland's stock of semistarved peasants. Rooting out this enormity, Mill argued, would require a revolutionary measure, though not a violent or unjust one.

But the proposal would be a shock, and so Mill carefully prepared his audience for it. A bit of praise, first, for England's ability to rule India successfully in the context of Eastern institutions. Why not put the old British know-how to work in Ireland? Then an appalling alternative: was England really prepared to undertake a military occupation of Ireland? For it would come to that, Mill predicted. Next, some arguments to show he was no anti-British extremist: separation of the two countries was undesirable. Ireland especially had too much to lose, deprivation having rendered her unready for stable representative self-government. Finally, a call to justice: better that the Union should be broken than that England should persist in enforcing oppressive social arrangements:

> Let separation be ever so complete a failure, one thing it would do: it would convert the peasant farmers into peasant proprietors: and this one thing would be more than an equivalent for all that [Ireland] would lose.

Yes, peasant proprietorship was again the key to the problem. Formerly, Mill had suggested selecting the proprietors from Ireland's surplus population and setting them to work on uncultivated waste lands. Famine and emigration, alas, had taken care of much of the surplus population. Now the only thing for it was to convert the present tenants into proprietors right under their landlords' noses. And so Mill dropped his bombshell. "What is wanted in Ireland is a commission . . . to examine every farm which is let to a tenant, and commute the present variable for a fixed rent." Then the farmer would have some security against ever-rising rents, some interest in the land he worked, some reason for making improvements, some hope of bettering his lot. But of course Mill's proposal flew in the face of British superstitions concerning the sacredness of private property and the landlord's inviolable right to do as he liked with his own. Still, if Englishmen could not outgrow such idolatry, Mill was adamant about the Union: "It is our duty to retire from a country where a modification of the constitution of landed property is the primary necessity of social life." (A remark to remember, especially when one recent historian concludes an assessment of Mill on the Irish question by labeling him "a convinced 'imperialist.'") The pamphlet closes with a brief promise of harmony, but only if action is taken "in time permanently to reconcile the two countries."

Looking at the pamphlet nowadays, one is most struck by Mill's awareness that time was rapidly running out for the Union, that left to itself Ireland might well be torn apart by religious and civil wars. But back in 1868 *England and Ireland* was merely denounced as a treasonable tract. "Mill ought to be sent to penal servitude as a Fenian," blustered Lord Bessborough, himself an Irish landlord. The press was equally aghast. The *Saturday Review* labeled Mill "the most recent and most thoroughgoing apostle of Communism," while the *Times* accused him of teaching "Property is Theft." When debate on the Irish question raged through Commons in March 1868, he was likened to Jack Cade. His proposal for fixed rents left even Gladstone stuttering: "I own I am one of those who are not prepared—I have not daring sufficient—to accompany my hon. Friend the Member for Westminster." Yes, it was a daring proposal, and of course nothing came of it at first. But its shock value was salutary. Less extreme measures became acceptable, and Mill had the satisfaction in 1870 of seeing the Irish Land Act provide the first deliberate government interference with landed property rights in Ireland.

Indeed, he had the satisfaction of seeing many of his pet proposals (albeit in diluted form) carried during Gladstone's first great ministry —the disestablishment of the Anglican Church in Ireland, the Married Women's Property Act, the National Education Act, the abolition of religious tests at the universities, the abolition of bought commissions in the army. But by that time he was no longer a member of Parliament. His views on Jamaica and Ireland were resented exceedingly, and when he subscribed money for the campaign of an avowed atheist, his own career in politics was finished. After losing the November 1868 election he sighed disappointedly—and turned down offers to stand for other seats. Having propounded his heresies in the House for nearly two years, he was glad to be dismissed from the work. Gratefully, he set out for Avignon once more.

Mill's parliamentary years were ones of hurry and vexation of spirit. Still, he was used to hard work and, though just turned sixty, he throve splendidly. He even found time in the midst of the hurly-burly to compose one of his most serene and thoughtful masterworks, the Inaugural Address to the University of St. Andrews.

Each year the students of the Scottish university elected a Lord Rector whose main chore was to deliver an address in person. Mill was chosen at a most inopportune time, late November 1865, when Parliament was shortly to convene. At first he respectfully declined, but the university persisted, quite willing to put off the address to suit his convenience. Ultimately, the students had to wait over a year to hear Mill's speech.

As fate would have it, Carlyle had simultaneously received a similar honor, being elected Lord Rector by his old alma mater, Edinburgh University. On 2 April 1866 he had delivered his address to an assemblage of students who guffawed obligingly at the jokes and mobbed the old mystic afterward. The speech itself was an extempore rerun of some favorite themes—the virtues of dictatorship, the benevolence of old England's aristocratic paternalism, the hopelessness of democracy. Silence was praised with the usual prolixity: "At the same time, I must say that speech, in the case even of Demosthenes, does not seem, on the whole, to have turned to almost any good account." The address was quintessential latter-day Carlyle, with a difference. The old opinions were there, the old sparkle and sputter were not. At seventy-one, the famous Carlylean cussedness had either mellowed or, more likely, exhausted itself. To make matters more melancholy, Jane Carlyle died suddenly in London while her husband was away in Scotland.

When Mill finally spoke at St. Andrews on 1 February 1867, Carlyle's mournful address was in the back of his mind. Mill's topic was university education, its content and aims. Brushing aside all petty, practical obstacles to perfection, Mill instead dreamed dreams and asked, why not? His address conjured up an ideal university curriculum and glowingly showed its value to both individual and race. In the process, the major areas of knowledge were surveyed so succinctly that the St. Andrews address can serve newcomers to Mill's thought as a handy guide to much of it. Not that he merely repeated himself or paraded past experiences, as Carlyle had done. Rather, everything was subordinated to a comprehensive vision of what an ideal course of university studies ought to be. And while arguing his curriculum's value, he produced a rationale and defense of liberal

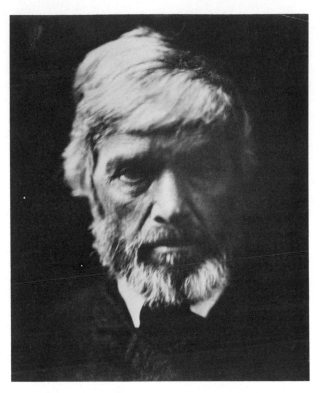

Thomas Carlyle. Photograph by Julia M. Cameron (ca. 1867).

education worthy of comparison with J. H. Newman's landmark lectures on *The Idea of a University* (1852).

Like so much of Mill's work, the St. Andrews address has grown more relevant with the years. To our own world, so enamored of specialization and professional training at the university level, the danger is disillusionment and frustration, that *angst* pervading T. S. Eliot's "Choruses from 'The Rock' ":

> *Where is the wisdom we have lost in knowledge?*
> *Where is the knowledge we have lost in information?*

To the fragmented modern consciousness, Mill's address is a stirring reminder of the university's ancient obligation to seek beyond data for wisdom.

Right from the start, Mill's aims are high. Education's purpose is to bring us "somewhat nearer to the perfection of our nature." Rejecting the narrow utilitarian view of universities as vocational training centers for business and the professions, Mill affirms that "their object is not to make skillful lawyers, or physicians, or engineers, but capable and cultivated human beings." Of course he does not reject schools of law, medicine, or engineering, but the genuine university exists to lift its students above specialization to an overview of the various fields of learning. Nor is general knowledge superficial knowledge; it is knowing systematically the leading truths of many disciplines, leaving the details to specializers. This kind of general knowledge, widely diffused, gives nations an enlightened public, capable of deciding intelligently whom to listen to on crucial questions.

Tackling directly the perennial problem of whether a university should stress the ancients or the moderns, the humanities or the sciences, Mill responds with characteristic many-sidedness: "Why not both? Can anything deserve the name of a good education which does not include literature and science too?" And to dissidents who reply it cannot be done, Mill answers that past educational performance is no gauge of what is possible. "Let us try what conscientious and intelligent teaching can do, before we presume to decide what cannot be done."

While on the subject of the ancients, Mill launches into a full-scale defense of Greek and Latin in the curriculum. With all his boyhood love of the classics flooding back in upon him, he extols translating for the way it exorcises that fundamental blunder of confusing words with things, for the way it demonstrates basic relationships between grammar and logic. Besides offsetting chauvinism of nation and time, the classics provide students with the foundations of philosophy and history, some fragments from "the wisdom of life," and examples of perfect artistic finish. With a probable glance at Carlyle's speech, he exclaims:

> Look at an oration of Demosthenes; there is nothing in it which calls attention to itself as style at all: it is only after a close examination we perceive that every word is what it should be, and where it should be, to lead the hearer smoothly and imperceptibly into the state of mind which the orator wishes to produce. . . . But then (as has been well said) it was not the object of Demosthenes to make the Athenians cry out, "What a splendid speaker!" but to make them say, "Let us march against Philip!"

The passage describes perfectly Mill's own artistic goals, perhaps no-where more superbly realized than in this eloquent address.

Turning to scientific knowledge, Mill praises it as a key to the world around us, as a discipline for ascertaining truth. Following Comte, he traces out a hierarchy of the sciences, beginning with those relying primarily upon either reasoning or observation, and closing with those requiring an increasingly complex integration of the two. Logic is the science of reasoning, either ratiocinatively from the general premises to particular conclusions, or inductively from particulars to general laws. Mill always enriches his scientific catalogue with tolerant and shrewd observations, with stirring illustrations. Newton is sketched in as an image of the scientific mind at its best, working from a few observed facts to general laws which explain a myriad of other facts. Unlike Comte, Mill sets aside a prominent niche in his hierarchy for psychology. And logic is stoutly defended against antirationalists who sneer at thinking by rule: "But if the practice of thinking is not improved by rules, I venture to say it is the only difficult thing done by human beings that is not so."

The true, the good, the beautiful. Mill finds room for all three in his ideal university. Besides humanistic and scientific truth, the university must foster the ethical and aesthetic dimensions of human existence. Not that Mill attempts to convert his university into a seminary, secular or otherwise. He knows the university cannot displace the home as primary molder of values. Still, dedicated teachers can disperse a tone of elevated sentiment which students may absorb, and some studies—like political economy and jurisprudence—directly impinge upon moral concerns. If ethics and politics themselves are not sufficiently advanced to be taught as sciences, the conflicting viewpoints in both fields can, and should, be studied tolerantly. Even that most tindery of subjects—religious beliefs—might be profitably approached in such manner. And though Mill declares that "a university ought to be a place of free speculation," he is far from advocating "an essentially skeptical eclecticism." As always in Mill, open-mindedness does not imply irresolution; it is instead a means of getting past ethical half-truths to fuller knowledge of human virtue. At the back of his mind there glows a vision of human history as "a great epic or dramatic action, to terminate in the happiness or misery, the elevation or the degradation, of the human race." In this all-important moral struggle, the actions of each person are fraught with momentous implications—for himself, for his society, for the future of his species.

Turning to aesthetic matters, Mill argues that "the education of the feelings and the cultivation of the beautiful" can be ends in themselves, but ideally they should mesh with the intellectual and ethical dimensions of life. It is through art and natural scenery that our loftiest sentiments are nurtured, our mental disturbances calmed. The arts can conjure up idealized visions of human excellence, models that we grow to love and imitate. "He who has learned what beauty is, if he be of a virtuous character, will desire to realize it in his own life—will keep before himself a type of perfect beauty in human character, to light his attempts at self-culture." A moral aesthetic, yes; but an open-hearted one that rejoices in Dante and Wordsworth, Handel and Italian Renaissance painters, Gothic cathedrals and mountain scenery. Gone completely is Mill's old concept of the poet as prisoner singing soulfully to himself in solitude. Now the artist takes his rightful place beside humanist, scientist, and moralist—all working together toward the betterment of humanity.

His journey through the realms of knowledge completed, Mill urges his listeners, in a final paragraph of sublime power, to cultivate the kind of knowledge he has so eloquently outlined.

Once again, the persona is the message. Like Newman in *The Idea of a University*, Mill speaks here with the voice of an "imperial intellect," a mind that has taken an overview of the various fields of knowledge, a heart that has responded to noble beauty. Because the love of liberal knowledge can be caught only from someone who already has it, Mill becomes in the St. Andrews address a supremely attractive image of what he is advocating—the liberally educated person.

The address abounds in Millian riches. Its art is unobtrusive but sure. Contrasting ancient directness with modern uncertainty, Mill's grammar shifts adroitly from the concise to the convoluted:

> The great ancients could express a thought so perfectly in a few words or sentences, that they did not need to add any more: the moderns, because they cannot bring it out clearly and completely at once, return again and again, heaping sentence upon sentence, each adding a little more elucidation, in hopes that, though no single sentence expresses the full meaning, the whole together may give a sufficient notion of it.

It is an eminently quotable talk. Here is Mill on social apathy:

> Bad men need nothing more to compass their ends, than that good men
> should look on and do nothing.

His own extraordinary education (though never cited specifically in
the talk) supplies a clutch of intriguing suggestions—children can
learn much more (especially languages) than most schools suspect, the
facts of history and geography can be picked up largely from private
reading (though a connected view of those facts may not), and foreign
languages should be studied abroad in their native setting, with international colleges providing such opportunity.

Though it reportedly took three hours to deliver, the speech was
well received, with students cheering the passage about free speculation. Probably Carlyle's address provoked greater contemporary
clamor, but time has vindicated Mill's. The Edinburgh speech has long
since vanished from the canon of Carlylean classics, while—as one
writer recently noted—"every liberal arts college president has at least
one quote from Mill's St. Andrews address in his repertoire."

Better yet, Mill provided an enduring portrait of an ideal university,
one to which later generations of educators can turn for ideas and
inspiration.

CHAPTER ELEVEN

SEXUAL POLITICS:
The Subjection of Women

It should be remarked that, as the principle of liberty is better understood, and more nobly interpreted, a broader protest is made in behalf of woman.
—MARGARET FULLER, *Woman in the Nineteenth Century*

 "I THINK it will be useful, and all the more, as it is sure to be very bitterly attacked," Mill wrote to a friend shortly before *The Subjection of Women* was published in 1869. The event proved his prediction resoundingly accurate, but Mill sat serenely through the blizzard of contempt that greeted the book. Why should he be perturbed? He had at last fixed the capstone on his lifelong commitment to women's rights.

Exactly how this commitment originated is not clear. It seems unlikely that he imbibed it at his father's knee. Disappointed with his wife, James Mill was most likely no enthusiast for women's suffrage. Perhaps it rubbed off from kindly old Jeremy Bentham. No doubt the energetic examples of his sister-in-law, Lady Bentham, and of Sarah Austin helped foster it. However that may be, young John seems to have been an early dissenter from his father's views on women's rights. His first article in the *Westminster Review*, largely a rehash of James Mill doctrine, nevertheless contains some apparently heretical passages scouting the glorification of feminine helplessness. At first, however, his devotion to the cause was quixotic and confused. In 1823 he went tearing about London flinging birth-control tracts to working women and getting arrested for his efforts. As late as 1832 he was arguing in

Mill's Logic; or, Franchise for Females. Punch (30 March 1867) kids women's suffrage. Mill is saying to John Bull, "Pray clear the way, there, for these—a—persons."

the press that women and children should be disbarred from factory work. His proposal was gallant enough, but when some female operatives pointed out that it would curtail their livelihood, he had to backpedal hastily and assure them he had meant only married women with working husbands. Definitely, Mill's chivalry needed sorting out.

It was Harriet Taylor who took the situation in hand. Chafing at her role as the doll in John Taylor's dollhouse, she had first been attracted to Mill partly because of his feminist views. Within two years they were exchanging essays on marriage and divorce with all the fervor of two lovers exchanging lockets of hair. And very liberated ideas on these topics they had, too. From this point on, women's rights became their special joint cause. In 1850 not even the aftermath of John Taylor's death prevented their firing off indignant letters to the newspapers on recent cases of child and wife abuse. The following year Mill saw to it that their "Enfranchisement of Women" appeared in the

Westminster, and among his wedding preparations he had drawn up a formal refusal of the legal powers over his wife that Victorian marriage would confer upon him. Once settled at Blackheath Park, the two contemplated a *magnum opus* on women's liberation. Their discussions later materialized in Mill's *Subjection of Women*, but the 1850s seemed the wrong time for writing such a book: England was slumbering through the prosperous complacency of mid-Victorian equipoise.

By the middle of the 1860s, however, matters had changed dramatically: workingmen were agitating for the vote, and a full-fledged women's rights movement was ready to break from cover and proclaim itself. Harriet had died in the interval, but John and Helen were prepared to carry the banners. Before agreeing to stand for election, Mill had warned voters he would push for women's suffrage if elected. True to his word, he hauled into the House of Commons a womanhood suffrage petition with fifteen hundred signatures on it. During debate on the 1867 Reform Bill, he mustered his finest eloquence in defense of amending the word "man" to read "person," thereby including women among the newly enfranchised. His amendment lost, but the seventy-three votes it received showed that the issue was neither patently absurd nor dead. Mill's defeat at the polls in 1868 only provided greater leisure to prepare his next thunderbolt. The time had come to print *The Subjection of Women*, which he had drafted in 1860–61. John and Helen took it out of storage, put some finishing touches to it, and published it in 1869. Its message was startling but sorely needed.

On the books, a Victorian woman's lot was not a happy one. Politically, legally, economically, socially—everywhere she turned there were disabilities. She could cast no vote, hold no public office. Should she marry (as she was expected to), she practically ceased to exist legally. "My wife and I are one, and I am he" sums up the situation neatly. The law classified wives with minors and idiots. She had no legal right to her property, her earnings, her children. She could sign no contract, make no will. Should her husband thrash her, she might (if she had the temerity) have him locked up for a time. Upon release, however, he was free to exact his revenge. Before 1852 it was practically impossible for her to separate from him—and extremely difficult after that. Before 1857 divorce required no less than a special act of Parliament. She could be jailed for denying him his conjugal right. Lower-class women sweated in factories, mines, and the homes of the wealthy; their earnings technically belonged in their husbands' pockets. The middle-class woman was expected to marry and spend the rest of her days raising a family. The universities were closed to her, the professions—medicine, law, the church—denied to her. Because her brain was supposedly smaller and her body weaker, nearly everyone (herself included) assumed she was mentally and physically inferior to man. The wealthier woman was required to devote her life to social calls, dinner parties, and various other forms of conspicuous consumption. With luck, a woman of any class might be tolerably happy within the system, but it was hardly a stimulus to her independence and growth, to say nothing of its injustice.

Behind all this inequity was an ambivalent, though frequently sincere enough, worship of womanhood. Womanly virtue was a precious civilizing force, an echo of pristine childhood, a last remnant of prelapsarian innocence in a world necessarily given over to the Mammon of male unrighteousness. The very idea of permitting women free access to the corrupt male world bordered on the obscene. On the contrary, to isolate this purity was a sacred duty—performed, often enough, with grim rigor. "Ladies" of the middle and upper classes were required to be genteel, asexual, and clever in an inconsequential way. Any frowardness was subject to immediate reproof or ridicule, frequently from powerful matrons. In an enormously popular *Saturday Review* article of 1868, Elizabeth Lynn Linton pilloried "the girl of the period." Entirely too snippy, Mrs. Lynn Linton concluded snippily. Where were the girls of yesteryear, she lamented, the old-fashioned homebodies who knew their place? "The girl of the period" was annoying, but the suffragist was positively dangerous, groveling as she was in the last stages of some wild disturbance of the female mind. It was, in short, not exactly the most congenial moment for anybody publishing a book on the subjection of women, however badly the book might be needed.

In fact, nothing Mill published during his lifetime occasioned greater animosity. Shortly after the *Subjection* showed itself in May 1869, the reviewers were after it in full cry, with unliberated women leading the pack. In *Blackwood's* Anne Mozley set the tone of contemptuous condescension: the book was insulting because it criticized women "as we love and admire and desire to keep them." Not to be outdone, Margaret Oliphant in the *Edinburgh* systematically argued against women's natural equality, womanhood suffrage, and equal education. Scenting blood, the male reviewers were quickly on the scene, most of them painfully splitting logical hairs with Mill and agreeing that this time he had really gone too far. Even when a stray

THE LADIES' ADVOCATE.

Mrs. Bull. "LOR, MR. MILL! WHAT A LOVELY SPEECH YOU *DID* MAKE. I DO DECLARE I HADN'T THE SLIGHTEST NOTION WE WERE SUCH MISERABLE CREATURES. NO ONE CAN SAY IT WAS *YOUR* FAULT THAT THE CASE BROKE DOWN."

The Ladies' Advocate. After Mill's unsuccessful efforts to amend the 1867 Reform Bill to include voting rights for women, *Punch* (1 June 1867) portrayed Mrs. Bull addressing him: "Lor, Mr. Mill! What a lovely speech you *did* make. I do declare I hadn't the slightest notion we were such miserable creatures. No one can say it was *your* fault that the case broke down."

loyalist stood by Mill, the help was sometimes of questionable value: Charles Kingsley, still smarting from his skirmish with Father Newman, kept hinting darkly in *Macmillan's* that antifeminism was all the doing of some Romish celibates. For years afterward, the *Subjection* and its views continued to draw fire. To Alexander Bain, Mill's feminism was the last infirmity of a noble mind. James Fitzjames Stephen disagreed with the book from "the first sentence to the last." Translating Mill for a German edition, none other than young Sigmund Freud was scandalized by the idea of sex equality. "If, for instance, I imagined my gentle sweet girl as a competitor," Freud cooed to his fiancée, "it would only end in my telling her, as I did seventeen months ago, that I am fond of her and that I implore her to withdraw from the strife into the calm uncompetitive activity of my home." The *Subjection* was a stumbling block to many a Mill admirer, numbers of whom preferred to pass it by with eyes discreetly averted.

Mill had expected as much, but he had also anticipated a different reaction from another quarter. And he got what he was looking for. "I lay the book down with a peace and joy I never felt before," the American feminist Elizabeth Cady Stanton wrote to him, "for it is the first response from any man to show he is capable of seeing and feeling all the nice shades and degrees of woman's wrongs. . . ." Other letters of gratitude began trickling in. "The most important thing we now have to do, is to stir up the zeal of women themselves," Mill trumpeted. "This is more important now than to conciliate opponents." On this score, the *Subjection* was a triumph. Mill became the rallying point of the feminist cause in England, the book remaining as the Bible of the suffrage movement long after his death. Translated into numerous languages, it was read around the world and created the first global stirrings for women's liberation.

With the temporary fading of the women's rights movement in the twentieth century, the *Subjection* was relegated to obscurity. In 1918 womanhood suffrage (for women over thirty, anyway) had been attained in England. The United States soon followed suit. The Western world was preoccupied with its wars and depressions. Surely, Mill's book could be safely ignored as a Victorian curiosity. That attitude, however, was shattered by the women's liberation revival of the late 1960s. In *Sexual Politics* (1970) Kate Millett drew almost cruel contrasts between Mill's enlightened views and the more representative male chauvinism found in a particularly cloying address by John Ruskin. Out of print for years, the *Subjection* was soon proliferating in gleaming new paperback editions. Far from being dated, the book was found to epitomize women's still unfulfilled aspirations for social, political, legal, and economic equality.

As a source of modern consciousness raising, *The Subjection of Women* can hold its own with anything in print.

In arguing for sex equality, Mill knew he was taking on a Goliath of awesome proportions. On the face of it, nothing could be more reasonable than contending that men and women ought to be equals in the eyes of the law and society; anyone arguing for the subjection of one sex to the other ought to bear the burden of proof. But Mill knew better. The patriarchal bias of society was of such venerable status, was so tightly interwoven with people's emotions, that to question it was to waken the sleeping dogs of nearly everybody's secret fears and hostilities. To get even a respectful hearing of his case would require every particle of logic and rhetoric he could muster.

The opening paragraph of *The Subjection of Women*, one long splendid sentence, shows that Mill had marshaled his resources with consummate skill. It is one of the most impressive paragraphs that Mill ever wrote:

> The object of this Essay is to explain as clearly as I am able, the grounds of an opinion which I have held from the very earliest period when I had formed any opinions at all on social or political matters, and which, instead of being weakened or modified, has been constantly growing stronger by the progress of reflection and the experience of life: That the principle which regulates the existing social relations between the two sexes—the legal subordination of one sex to the other—is wrong in itself, and now one of the chief hindrances to human improvement; and that it ought to be replaced by a principle of perfect equality, admitting no power or privilege on the one side, nor disability on the other.

With clarity and brevity the paragraph outlines Mill's subject, establishing at once the author's dignity and integrity. This is no enthusiast parading his latest whim before the public: Mill deliberately puts his entire career on the line, proclaiming an opinion that has withstood a lifetime of testing. For the sensitive ear, the paragraph contains verbal echoes of *On Liberty*'s opening sentence and its "one very simple principle"—Mill's hint that the *Subjection* is *On Liberty*'s companion piece. Whereas the *Liberty* lays siege to the general evil of oppression, the *Subjection* assaults the particular evil of society's most prevalent form of oppression. Indeed, underlying all the arguments in the *Subjection* is the basic thesis of *On Liberty*: the only means to human improvement is rational liberty for the individual.

Having startled us into respectful attention, Mill enumerates the difficulties of the task in hand, especially with patriarchy having achieved the status of sacred dogma. Nothing daunted, however, Mill challenges it, devoting the bulk of his first chapter to a two-pronged "philosophical" attack consisting of a historical survey and an exploration of feminine nature.

Remembering his Coleridge, Mill first questions whether patriarchy's long survival is an argument in its favor. The argument would be sound, he says, only if other power arrangements between the sexes had been tried and patriarchy found most suitable. But such a trial had not occurred. Instead, male dominance is an early form of primitive oppression that has managed to drag its fossilized remains into the present age. Taking a sweeping view of Western history, Mill sees again the drama of force gradually yielding to justice, surrendering to concepts of human equality. What characterizes modern life, Mill argues, is that people are no longer born into their stations in life, as slave and serf once were. Only the subjection of women lingers on, an anachronism left over from the days of force. And of course it would be more durable than other forms of oppression: "The subjection of women to men being a universal custom, any departure from it quite naturally appears unnatural." There are, moreover, plenty of parties interested in its upkeep. But it is doomed, Mill concludes (with almost Marxian inexorableness): "So far as the whole course of human improvement up to this time, the whole stream of modern tendencies, warrants any inference on the subject, it is, that this relic of the past is discordant with the future, and must necessarily disappear." Clearly, history is on the side of women's liberation.

Never one to leave logic naked to its enemies (and especially not in the present case where emotions are sure to run high), Mill carefully drapes it in the most persuasive images and allusions he can stitch together. To convey his vision of patriarchy as anachronistic superstition, he associates it with idol worship, paganism, and false religion. The persistence of patriarchy, he says, is "as if a gigantic dolmen, or a vast temple of Jupiter Olympius, occupied the site of St. Paul's and received daily worship, while the surrounding Christian churches were only resorted to on fasts and festivals." In these religious allusions, Mill seldom fails to enlist his audience's Christian allegiance: "To pretend that Christianity was intended to stereotype existing forms of government and society, and protect them against change, is to reduce it to the level of Islamism or of Brahminism." Once again, the status quo of male dominance is linked with "false" religion. That all men are fit to exercise power over women, Mill contends, is as unlikely as the return of the pagan goddess Astraea. By essay's end, male ascendency has been proscribed as a form of idolatry that should have gone out with nymphs and fauns.

Idolatry is not the only relic scored in the essay; the *Subjection* is crowded with other forms of barbarism—tyranny, slavery, serfdom. Repeatedly Mill makes us imaginatively witness the despot torturing rebels, the slaveowner working his victims to death, the monarch listening to his subjects' groans. Carefully he links our revulsion to these horrors with the subjection of women: "Meanwhile the wife is the actual bond-servant of her husband." In particular, frequent allusions to slavery constitute Mill's version of the "woman as nigger" idea. In a daring analogy he brands marriage (at least Victorian marriage) as an especially insidious form of slavery. Anticipating Virginia Woolf, Mill observes that Uncle Tom at least had his cabin, but the wife lacks a room of her own, a private life apart from her master's. Drawing us away from these horrors, Mill points to a more liberated future: "We have had the morality of submission, and the morality of chivalry and generosity; the time is now come for the morality of justice."

With history enlisted in the cause, Mill next explores that most prickly of problems—woman's nature. What he is out to demolish, of course, is the widespread notion that women are "naturally" sweet, submissive, and simple-minded. With one dazzling observation, he stops the mouths of all chatterers on the subject: "Standing on the ground of common sense and the constitution of the human mind, I deny that any one knows, or can know, the nature of the two sexes, as long as they have only been seen in their present relation to one another." Or, as modern feminists have been pointing out, humanity has yet to evolve an adequate psychology of the sexes. Meanwhile, women (and men) are shaped by society to fit certain patterns, and the result is labeled "feminine (or masculine) nature." Mill wasn't fooled for a moment: "What is now called the nature of women is an eminently artificial thing—the result of forced repression in some directions, unnatural stimulation in others." The only important thing we know about the nature of woman is that she—like man—is an organic creature who needs to develop herself on all sides. One of Mill's most striking organic images clinches the point:

> But in the case of women, a hot-house and stove cultivation has always been carried on of some of the capabilities of their nature, for the benefit and pleasure of their masters. Then, because certain products of the general vital force sprout luxuriantly and reach a great development in this heated atmosphere and under this active nurture and watering, while other shoots from the same root, which are left outside in the wintry air, with ice purposely heaped all round them, have a stunted growth, and some are burnt off with fire and disappear; men, with that inability to recognise their own work which distinguishes the unanalytic mind, indolently believe that the tree grows of itself in the way they have made it grow, and that it would die if one half of it were not kept in a vapour bath and the other half in the snow.

It is again Mill's old enemy—nurture posing as nature and thereby blocking human development.

Perhaps the most compelling aspect of the *Subjection* occurs in its discussion of what might be called a dead issue—the wife's legal position in Victorian marriage. Though hardly equitable today, woman's legal status is no longer the unmitigated outrage it once was. But in portraying the desperation of the working-class wife imprisoned in an unhappy marriage, Mill reveals a startling awareness of the perverted eroticism that invests male dominance, a concept superbly explicated in our own time by Millett in *Sexual Politics*. Citing steamy passages from modern novelists (Mailer, Miller, Lawrence, *et al.*), Millett demonstrates that the male protagonists are busy making war not love. Confusing sexuality with cruelty, they derive their biggest thrills from debasing, not loving. For them sex is violation, violence is sexy. Millett makes a depressingly convincing case for the extensiveness of this malign machismo, not to mention the literature pandering to it. Mill sees the same sordid vision: behind the subjection of women lurks a perverted sexuality in which power is pleasure. To proclaim this vision from the rooftops was of course impossible in Victorian times; Mill has to suggest it almost subconsciously through low-definition images or linguistic hints:

Not so the wife: however brutal a tyrant she may unfortunately be chained to—though she may know that he hates her, though it may be his daily pleasure to torture her, and though she may feel it impossible not to loathe him—he can claim from her and enforce the lowest degradation of a human being, that of being made the instrument of an animal function contrary to her inclinations.

Though couched in carefully restrained terms, the link between power and sadistic sex is fairly explicit here. More often, Mill resorts to subtle *double entendres:*

Such being the common tendency of human nature; the almost unlimited power which present social institutions give to the man over at least one human being—the one with whom he resides, and whom he has always present—this power seeks out and evokes the latent germs of selfishness in the remotest corners of his nature—fans its faintest sparks and smouldering embers—offers to him a license for the indulgence of those points of his original character which in all other relations he would have found it necessary to repress and conceal, and the repression of which would in time have become a second nature.

In no other work by Mill are the sexual undertones of language and image so pervasive. But unlike, say, the spectacle of Bill Sikes murdering Nancy in *Oliver Twist,* Mill's nightmare images of sexual violence are clearly designed not to fascinate but to repel.

Seen from this angle, the book's sexual aspects are positively refreshing, probably because Mill—whatever else may be said of his sexuality —was at least free from the grotesque obsessions of modern machismo. "I suspect it is the second-rate people of the two sexes that are unlike —the first-rate are alike in both," he once observed to Carlyle (whose ears no doubt were tingling). The only passage in the *Subjection* which celebrates phallicism is a tribute to the man of "high nervous sensibility," that is, the man most people would regard as possessing a "feminine" temperament.

In Mill's discussion of marriage in chapter two of the *Subjection,* two points may cause a modern reader mild surprise. The first is his refusal to commit himself on divorce. No doubt he saw the topic as too hot to handle publicly in 1869, and sex equality would have enough trouble getting a hearing on its own merits without an additional fuss over the

Mr. Morley of Blackburn, on an Afternoon in the Spring of '69, Introduces Mr. John Stuart Mill.
"It has recently," he says, "occurred to Mr. Mill that in his lifelong endeavour to catch and keep the ear of the nation he has been hampered by a certain deficiency in—well, in warmth, in colour, in rich charm. I have told him that this deficiency (I do not regard it as a defect) might possibly be remedied by *you*. Mr. Mill has in the press at this moment a new work, entitled 'The Subjection of Women.' From my slight acquaintance with you, I gather that women greatly interest you, and I have no doubt that you are incensed at their subjection. Mr. Mill has brought his proof-sheets with him. He will read them to you. I believe, and he takes my word for it, that a series of illustrative paintings by you would" etc., etc.

Max Beerbohm's cartoon capitalizes on the early-twentieth-century stereotype of Mill as undersexed intellectual. Here, a rather attenuated Mill is being introduced by John Morley into the fleshly world of Victorian poet-painter Dante Gabriel Rossetti.

divorce question. Also, as Mill kept assuring correspondents, he wished speculation on divorce deferred until liberated women had had their say about it. On the second point, he didn't hesitate to speculate —though some may wish he had. On the question of breadwinning, he argues that the usual pattern of husband as wage-earner and the wife as housekeeper-child raiser is preferable in most cases. Freud and others were appalled that any married women would be let out of the house to compete with men; more recently some feminists have attacked the opposite flank, faulting Mill for a failure to envision alternate marital life-styles. In any event, Mill's conjecture is not essential to his argument and must be weighed with his support of married women's property rights and with his observations that "the *power* of earning is essential to the dignity of a woman" and "the utmost latitude ought to exist for the adaptation of general rules to individual suitabilities."

Turning from marriage, Mill in the third chapter of the *Subjection* plunges into yet another maelstrom of controversy—the question of women's exclusion from political life, higher education, and the professions. Beneath all these interdictions, he locates a common villain: the widespread conviction that, mentally, women are a lesser breed. But to defend women's potential in all these areas forces Mill to grapple with a veritable octopus of entrenched bigotry. He puts up a spirited fight, to say the least. He takes on political matters first, with history as his weapon. Where in the past women have been allowed to rule, some women have shown extraordinary ability. On the score of political acumen, then, woman's record is at least as good as man's: she can be safely entrusted with the right to vote and hold public office. He next rushes to the defense of women's intellectual capabilities, easily annihilating the idea that women are stupider than men because their brains are supposedly smaller. If so, Mill counters, then bigger men must be more intelligent than smaller men. But victory in this area is not so easily won, and Mill resorts to a dissertation upon women and men as each other's intellectual completing counterparts. He is soon rhapsodizing on the subject, the memory of his own relationship with Harriet warming the prose:

> Hardly anything can be of greater value to a man of theory and speculation who employs himself not in collecting materials of knowledge by observation, but in working them up by processes of thought into comprehensive truths of science and laws of conduct, than to carry on his

speculations in the companionship, and under the criticism, of a really superior woman.

It is yet another portrait of Scientist and Artist, of John and Harriet, working together toward philosophic vision. The male is the speculative partner, the woman the practical intuitionist. The portrait might at first seem to clash with Mill's idea that the first-rate women and men are alike. But not really: alikeness is not identity. Moreover, Mill specifies that the male/scientist and female/artist equation is a description of how matters are apt to fall out under present social conditioning; the division is probably not inherent in the "nature" of men and women. But should it turn out that women's minds are inherently different from men's, Mill has already demonstrated that both kinds of intellect are valid and complementary. All the more reason, then, for opening up those hallowed halls of higher education to women.

Mill next assaults the evidence that women are unfit for the arts and sciences: after all, there have been no female Mozarts or Michelangelos. In a vindication that would do Virginia Woolf proud, Mill first notes that "it is scarcely three generations since women, saving very rare exceptions, have begun to try their capacity in philosophy, science, or art." Also, deficiency of education has cut off women from the great traditions of thought and art. Even when a woman hits upon a lucky insight, it is frequently lost, Mill points out (waxing autobiographical again), for want of a husband or friend to evaluate and publicize it. "Who can tell," he wonders, "how many of the most original thoughts put forth by male writers, belong to a woman by suggestion, to themselves only by verifying and working out? If I may judge by my own case, a very large proportion indeed." Finally, women have little time for the concentrated effort that produces proficiency: "Everything a woman does is done at odd times." Mill finishes off the adversary with some bracing remarks on the supposed moral differences between women and men, deftly exposing the hypocrisy of those who extol female goodness while systematically excluding it from public life. All in all, it is a frantic, heroic performance that Mill provides in this section of the *Subjection*. He emerges a bit breathless but unbowed.

Mill can denounce injustice as well as any social critic; he can also envision order and equality—and this is a rarer ability. But just such a capacity is one of Mill's hallmarks and the clearest indication of his healthy-mindedness. Unlike, say, Carlyle's latter-day fulminations,

Mill's works are not obsessed with evil and decay. They may reproach vehemently, their final words may recall the evil at hand, but they seldom fail to refresh with a portrait of the good to be striven for.

The *Subjection* is no exception. In its final chapter Mill asks what good can be expected from the social revolution he is proposing. He finds more than enough to warrant the dislocations involved. The terrorized wife would at last find a refuge. Moreover, the advantages of a just system over an unjust are not to be sniffed at: people growing up under a system of injustice learn to accept and perpetuate it. "Think what it is to a boy," Mill challenges us, "to grow up to manhood in the belief that without any merit or exertion of his own . . . he is by right the superior of all and every one of an entire half of the human race." Also, though many women would probably choose not to compete, the change would theoretically double the amount of talent available for public office and the professions—no mean consideration, what with talent in these areas seldom constituting a flood upon the market. And, finally, a race of liberated and educated women would raise the whole level of civilization. As it is now, too many women are worshipers at the shrine of middle-class respectability, sacrificing to it whatever social conscience their husbands may have. Mill is at his satiric best here, caricaturing such women. (Did he, one wonders, have his mother in mind?)

> Many a woman flatters herself (nine times out of ten quite erroneously) that nothing prevents her and her husband from moving in the highest society of her neighbourhood—society in which others well known to her, and in the same class of life, mix freely—except that her husband is unfortunately a Dissenter, or has the reputation of mingling in low radical politics. That it is, she thinks, which hinders George from getting a commission or a place, Caroline from making an advantageous match, and prevents her and her husband from obtaining invitations, perhaps honours, which, for aught she sees, they are as well entitled to as some folks.

But true to his sense of balance, Mill goes on to envision, not only liberated women, but liberated men and women in a true marriage of equals:

> What marriage may be in the case of two persons of cultivated faculties, identical in opinions and purposes, between whom there exists that

best kind of equality, similarity of powers and capacities with reciprocal superiority in them—so that each can enjoy the luxury of looking up to the other, and can have alternately the pleasure of leading and of being led in the path of development—I will not attempt to describe. To those who can conceive it, there is no need; to those who cannot, it would appear the dream of an enthusiast.

But he has already described it, here and elsewhere in the essay—and so effectively that even a fuming opponent like *Blackwood's* Anne Mozley could sigh: "But we cordially enter into the charm of the union he pictures."

Mill concludes the book with a favorite insight cast in fascinating new terms. He describes liberty almost as Freud described sex, as a basic human need that, if thwarted, will reemerge malignantly. Deny people liberty, Mill says, and they will seek power, they will bully and scheme, they will find their pleasure in tyrannizing others. Only between equals can liberty exist, he argues, providing by way of illustration some autobiographical insights too revealing to ignore:

> As between father and son, how many are the cases in which the father, in spite of real affection on both sides, obviously to all the world does not know, nor suspect, parts of the son's character familiar to his companions and equals. The truth is, that the position of looking up to another is extremely unpropitious to complete sincerity and openness with him. The fear of losing ground in his opinion or in his feelings is so strong, that even in an upright character, there is an unconscious tendency to show only the best side, or the side which, though not the best, is that which he most likes to see: and it may be confidently said that thorough knowledge of one another hardly ever exists, but between persons who, besides being intimates, are equals.

> Let any man call to mind what he himself felt on emerging from boyhood—from the tutelage and control of even loved and affectionate elders—and entering upon the responsibilities of manhood. Was it not like the physical effect of taking off a heavy weight, or releasing him from obstructive, even if not otherwise painful, bonds? Did he not feel twice as much alive, twice as much a human being, as before? And does he imagine that women have none of these feelings?

Evidently, Mill's compassion for women is rooted in home soil.

Liberty denied also leaves the individual in lifelong checkmate. The book's final image is memorably poignant: the widow or single woman, middle-aged, denied larger participation in public or professional concerns; her life unfulfilled, empty. Like Dürer's *Melancholia*, she broods despairingly amid the symbols of worldly progress, a disheartening image of human capability paralyzed.

One closes *The Subjection of Women* with a feeling of awe at its achievement—and more than a twinge of dismay at its fate. How, one wonders, could such a wise and perceptive book be so misunderstood, abused, ignored? Granted, Mill's concept of sex equality was heady stuff in 1869 (not to mention a century later), but even on the presumably neutral question of style, earlier critics seem to have been struck deaf and blind while reading it. Though recognizing the work's emotional power, Bain mostly fussed about its departures from prim grammatical correctness—and never surmised the connection between the two. Freud once felt that Mill was never quotable. How unfortunate that he missed a gem like this comment on middle-class marriage: "Whoever has a wife and children has given hostages to Mrs. Grundy." Oscar Wilde would have given his green carnation to have penned it. And there are others, equally astute. Fortunately, time has brought consolation: few critics nowadays would fail to rank the *Subjection* with *On Liberty* as an example of Mill's impassioned prose at its best, addressing mind and heart in a superb coordination of thought and language.

Viewing the book as a whole, one hardly knows what to admire most —its compassion or its comprehension, its argument or its art. However acquired, Mill's understanding of women's feelings is a triumph of sympathetic imagination. That this most significant of works on women's rights was written by a man is in itself an important symbol of goodwill between the sexes, a sign of hope for their future development together. To summarize the *Subjection* is to be astonished anew at how much Mill anticipated: his goals read like the latest list of demands from modern feminists, his arguments like the latest analysis of male chauvinism. His insights still startle with their relevance and maturity: he knew and despised, for example, the male tendency to view woman as sex object—or "odalisque" or harem "favourite." Finally, he saw that the women's cause was the cause of everyone concerned with human betterment; the emancipation of women was also

Albrecht Dürer, *Melancolia I*

the business of emancipated men. As we listen to Mill in the essay, we hear the voice of a genuinely liberated man, sure in his rejection of privileges and prejudices that lesser men have clung to for centuries.

The tempest over *The Subjection of Women* was but one squall in the general tornado Mill was whipping up for womanhood suffrage. Helen and John created the principal storm center, a National Society for Woman's Suffrage, and together they kept a number of local thunderstorms brewing. "I am in great spirits about our prospects," he clarioned to a falterer in the cause, "and think we are almost within as many years of victory as I formerly thought decades." He had reason to be optimistic. Almost unnoticed, a bill permitting women to vote in municipal elections had passed both Houses shortly after the *Subjection* appeared. A tepid Married Woman's Property Act had also passed in 1870, with the promise of stronger measures on the matter in the not-too-distant future. If only the right to vote could be secured, Mill felt, then everything else—equal education, job opportunity, fuller property rights—would follow. More than anything, he wanted to see womanhood suffrage achieved before he died.

It was not to be. Opposition to the movement stiffened, and its adherents split in a nasty dispute over tactics. It was a question of moderation versus radicalism, John and Helen being adamant moderates. To them, only one method would overcome public revulsion to womanhood suffrage: make the outrageous respectable. Any pushy language or demonstrations would automatically ruin everything. For the same reason, the movement had to be isolated from universal suffrage, the question of divorce, and opposition to the Contagious Diseases Acts—however worthy in themselves these efforts might be. With bristling animosity, Mill maneuvered against the society's militants. But the suffragist movement, contending with external opposition and internal friction, inevitably faltered. When Mill died in 1873, its moment had passed.

And a calamitous passing it was. The enfranchisement of women was successfully blocked for the next forty-five years, and then was achieved only at an appalling cost of civic disruption, political betrayal, property damage, imprisonment, and death—for the movement eventually claimed its martyrs. Small wonder that after suffrage was attained in 1918 (in England) and 1920 (in America), the women's rights movement collapsed in exhaustion, to be revived only after nearly a half-century of dormancy.

The continued relevance of *The Subjection of Women* in our own time is a sad reminder of society's failure to heed its most enlightened prophet of sex equality.

CHAPTER TWELVE

PHILOSOPHIC COMEDY:
The Autobiography

The Eternal-Feminine
Draws us onward.
—GOETHE, *Faust*, Part II

 HAVING done what he could for women, John Mill now turned to do what he could for Woman—that is, Harriet. In short, he had to finish his *Autobiography*, somehow indicating to the world what her role in his life had been. It was a task to test all his emotional resources.

Writing about his early life had been bad enough. Around 1853, when he and Harriet were sure fate would consign them to premature consumptive graves, they had determined to write the Life forthwith. They had to explain the growth of John's mind, the influences acting upon it, and above all the lofty nature of their relationship—"to stop the mouths of enemies hereafter," as John put it. Nervous but resolute, he got out the paper, folded it lengthwise, began writing in the right-hand columns. Those on the left were mainly for Harriet's improvements.

Carefully, she inspected the whole work—commenting, revising, excising. Oddly enough, she who only a few years before had demanded the demythologizing of women ("What is wanted for women is equal rights, equal admission to all social privileges; not a position apart, a sort of sentimental priesthood") now put her own finishing

(224)

touches to John's elaborate icon of her as a paragon of virtue, feeling, and intellect. But such was his vision of her, as she must have realized early in their affair. Indeed, in the first fine careless rapture of the relationship, he had actually let slip that "the less human the more lovely" she seemed to him. Surely a peculiar compliment for one ardent humanist to pay another, but in rejecting the scandalous possibilities of their relationship, they both seem to have taken refuge in its spiritualized potential. So, to the world's eyes, as well as their own, she was to play heavenly muse to his earthly genius. "I should like every one to know," he gushed to her in 1853, "that I am the Dumont and you the originating mind, the Bentham, bless her!"—an effusion prompted no doubt by memories of how the Frenchman's redaction of the old utilitarian sage had rapt him into teenage ecstasies.

When at last they had finished reworking the Life, the story of John's intellectual growth closed with the two philosophers united in the rosy sunset glow of marital bliss. As a conclusion, it was almost too pat.

And of course the story didn't end there. After seven and a half years of marriage, Harriet had died. Reluctantly, John picked up the Life again in 1861 but could add only a few sorrow-sodden paragraphs recording her death and his worship of her memory. In its own secular sort of way, the revised ending now resembled that of Dante's *Vita Nuova (The New Life)* with the poet determining "to say nothing further of this most blessed one, until such time as I could discourse more worthily concerning her. And to this end I labour all I can; as she well knoweth."

To this end Mill labored through the sixties, publishing from the pemican, composing new works, fighting the good fight in Parliament and the periodicals. At last, during the winter of 1869–70 in Avignon, the time had come to discourse more worthily of the blessed one. In lengthy additions to the Life, John showed how her spirit had re-emerged in her daughter, how it had guided him through crises of politics and public service. When he was finished, the completed Life was a humanist *Commedia*, with Harriet as the new Beatrice.

Published less than six months after his death in 1873, the *Autobiography*'s tributes to Harriet, coupled with its glaring evidence of Mill's radicalism and religious unorthodoxy, touched off predictable fireworks. Braced for the backlash, Bain was sure Mill's exhibition of uxoriousness would sink his reputation for clear-headedness. To be sure, some enemies were quick to seize the opportunity. "Mill had no

Statue of John Stuart Mill in the Embankment Gardens near Temple Station

great faith in a God," the *British Quarterly Review* pronounced icily; "he had unbounded confidence in a goddess." As the howls increased, however, John Morley and other admirers mounted a counteroffensive, and though Gladstone himself faltered in the fray, they bore

(226)

down the opposition and crowned the victory by erecting a statue of Mill in the garden near Temple station. There it stands to this day.

And to this day the controversy surrounding the *Autobiography* goes on—particularly on two counts. One, of course, is John's intellectual debt to Harriet. For three-quarters of a century, his claims on that score were written off as the excesses of a too-fond widower. Then in 1951 F. A. Hayek's *John Stuart Mill and Harriet Taylor* took a new look at their relationship and concluded that her influence on his thought and outlook was as great as Mill asserted, though it was the rational, not the sentimental, element she reinforced. Reopened in these terms, the question of her influence has not been closed since.

The second controversy over the *Autobiography* flares periodically between those who regard the book as dehydrated intellectual history and those who find it moving and memorable. "Autobiography of a steam-engine," snarled the aged Carlyle, his old wounds reopened by the book's rating Harriet as a greater poet than he. Less hostile critics have since picked up the refrain: the *Autobiography* is a mere recital of philosophic influences, barren of human details.

But how to account for the book's impact and appeal? For all its seeming shortage of human detail, it somehow remains one of the great human documents of Victorian England. Nowadays, it is more widely accepted that Mill somehow structured his life story into a moving tale of man's search for meaning and fulfillment in a world where divine love can no longer be seen as moving the sun and the other stars. Yet such a world can have its *Commedia*, its story of human hell, purgatory, and paradise. Such a world can have its Beatrice, its pilgrim seeker of truth.

In telling this story, Mill managed to fashion a supreme example of creative autobiography, a personal *Commedia* disguised as intellectual chronicle.

The *Autobiography* gets off to as orderly and forthright a start as any of Mill's works. The seemingly artless opening paragraph unobtrusively forecasts much of the book's structure and substance.

In Mill's usual systematic way, the paragraph lists his three main reasons for writing the memoir. First, at a time when everyone is rethinking educational methods and goals, a record of his own peculiar education might be instructive. Second, in a transitional age of opinions, the record of a mind ever pressing forward in its quest for many-sidedness might be interesting. Finally, and most important, the author wishes to acknowledge publicly his intellectual and moral debts to others, "some of them of recognized eminence, others less known than they deserve to be, and the one to whom most of all is due, one whom the world had no opportunity of knowing."

Beneath the orderly exposition, the paragraph is quietly laying out the book's main divisions. The first third of the *Autobiography* depicts John's youthful education, the middle part shows his mental crisis and the ensuing search for many-sidedness, and the final third concerns his progress under the guidance of "the one," that is, Harriet. This last section has its own tripartite pattern, as friendship is followed by marriage, and then by spiritual communion after her death.

Like the book, the paragraph climaxes in a vision of Harriet sailing on a cloud of religious allusions. When Mill refers to her mystically as "the one," he begins to suggest her human holiness. And that phrase "one whom the world had no opportunity of knowing" is his reworking of John 1:10: "He was in the world . . . and the world knew him not." Such echoes from the cathedral are no accident. They recur throughout the *Autobiography* for a deliberate reason: Mill is depicting his life as nothing less than a religious quest in which his wife emerges as both guide and goal. As the *Autobiography* tells it, young John starts life with Benthamism as the religion of his youth, moves on to a religion of poetry and feeling after the mental crises, and—with Harriet as guide—enters a humanist paradise of successful service in the cause of progress. To be sure, Mill discreetly veils this exalted interpretation of his life with the prosaic details of intellectual history. Still, it is there—and sufficiently obvious to most readers. Small wonder, then, if the *Autobiography* has drawn its share of startled and strong responses.

For perhaps entirely different reasons, however, the first four chapters of Mill's memoir possess an absorbing interest all their own. These are the sections devoted to childhood and youth—specifically, John's early education at home, the moral influences on his character, the first stages of self-education, and his time of youthful propagandism. Not only does the astonishing nature of the education grip one's interest, but James Mill emerges as a memorable, if menacing, presence throughout. The whole account resembles an intellectual *Bildungsroman*, eerily illuminated from time to time with quiet flashes of an almost Dickensian vision of loveless childhood.

"I was born in London, on the 20th of May 1806, and was the eldest son of James Mill, the author of the History of British India." Thus

Mill's life story begins—with crashing matter-of-factness. Soon, however, this seemingly pedestrian account has become shot through with quiet ironies. For instance, the total absence of any reference to Mill's mother silently registers a lack in the Mill household—the absence of warmth, feeling, poetry. Both she and the feminine principle seem to have been reduced to nullity by James Mill's dominant masculinity. Further, James's character emerges as a bundle of bizarre contradictions. In defiance of all prudence and even his own convictions, he produces an enormous brood of young Mills. And with his unsteady income derived solely from writing, he yet insists upon lacing everything he writes with every offensive opinion he can muster for the occasion. In his thought and practice, the admirable and the absurd jostle each other continually. Clearly, a home education conducted by a man of such energetic contradictions will produce a mixed bag of unusual results.

And so it turns out. The educational narrative in chapter one opens with little John lisping his Greek vocables at three, proceeds through astonishing recitals of the works that he studied in several languages, and closes with the young lad in his early teens plowing through logic, political economy, and the higher branches of mathematics—and of course the history of British India. Mill mercifully pauses at chapter's end to assess this prodigious educational experiment. Yes, it demonstrated how much more factual information children can imbibe than they usually do, how wasteful most schooling is. On the other hand, something went drastically wrong somewhere. In the chapter's long closing paragraph, the drawbacks are listed, in a tone suddenly bitter and personal. He was, Mill reports, cut off from children his own age, from physical play. His motor development suffered. His father was harsh, dominating him into passivity. He was taught to know, not to do. He was left helpless in mastering practical matters. His father expected too much. By paragraph's end, one's initial enthusiasm for the education has diminished considerably.

A similar subversion is at work in Mill's portrait of his father. Somehow, James's dedication to his son is always offset by his damaging dominance. The interplay of these conflicting qualities produces several poignant scenes—such as the one in which young John is learning Greek in the same room and at the same table where his father is writing articles and wrestling with the behemoth of British India. With no Greek-English lexicons in existence, the boy must trouble his father for every word he does not know. The father, "one of the most impatient of men," submits (with how much grace we are not told) to this incessant interruption. One's admiration for the father's resoluteness is neatly offset by pity for the child's plight. Later, father and son are taking vigorous constitutionals through rustic lanes. "In these walks I always accompanied him," Mill reports, "and with my earliest recollections of green fields and wild flowers, is mingled that of the account I gave him daily of what I had read the day before." The reader is impelled simultaneously to praise James's diligence and to damn the insensitivity that allows green fields and wildflowers to be blighted by book-learning "accounts"—a word of chillingly unromantic connotations. But it is ever the case with father-and-son walks: nature is overwhelmed by James's looming presence. Elsewhere, James tries to trigger his son's thinking by engaging him in Socratic dialogues—and then loses his temper most un-Socratically when the boy fails to produce the desired reasoning. Indeed, all the way through chapter one, eulogy and irony blend to make James Mill one of the most admirable and exasperating of father figures.

The ambivalence continues into chapter two, where Mill depicts the moral influences on his character. James's zealous agnosticism ruled out ordinary religious belief for his son; it did not, however, prevent generous helpings of morality from being served up during school hours. Taking the Greek philosophers as models, James inculcated enough humanistic earnestness to satisfy even the most demanding Victorian standards. But, Mill remarks, his father's teachings were a less significant moral influence than his character—and, as Mill embarks upon an assessment of that character, the *Autobiography* takes another of its more dramatic swerves into devastating irony. For all his preachments on pleasure-pain, James had scarcely any belief in pleasure. For someone who placed the benevolent affections high in the scale of pleasures, he managed to be singularly unaffectionate toward his elder children—thereby nipping their affection for him. (Even as he is writing, the best Mill can muster are loyalty and pity for his father.) For someone who hated passion, James was driven by strong and devious passions. With his contempt focused on an unusually full range of subjects, James was a remarkable hater whose vials of wrath (Mill suggests) were distilled from bottled-up benevolent feelings.

With a father so crucially warped, one would expect his son to be morally maimed for life. Luckily, the damage was offset by another force, one which dominates the latter half of chapter two. Frequenting

Ford Abbey and grounds

the Mill household were kindlier acquaintances (David Ricardo, Joseph Hume, Jeremy Bentham) who mitigated James's grim earnestness; these three men serve as a glide in Mill's narrative to that even stronger liberating force—Nature. First at Bentham's Barrow Green House, then at gloriously rustic Ford Abbey, this new source of moral impulse begins to stir John's poetic emotions. As if in imitation, the *Autobiography*'s hitherto sober prose breaks into lyricism over the Abbey environs:

> The middle-age architecture, the baronial hall, and the spacious and lofty rooms, of this fine old place, so unlike the mean and cramped externals of English middle class life, gave the sentiment of a larger and freer existence, and were to me a sort of poetic cultivation, aided also by the character of the grounds in which the Abbey stood; which were riant and secluded, umbrageous, and full of the sound of falling waters.

But the chapter's climax is fourteen-year-old John's visit with the Samuel Benthams in southern France, where he finds just about everything his own home lacks—a strong mother figure, siblings who are not just his pupils (indeed *they* teach *him*), and an appreciation of beauty, feeling, and liberty. Under this tutelage, John thrills to mountain glory in the Pyrenees and rhapsodizes over French freedom.

The reprieve, alas, is only temporary. On his way back to England, John visits Monsieur Say, Saint-Simon, and "an old friend of my father's," the three men serving as corresponding glide for the return from Nature's domain to his father's. After the exhilarating language of the French interlude, the *Autobiography*'s prose turns glumly factual again: "I returned to England in July 1821; and my education resumed its ordinary course."

The gloom, however, is soon dispelled. In one of the book's most surprising twists, chapter three shows John reembracing orthodox Benthamism with ecstatic fervor. His father puts into his hands (here and elsewhere in the *Autobiography* the phrase suggests priestly ceremonial) a Dumont redaction of Bentham, and soon the boy is illuminated with philosophic vision. The principle of utility flashes upon him with blinding revelation. Suddenly all the scattered fragments of his learning fall into place; suddenly he has a moral imperative to preach the gospel of utility to a fallen world. Suddenly he has "opinions; a creed, a doctrine, a philosophy; in one among the best senses of the word, a religion."

Fired with apostolic zeal, young John rushes out to inflame the world with Benthamite doctrine. For the first time in the *Autobiography* he begins to act independently—dashing off essays for the journals, conversing on his own with his father's friends, infiltrating a group of young Cambridge intellectuals. He even founds his own utilitarian cell. Ironically, though, these first efforts at independence only mark him as a carbon copy of his radical father, a point made clear at chapter's end by John's assuming a minor position under his father at East India House.

In chapter four, "Youthful Propagandism; the Westminster Review," Mill provides a marvelous first-hand account of the beginnings of the 1820s reform movement. Clearly, it was joy to be alive in that dawn, at least for a radical enthusiast caught up in the first stirrings of the push that would lead to the great reform bill of 1832. On the personal level, however, the chapter is a bit less exhilarating: John still seems destined to become merely a pocket-size version of his father.

Only at the very end are there tremors of his impending philosophic upheaval.

The chapter's first half focuses on James Mill's heroic doings, as he rallies support for reform. Though neither founder nor editor of the *Westminster*, James actually launches it with an explosive article in the first issue. A sort of intellectual mana radiates from him in all directions, stimulating others to write, shaping periodical policies, charming bands of disciples. By comparison, poor John is bumptious immaturity itself. In the *Westminster* his follow-up article to James's comes off a resounding fizzle, and his youthful zeal seems to hinder the movement as much as help it. Worse, he declines into "a mere reasoning machine," once again impervious to poetry and feeling.

In the chapter's second half, John does grow up considerably, but his actions merely repeat his father's. Serving as Bentham's oracle, launching a radical review, retrieving the Debating Society—in all this, John duplicates James's successes. Only in the chapter's final paragraph are rumbles of oncoming thunder heard: Mill mentions his interest in the French Revolution, the usefulness of his researches to Carlyle. The chapter that had begun dominated by a utilitarian father figure closes with references to a violent overthrow of the old order and to a mystical father figure whom the son will serve.

In chapter five the gathering emotional storm breaks in fury. Here Mill recounts his mental crisis and its aftermath, making them literally and metaphorically central to his autobiography. Occupying the book's crucial middle section, these events irrevocably divide John's childhood from his maturity.

The time is autumn 1826. John is just twenty years old. The first bloom of enthusiasm has withered from his crusade to reform the world. "In a dull state of nerves" he asks the fatal question: suppose all your reforms could be achieved this instant; would that make you happy? When an irrepressible self-consciousness answers "No" in thunder, John's whole world collapses. Having taken up Benthamite doctrine as a religion, having staked his happiness on evangelizing the nonutilitarians, John discovers that dedication to the greatest happiness principle brings no happiness. The principle itself must thus be doubted. It is a religious crisis of the first magnitude, the sort of spiritual cataclysm (Mill observes) that usually follows "conviction of sin" and oftens precedes religious conversion.

It was typical of John at the time that he could not suffer a nervous breakdown without analyzing it on the spot—and in terms of associationist psychology. Accordingly, the *Autobiography* pauses in midcrisis to present his elucidation of it. By resorting solely to praise and blame, reward and punishment, his father had instilled in him an artificial link between pleasure and the desire for human improvement. If only James had let benevolent feeling also weave a natural link between the two! And then, when John neglected feeling, when he gave himself up to wholesale analysis, the link disintegrated completely, lacking any affective glue to hold it together. Intellectually, then, John's commitment to human progress remained in high gear; emotionally, it was out of fuel. Or, to quote Mill's own metaphor:

> I was thus, as I said to myself, left stranded at the commencement of my voyage, with a well equipped ship and a rudder, but no sail; without any real desire for the ends which I had been so carefully fitted out to work for: no delight in virtue or the general good, but also just as little in anything else.

In short, just the opposite of the natural poet like Shelley, whom he had described so many years ago in "The Two Kinds of Poetry." His crowd of sail filled with emotional gusts, but lacking philosophical ballast, the poet of nature often plies splendidly into "the most utter wreck." No wonder John felt his "was not an interesting, or in any way respectable distress."

Picking up the narrative thread again, Mill records the event that overturned the crisis—his accidental reading of Jean François Marmontel's *Memoires*. The episode is an armchair psychologist's delight, hinting darkly of Freudian death wishes. Reading away in Marmontel, John comes to a passage in which the author as a boy returns home after his father's death, confronts his distraught family, and in a burst of exhilarated self-confidence comforts them by proclaiming that he will take his father's place in their lives. (He even crowns the event by sleeping in his father's bed, but Mill omits this indecorous detail.) Dissolving in tears, John discovers he is no longer a stock or stone. But why did this particular scene move him to tears? As a persuasive answer, the Freudian one has much to recommend it: the episode dramatized John's own repressed death wish against his father, reminded him that fathers die, that sons displace them. In support of the theory it can be noted that Mill echoed his account of the Marmontel scene when he later recounted James's death. Or at least he did in the early draft of the *Autobiography*. Apparently catching himself, he excised the give-away phrase for the final version.

The worst over, John now seeks support from the arts. Recognizing that he must cultivate feeling or lapse anew into spiritual dryness, he luxuriates in music and turns to poetry. Unluckily, he first lights upon Byron, whose antiheroes seem only burnt-out cases of romantic passion—not exactly the sort of thing to perk up a world-weary young despairer. With better luck next time, John encounters Wordsworth's verse. The mountain scenery, the tranquil emotions, the serene acceptance of life—all pour soothing oil on his soul's troubled waters. In a glow of gratitude, Mill once more pays tribute to the Lakeland poet: "Compared with the greatest poets, he may be said to be the poet of unpoetical natures, possessed of quiet and contemplative tastes." Like many another storm-tossed Victorian, Mill prized Wordsworth less as artist than as spiritual therapist.

At this point in the *Autobiography* occur two almost symbolic episodes, crystallizing the two major divisions of John's life. As he moves from his father's influence to his wife's, these incidents represent the point of no return. The first episode, John's debate with Roebuck, epitomizes his disaffection with his father's character and teachings. The other event, his friendship with Sterling, looks ahead to his special relationship with Harriet Taylor. One incident serves as coda to the first half of John's life, the other as prelude to the second half.

In debating John Arthur Roebuck, John was up against a daunting opponent. In the heyday of his later parliamentary career, Roebuck became such a byword for aggressive forensics that he was dubbed "Tear 'Em," and as late as the 1930s "Don't John Arthur Roebuck me" was still used in England to fend off a heated opponent. As Mill describes him in the *Autobiography*, Roebuck bears more than a passing resemblance to the starchy James Mill. A go-ahead philistine of liberal stripe, Roebuck undervalues art, represses feeling, and scouts Wordsworth's poetry as so much "flowers and butterflies." As fate would have it, his favorite writer is Byron. All this is too much for John soaring in the first flights of Wordsworthian enthusiasm, and so the two young men have it out on the floor of the Debating Society. Stoutly defending the compatability of intensest feeling and practical reason, John is clearly defying his father's buttoned-up views on the question, is indirectly denouncing James's failure to cultivate feeling through art. But, as far as no-nonsense Roebuck is concerned, the passionate persuasion is all in vain. And so John's friendship with him begins to dissolve. So also does John's wholesale allegiance to his father's views.

Into the resulting friendship gap step the two Coleridgeans, F. D. Maurice and John Sterling, living proof of John's argument that thought and feeling are compatible. "Maurice was the thinker, Sterling the orator, and impassioned expositor of thoughts which, at this period, were almost entirely formed for him by Maurice."

When John enters their lives, however, a curious triangle forms, gingerly prefiguring that of John, Harriet, and her husband.

If Mill depicted Roebuck in the image of his father, he portrays Sterling as a forerunner of Harriet. Like her, Sterling possesses a poetic nature, which he supplements by attaching himself to a thinker. Alas, his first thinker turns out to be inadequate for the task. Maurice, Mill says, wastes his intellectual power, thereby lagging behind in cultivation—rather like the well-meaning but mentally sluggish John Taylor. Winning poet away from thinker, John conjoins with Sterling in a more viable union of logician and artist. Even Sterling's early death anticipates Harriet's. Ever so briefly, then, the crucial relationship between John and Harriet is played out before our eyes in this Mill-Sterling interlude.

Meanwhile, John's already tottering faith in Benthamism receives yet another blow from the clash between Macaulay and his father. Enlivening the March 1829 *Edinburgh*, Macaulay's playfully pontifical assault upon the hallowed *Essay on Government* had provoked James to a reply that, to John, had as many holes in it as the original attack. Despairing of light from either quarter, John at last flees the confines of orthodox utilitarianism. The philosophic world is all before him.

First stop on the journey to many-sidedness is the Germano-Coleridgean school where Mill learns a philosophy of history, an awareness that different times require different social institutions. Then the Saint-Simonian theory of alternating organic and critical ages; then Comte's vision of theological, metaphysical, and positive stages of society succeeding each other in a grand march toward truth and harmony. Setting his own philosophic house in order, John had earlier formed an antiselfconsciousness theory: instead of seeking frantically for personal happiness, he had learned he must work for a worthy goal (such as general happiness) and thereby attain personal happiness as by-product. Now another gain is made when he manages to reconcile free will with scientific predictability of human behavior.

Amid the heady swirl of new thought, John also revises his thinking on politics, though he remains a radical on the grounds that representative government (for all its drawbacks) is what is most needed for human progress at this stage of European history. Accordingly, he rushes off to cheer the 1830 French Revolution, seconds the English reform movement, and takes up with the radical mystic Carlyle.

On the whole, the passage assessing the old mystic's influence is cautiously cordial. Walking a tightrope here, Mill commends his old friend-enemy not as an original thinker, but as a powerful poet. Only at the very end does Mill touch off an explosion. "And I never presumed to judge him with any definiteness," he concludes, "until he was interpreted to me by one greatly the superior of us both." Again it is Harriet, the sacred "one," who was "more a poet than he, and more a thinker than I—whose own mind and nature included his, and infinitely more." There, he had said it. Carlyle would never forgive him, but Mill was past caring. Besides, he was only paying his intellectual debts as exactly as he could; the chips could fall where they would.

To wrap up the tale of his mental crisis, Mill introduces a full-length portrait of John Austin. A rather odd choice at first glance, but soon it becomes clear that in describing Austin ("one with whom I had now most points of agreement"), Mill is describing himself after rebounding from the mental crisis. Austin, it seems, "cultivated more and more a kind of German religion, a religion of poetry and feeling." Clearly, young John did likewise. To such an extremity had the backlash from Benthamism brought him.

But he begins to correct the imbalance, as chapter six surveys the years 1830 to 1840. Harbinger of true philosophic symmetry, Harriet Taylor now takes her place in the narrative. In a prose clogged with reverential superlatives, the *Autobiography* attempts to convey the quasi-sacred nature of her character and their relationship. When John first met her, she was a natural poet like Shelley, all feeling and intuition. Her husband—for all his upright qualities—was an inadequate logical and artistic helpmate. Worse, the prevailing subjection of women relegated her to a small circle of friends. John now enters the magic circle. After a respectable interval, the two became friends. She eventually develops into a full-fledged philosopher, combining logic and lyricism, surveying long-run goals as well as short-run means of securing them. Thus, she becomes a sacred human, because a most highly developed one. As for John, he at last finds the poetic counterpart to give human substance to his airy speculations. Together they act out the drama of Art and Science that had closed the *Logic* in a blaze of light. As seal of their union are his writings, "not the work of one mind, but of the fusion of two."

To be sure, few modern readers have been able to bend the knee to Mill's philosophic angel in the house. Some critics, hostile to Harriet to begin with, merely accuse Mill of attempting to create Dulcinea from a particularly unlikely Aldonza. Others, less hostile, question her excellence and influence, begin poking for corroborating evidence, and find little or none. Like most readers, they are left unable to suspend disbelief.

However that may be, the great gush of piety brought on by mentioning Harriet has swept Mill off course, and he now has to backpaddle rapidly to the early 1830s when she was but one of his many guiding lights. Under the impetus of her presence, however, John becomes reinvigorated intellectually and politically. We see him awakening to de Tocqueville on democracy. And when the Radicals elected after 1832 begin dawdling for lack of a leader, John takes over the *London and Westminster Review* in a heroic effort to supply that leadership from afar.

Called in to help launch still another radical journal, James Mill whips up a familiar storm of excitement and casts an even more familiar pall of intransigence. With his father about, John simply cannot express his heterodoxy freely. When James dies in midchapter, the *Autobiography* loses its most compelling yet constraining character. Dutifully pausing to pay tribute, Mill cannot resist concluding the eulogy with yet another allusion to Harriet as the sacred one. "In the power of influencing by mere force of mind and character," Mill intones, "the convictions and purposes of others, and in the strenuous exertion of that power to promote freedom and progress, he left, as far as my knowledge extends, no equal among men, and but one among women." It is very much the same punch line he had used earlier on Carlyle.

Once the narrative has safely laid James to rest, John springs into action with almost unseemly haste. In a trice he has opened up the review to the likes of Carlyle and Sterling, is financing it out of his own pocket, and making dramatic headway with the *Logic*. Soon he is deep in correspondence with Comte, defending Durham, and heading off the critical stampede that seems destined to trample Carlyle's *French*

Revolution. Still unwinded, he composes sweeping assessments of Bentham and Coleridge as the great seminal minds of the age. Now severing all ties with his sectarian past, he sells the *London and Westminster* and begins instructing the *Edinburgh*'s Whig readership with an article on de Tocqueville. The chapter contains not a hint of his breakdown following his father's death, not a whisper of the carelessness that burned Carlyle's manuscript. As chapter six tells it, once Harriet has entered his life and James departed it forever, John becomes a veritable fireball of energy and decision.

In the book's long concluding chapter, the achievements of John's mature life command the forestage, while the related drama of Harriet's death and rebirth occupies the shadowy background. Simultaneously matter-of-fact and mystical, Mill is at his most baffling here, offering startling glimpses into the religious experiences that shaped his vision and vocation.

The burst of creative energy that had closed chapter six carries over into chapter seven, with John publishing the *Logic* to great applause and writing out the *Political Economy* in record time. With similar finesse, he wins Harriet for himself and eventually marries her. Then, in a stunning reversal, her sudden death is reported, and the *Autobiography* comes grinding to a halt. John's creative impetus, his very life, come to a stop.

It is only "some years after closing the preceding narrative" that Mill is able to resume his story. The first thing he does is suggest how his creative torpor was dispelled. At first, he could publish only their finished joint productions. He dares not alter anything in *On Liberty* without her guidance. When he does add a new feature to *Thoughts on Parliamentary Reform*, that feature is speedily superseded by Thomas Hare's work. Without his "almost infallible counselor" he abandons revising his old articles and sends them off for republication almost as is. A few original articles trickle forth, but it is clear John's creative life is at low ebb. In a way, it is the mental crisis all over again—but worse. Then, his doubts about Benthamism had crippled his youthful propagandism. Now, the loss of his *femme inspiratrice* threatens permanent creative paralysis.

Soon, however, the tide turns. Harriet's influence is reborn. "And, though the inspirer of my best thoughts was no longer with me, I was not alone: she had left a daughter—my step-daughter, Miss Helen Taylor, the inheritor of much of her wisdom, and of all her nobleness of character." As the organ prose swells louder, Mill begins extolling Helen's "original thought and soundness of practical judgment"— exactly her mother's strong suits. And then we learn that henceforth all his writings are the product not of one mind, but of three—himself, Helen, and Harriet. The clouds of religious language that had previously wafted in with every mention of Harriet now begin clustering about Helen. In brief, Harriet has been resurrected in Helen, who becomes John's instructor and guide.

As soon as Harriet-Helen's presence has been established, John is out of the doldrums and into the thick of things again. In short order he composes three new major works—*Representative Government, Subjection of Women, Utilitarianism*—and helps head off British support for the slave states at the start of the American Civil War. Getting his second wind, he embarks upon full-scale assessments of Sir William Hamilton and Auguste Comte, fixing their philosophic niches as he had done with Coleridge and Bentham. And, most marvelous of all, he comes bounding out of the library to win a seat in Parliament.

Describing this energetic outburst, the *Autobiography* utilizes a repeated pattern. John's later career is depicted as a series of episodes, each containing three elements—an announcement that he has a duty to perform, an account of the crisis enjoining that duty, and a statement of his success in performing it. Trained to know rather than to do, John hits his stride in this chapter. But he is not preening himself. Rather, the guiding presence of Harriet-Helen is constantly suggested or cited for whatever success there is. Indeed, his later career becomes dynamic evidence of Harriet's ability to survive death and reinvigorate her lover-worshiper. For all its seeming factuality, the *Autobiography*'s final chapter represents Mill's exultant *Paradiso*, a successful career of philosophic writing and public service carried out under the eye of a Beatrice who dies and ascends to a new life.

And so his parliamentary career passes in review, a wild parade of idealism and integrity. There is John refusing to incur a farthing of campaign expenses, spelling out in writing his most controversial views, and publicly admitting he once wrote that workers are generally liars. After this grandly implausible start, the career rises to evergreater heights of heroic folly, with John championing every honorable lost cause in sight. Needless to say, any success under the circumstances seems little short of miraculous, and even outright failure is a victory of sorts. At least John has given the outrageous a

Before the Tournament. Gladstone and Disraeli face off in this *Punch* cartoon, while Mill prepares for parliamentary battle at the far left, beside Punch on his hobbyhorse.

creditable public airing, mustered some support, and thereby asserted the claims of the future.

While tilting at full gallop in Parliament, John yet finds time for an outside philosophic joust or two. He delivers the magisterial St. Andrews address and—with Bain, Grote, and Andrew Findlater—edits and updates his father's *Analysis of the Phenomena of the Human Mind.* This is the *Autobiography*'s last tribute to James Mill, and running true to form it contains an ambiguous twist. While Mill lavishes high praise on his father's pioneering book, he acknowledges that it did need to be "enriched, and in some cases corrected." As one psychological Mill-watcher, Howard R. Wolf, argues, the man who introduces himself in the *Autobiography* as "the eldest son of James Mill, the author of the History of British India," saw his father's works as rival siblings to be outperformed by his own greater works.

As if his parliamentary performance were not quixotic enough, John decides during the next election to subscribe money for the abrasively atheistic Charles Bradlaugh—the last straw as far as Westminster voters are concerned. His bid for reelection lost, John serenely ends his brief career in Parliament. At this point in the book John has evolved into that steady-minded philosopher whose calm voice has narrated the *Autobiography* from the start, a philosopher whose logical bent of mind has been tempered with profoundest feeling. To this philosopher, losing an election is the merest of trifles compared with the losses he has already suffered and survived.

A backward glance at the *Autobiography* now shows that John has traveled a path through three distinct realms, roughly resembling those in Dante's great *Commedia*. As a child, John awakens in a dark wood of Benthamism: he says he has "no remembrance of the time" when his Benthamite education began. His childhood is a sort of loveless *Inferno*, where a heroic but inadequate father-guide introduces him to great knowledge and great sin. The mental crisis serves as his *Purgatorio*, where he stands convicted of the Benthamite sin of neglecting feeling and where he learns from a series of guides (Wordsworth, Coleridge, and others) how to purge himself of this sin. Having thus righted himself, John encounters the Beatrice of whole philosophy in Harriet Taylor, who before and after her death leads him into the humanist's *Paradiso* of active life devoted to human betterment. As in Dante, Virgil disappears; Beatrice endures.

The moment now approaches for the climactic vision in Mill's *Commedia*:

> Since that time little has occurred which there is need to commemorate in this place. I returned to my old pursuits and to the enjoyment of a country life in the South of Europe; alternating twice a year with a residence of some weeks or months in the neighbourhood of London. I have written various articles in periodicals (chiefly in my friend Mr. Morley's Fortnightly Review), have made a small number of speeches on public occasions, especially at the meetings of the Women's Suffrage Society, have published the "Subjection of Women," written some years before, with some additions by my daughter and myself, and have commenced the preparation of matter for future books, of which it will be time to speak more particularly if I live to finish them. Here, therefore, for the present, this Memoir may close.

Underlying the matter-of-fact prose is a quiet joy. With consummate subtlety the passage recalls the *Autobiography*'s most elevated images and themes, blending them into a single vision of human happiness—

the union of Harriet, Helen, and John, the philosophic work symboliz-
ing their joint creativity, Morley's discipleship indicating the endurance of their views, the crusade for human liberty with London as its
focal point, the wild beauty and free atmosphere of the Pyrenees. The
memoir may well close here. Mill has had his vision.

CHAPTER THIRTEEN

PATTERN OF CONVERSION:

Three Essays on Religion

There lives more faith in honest doubt,
Believe me, than in half the creeds.
—ALFRED TENNYSON, *In Memoriam*, 96, 11–12

FOR all the commotion it created, the *Autobiography* was not Mill's biggest posthumous bombshell. That honor went to *Three Essays on Religion*, published in 1874 by Helen Taylor.

Among her late stepfather's papers, Helen discovered "Nature" and "The Utility of Religion," written in the early fifties when John and Harriet were busy compacting their pemican. She also found a third related essay—"Theism"—composed during 1868–70, the last considerable work completed by Mill during his lifetime. Subjoining a brief introduction, Helen published the three works together in a single volume. Amid the outcries that greeted it, a few sighs of relief could be heard. Mill was not the atheist some had anticipated. To the end, he proved to be splendidly controversial and surprising.

His religious convictions had evolved unsteadily over the years. Apparently his father's belief in Christianity was on the point of final collapse just as young John's education got under way, and thus supernaturalism was effectively excised from his training program. Instead, James's indignation at universal injustice was burned vividly into his

(244)

son's imagination. Later on, the impression seems to have been reinforced by Harriet Taylor, who entertained much the same indignation —at least in her later years. Watching her first husband die of cancer prompted her to fierce outbursts against nature's senselessness, and she and Mill sometimes talked vehemently of "our atheism."

But his beliefs are not so easily categorized. As a youth, he had genuine faith in Benthamite doctrine and, later, the Religion of Humanity. In addition, he apparently harbored a capacity for myth-making and supernatural belief that logic never managed to exorcise entirely. Given James Mill's fatal harshness, John understandably resisted belief in an omnipotent deity addressed as "Our Father," but he exhibited imaginative skill in worshiping Harriet as Our Lady, a sort of Virgin Mary in the Religion of Humanity. To add to the situation, his Benthamite hostility toward reactionary Christian institutions was constantly pitted against his Coleridgean awareness of their enduring contributions to moral and social improvement. Like many another Victorian, he was thus torn between faith and doubt, between yearning for the wholeness of past Christian civilization and exulting in the advancing tide of disbelief. So when supernatural religion came up for discussion, one could never be sure whether Mill would bless or blaspheme it.

Not that he had much to say in public about theological matters. He had picked up his father's wariness about shocking middle-class religious sensibilities, and in the 1830s he even abandoned a projected history of the French Revolution rather than tip his disbelieving hand. Besides, the superheated world of Victorian religious controversy was well avoided by any social reformer wishing to be heard on other topics with some degree of calmness. Once a doctrinal issue had been raised, all other considerations were likely to be lost in the ensuing uproar. Mill was not one to flinch in the face of controversy, but why should he sacrifice his campaign to reform the world merely to score theological debating points?

Certainly the reception accorded *Three Essays on Religion* amply verified the wisdom of Mill's earlier reticence. Though a few believers rejoiced to discover that their worst fears concerning him had proved unfounded, the book was generally greeted with rancor and repudiations.

To be sure, *Three Essays on Religion* offered something to offend nearly everybody. For those who believed that religious beliefs were sanctioned by nature's laws, the opening essay ("Nature") portrayed their idol as more vicious than a demented criminal. No, Mill proclaimed, humanity could not march forward to a simple-minded chant of "Follow Nature." For orthodox believers, "The Utility of Religion" boldly argued that the world could do quite nicely without divine revelation, belief in God, or hope of an afterlife. But most offensive of all was "Theism." After ruffling believers by discrediting most of the traditional "proofs" for God's existence, as well as those for immortality and revelation, the essay then reversed field to scandalize unbelievers—many of them Mill's own disciples—who had counted on his being safely enlisted in the atheist or at least agnostic camp. No such thing. Instead, he gave dismaying credence to belief in a God and even encouraged people to hope for immortality. Once again the intricacies and alterations of his thought were too much for party-line thinkers. While the *Edinburgh Review* thundered away at his unbelief ("We do not remember that in the whole range of sceptical literature any writer ever adopted conclusions so atrocious"), John Morley was complaining in the *Fortnightly* of the book's excessive credulity. Having lost his own faith partly through reading *On Liberty*, Morley was aghast to find his teacher flirting with belief in his old age. To the disillusioned disciple, "Theism" represented an enormity worthy of Comte's final frenzies.

Now that religious skepticism and qualified belief are commonplaces, the shock value of the essays has much diminished, though not in all quarters. Instead, Mill's *Three Essays* can be viewed as a paradigm of their author's quest for religious meaning. Certainly they are the superb results of a sensitive mind probing the evidences for belief. And if the conclusions they reach at last are more tentative than the orthodox would prefer, they are also more believing than the rigid skeptic would like to admit.

Mill's publication plans for the essays were cloudy in the extreme. As late as 1873 he thought of releasing "Nature" as a trial balloon, perhaps to see if the wind was right for publishing the other two. Though the essays were not originally written to form a consecutive series, twice in "Theism" Mill refers the reader to "Nature," thereby hinting at some link between them. Whatever his intentions, when the essays were grouped together in a single volume, they fell into place as a fascinating version of the "pattern of conversion."

Victorian literature teems with examples of the pattern: loss of faith is followed by despondent skepticism, and at last resolved by new faith. In *Sartor Resartus* Carlyle had fixed the pattern for the age, in three grand and fiery chapters entitled "The Everlasting No," "The Centre of Indifference," and "The Everlasting Yea." In these pages Carlyle's hero (who bears the symbolic but jawbreaking name of Diogenes Teufelsdröckh) passes through a crisis of faith in which he fiercely rebels against the absurd universe he finds himself confronting. After simmering down to sullen quiescence, he goes on to attain new faith in a purposeful universe. After Carlyle, the pattern cropped up everywhere—in Tennyson's *In Memoriam*, in Newman's *Apologia Pro Vita Sua*, in scores of novels and poems. Indeed, Mill himself had already traced out the pattern in his *Autobiography*, depicting his "No" to old-line Benthamism, the ensuing mental crisis, and his final emergence with Harriet in the Religion of Humanity.

But in *Three Essays on Religion* the pattern is, if anything, more in evidence than ever. "Nature" peals Mill's resounding "No" to an absurd universe ruled by Nature red in tooth and claw. "The Utility of Religion" casts skeptical stones at monotheism, immortality, and the future usefulness of supernaturalism, though it does affirm belief in the Religion of Humanity. But "Theism," after a prolonged scrutiny of the evidence, pronounces qualified assent to a God of limited power. Rigorous investigation having done its worst, the concluding section of "Theism" gives its blessing to "supernatural hopes," such as belief in God's goodness, immortal life, and the divine mission of Christ. In a final burst of affirmation, such hopes are declared legitimate supernatural ingredients in the Religion of Humanity.

"Nature" opens with Mill setting out in his most coolly rational fashion to clarify the word "nature" and to discover if there is any validity to the ethical bromide "Follow Nature." Being calmly Socratic about the whole matter, he first decides that "nature" in this case means either one of two things. First, it means everything that happens in the world, because such things happen "naturally" or according to natural laws. But in this instance, any advice to follow nature is meaningless: disobeying nature's laws is not wrong but impossible.

In the second sense "nature" means everything that happens without man's intervention, such as acts attributed to an almost personified Nature. Indeed, some people hold up Nature's ways as a model for man's moral behavior, the word "unnatural" being just about the worst label that can be attached to certain acts. And so Mill begins scrutinizing Nature's ways to discover just what sort of morality they propound.

As he does, he rapidly loses his cool detachment. In the face of

J. M. W. Turner, *Snowstorm—Steamboat Off a Harbour's Mouth*, 1842

Nature's appalling atrocities, his language begins to surge with outrage. Nature is soon exposed as that most hated of Millian villains—a despot who delights in inflicting pain. The essay peaks in one of the most vividly impassioned passages Mill ever wrote. "In sober truth," he begins, "nearly all the things which men are hanged or imprisoned for doing to one another, are nature's every day performances." Nature is a murderer slaying everyone, sometimes with the most horrifying torments:

> Nature impales men, breaks them as if on the wheel, casts them to be devoured by wild beasts, burns them to death, crushes them with stones like the first christian martyr, starves them with hunger, freezes them with cold, poisons them by the quick or slow venom of her exhalations, and has hundreds of other hideous deaths in reserve, such as the ingenious cruelty of a Nabis or a Domitian never surpassed.

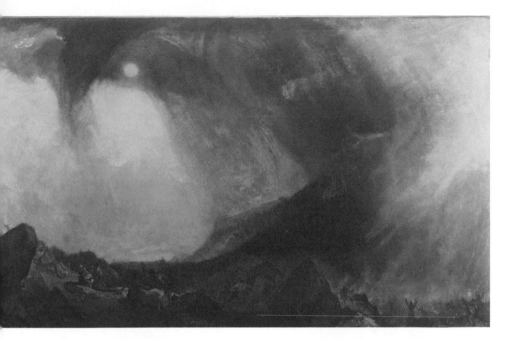

J. M. W. Turner, *Snowstorm: Hannibal and His Army Crossing the Alps*, 1812

As the passage progresses, other sinister names are added—Carrier, the Borgias—mere amateurs to Nature's accomplished villainy.

Completely lacking a moral sense, Nature strikes without rhyme or reason: "A single hurricane destroys the hopes of a season; a flight of locusts, or an inundation, desolates a district; a trifling chemical change in an edible root, starves a million of people"—a swift allusion to the nightmare of Irish famine. Mill's prose transforms itself into a series of terrifying images, almost like the cataclysms that sweep across the canvases of J. M. W. Turner. Storm, pestilence, hurricane—all spin with dizzying speed across Mill's page, much as Turner's snowstorms swirl about beleagured steamers, or his vortices of darkness gather ominously above cowering humanity. But Nature's awesomeness in Turner's work occasionally warns man of his littleness, gives him pause as he lifts the dagger of murder and rapine. In Mill, Nature merely enacts terrifying examples of cruelty and rapacity, examples that only the most depraved of people would think of emulating.

Shipwreck, that archetypal horror haunting the Victorian imagination, is here crystallized in one striking simile: "The waves of the sea, like banditti seize and appropriate the wealth of the rich and the little all of the poor with the same accompaniments of stripping, wounding, and killing as their human antitypes." In a flash Mill conjures up a comparison which recalls the Track-of-a-Storm metaphor that had raged through Dickens's *Tale of Two Cities:* "Anarchy and the Reign of Terror are overmatched in injustice, ruin, and death, by a hurricane and a pestilence."

Given such a vision of the world, the advice to follow Nature becomes perfectly grotesque. Far better to cultivate the artificial rather than the natural. "All praise of Civilization, or Art, or Contrivance, is so much dispraise of Nature," Mill snaps, "an admission of imperfection, which it is man's business, and merit, to be always endeavouring to correct or mitigate." Like the tormented Dr. Rieux in Albert Camus's *The Plague*, Mill refuses to love a scheme of things in which children are put to torture.

Nor will he love Nature's God either. At least not if that God is all-powerful. "If the maker of the world *can* all that he will, he wills misery, and there is no escape from the conclusion." The only acceptable theological theory is that the powers of good are limited and cannot altogether subdue the forces of evil—an idea that immediately recalls James Mill's partiality for Manichean belief. Indeed, James used to wonder in his son's presence why nobody revived the theory in modern times. In the first two of the *Three Essays on Religion* he got his wish.

At least on the Manichean view of things, humanity has a worthy purpose in life—to aid providence in its struggle with evil. But such a view also implies that not all "natural" impulses are to be encouraged. Certainly not that "voluptuous" love of cruelty which Mill denounced in *The Subjection of Women* and elsewhere. Certainly not that primitive behavior that had been rosily recommended by Rousseau and his followers since the late eighteenth century. And certainly not that fondness for preying on others that Social Darwinists would soon be hawking to the world in the late nineteenth century. As far as Mill was concerned, the less people behaved like animals, the better. The unfavorable animal imagery in his works had always implied as much.

"Nature," then, is Mill's searing *non serviam* to Nature and the natural theologians. His persona epitomizes civilized sensibility. His prose depicts a terrifyingly absurd universe, one in which humanity by itself must evolve a finer ethic than it sees at work in creation.

Though the essay's rebelliousness is clear enough, some of its other aspects remain a puzzle. What, for example, brought on this defiant cry of "No"? Was it written in protest against the consumptive deaths John and Harriet envisaged for themselves in the fifties? And where is that other concept of Nature as the beauty of the world that stirs the soul to ethical grandeur? What of Nature lifting the heart to new heights of freedom? What of Nature ministering to a mind diseased? In brief, what of Nature as the Pyrenees and the Lake District? Did Mill, as chapter two of the *Autobiography* suggests, take Nature as a father substitute, transferring to it the ambiguous feelings he felt for James Mill? Certainly "Nature" is the hardest essay to square with Mill's other works. His love of wilderness, his championing of spontaneity, even his perpetual use of natural organic imagery, belie the hostility toward Nature exhibited here. It is as if Mill's persona has plunged into such a Teufelsdröckhian crisis that the beauty and glory of the world are no longer visible to him.

Having assailed the worship of Nature, Mill next takes on Christianity—and indeed all other supernatural religions—in "The Utility of Religion." But his mood is more temperate now; no longer is Mill's persona able to sustain his defiance. Toward the essay's end he readily grants supernaturalism's great utility in the past, even while arguing its inutility for the future. For all its opening antisupernatural barbs, the essay at last becomes tinged with a melancholy reminiscent of Matthew Arnold's sad farewells to supernatural hopes.

The essay starts out cantankerously enough. The question of religion's usefulness, Mill notes, could arise only when its doctrines were seriously in doubt. Unable to win the case for belief, religious apologists had lately taken to suggesting that supernaturalism was needed to keep the population moral, those rambunctious lower classes in particular. Remove the fear of hell from people's hearts, and ethical pandemonium will be unleashed. Far better, apologists argued, for nonbelievers to muzzle themselves in the interests of social order. Far better for semi-believers to whistle hymns in the dark. Far better for everyone to refrain from airing nagging doubts in public. But before Mill will submit to such enforced hypocrisy, he will determine just how morally useful religion really is.

Predictably, he finds society has sufficient nonreligious means to keep up morality. The sheer weight of public opinion, the mere fact that "everybody" agrees on a point of morality, insure that the individual will take the matter seriously. And since early religious education has succeeded because it was early, not because it was religious, there is no reason to suppose that secular ethical training would be unsuccessful. Indeed, should supernatural religion depart the scene (as Mill seems to expect it to do at any moment), these resources could serve to keep people morally in line. (Nor is Mill here contradicting his views in *On Liberty:* there also he had stressed society's ability and right to inculcate and enforce moral behavior, that is, any behavior in which the rights of others are involved.) Looking at the other side of the coin, Mill wonders if fear of hell really works to deter sin. On the Benthamite calculus, the pains threatened by an angry deity are too remote and uncertain to influence behavior much, as the continual backsliding of the ancient Jews (who believed in divine wrath if anybody did) indicates.

During the essay's opening section, Mill's persona gleefully aims his venom-tipped sarcasms at supernatural belief. But his attitude soon changes. Religion is not to be dismissed so lightly. It has held up to humanity ideal visions toward which people could aspire—and for this it is to be honored. More, religion has addressed itself to those mysteries of human existence that defy answer, to those immortal longings —as understandable as they are futile. Before long Mill's prose has become quite solemn:

> Human existence is girt round with mystery: the narrow region of our experience is a small island in the midst of a boundless sea, which at once awes our feelings and stimulates our imagination by its vastness and its obscurity.

Religion—and poetry too—have unquestionably done (and do) great service to humanity by cultivating elevated feelings and offering comforting hope. At this point in the essay, the utility of religion has turned out to be—surprisingly enough—enormous.

But must religion be *supernatural* to be useful? Obviously not, and so Mill begins a solemn apologia for the Religion of Humanity. Though belief in immortal life is baseless, he says, we can still nourish our moral feelings on visions of future races who will indirectly immortalize us by achieving what we strove for. Meanwhile, the Saints of Humanity are there to guide and fortify us: "The idea that Socrates, or Howard or Washington, or Antoninus, or Christ, would have sympathized with us, or that we are attempting to do our part in the spirit in which they did theirs, has operated on the very best minds, as a strong incentive to act up to their highest feelings and convictions." And for humanists who still insist upon theological belief, there is the consolation that they need not bow down to an omnipotent Despot when they could be reverencing and aiding a God of limited power in his campaign against evil.

Closing with sad grandeur, Mill argues that once existence has been bettered in this world, people will be less anxious for life in the next. Indeed, such eternal life may eventually be seen as an unwanted burden. And so the essay ends, with an image of happily satiated people quietly laying down their full lives, peacefully consigning their consciousness to annihilation once the end is near.

Not entirely a center of skeptical indifference (and certainly no slough of despond), the essay yet ends sighing amid its affirmations. The Religion of Humanity at least is sure, though comforting supernatural hopes must be abandoned by the clear-headed: for Mill's persona, belief in a God of limited power is for "whoever can succeed in believing it," for "those who need it." As for himself, the persona is reconciled to doing without such supernatural consolations.

But can he maintain the posture? As the final essay demonstrates: not quite. Though hardly trumpeting an Everlasting Yea, "Theism" does manage to firm up Mill's belief in God and hope of immortality.

This time Mill sets out to test the truth of religious arguments for belief. But now he has regained his old sense of balance and proportion. In the conflict between believers and unbelievers, he takes no extremist position, charting instead a *via media*. As of old, he insists upon knowing both sides of a question: "For, whatever opinion a person may adopt on any subject that admits of controversy, his assurance if he be a cautious thinker cannot be complete unless he is able to account for the existence of the opposite opinion." A cautious thinker—it is Mill's old persona again. Indeed, his favorite word in "Theism" seems to be "consider."

And consider he does—exhaustively. The bulk of Part One of "Theism" is a thoroughgoing investigation of the traditional evidence for God's existence. Early on, Mill concludes that only monotheism is compatible with the universal order that modern science has discovered. Polytheism means chaos, not fixed natural laws. In this way, James Mill's Manicheanism—the very belief sanctioned in "Nature" and "The Utility of Religion"—is now rejected. And all in the name of science. So our author will be a monotheist if he can ever discover any reasons for believing in divinity at all.

The investigation now begins in earnest. Poking away at the evidence for God's existence, Mill duly rejects the argument from first cause, the argument from general consent of humankind, and the argument from consciousness—the latter being entirely too *a priori* for his tastes. But on the argument from design in nature, he pauses. Though hardly conclusive, there is something to be said for the way some things in nature, such as the eye, are designed to fulfill an end —such as seeing. (It is apparently one of the few points in William Paley's *Natural Theology* of 1802 that Mill found at all convincing.) Such teleology suggests, however tenuously, that some kind of Mind may be at work shaping the materials of the universe. Mill considers briefly the Darwinian theory of adaptation through "survival of the fittest" and admits that, though compatible with divine planning, it would greatly "attenuate" the evidence.

In this way, the discussion narrowly squeaks through to Part Two. Minimal evidence for belief in God having been unearthed, Mill goes on to consider the deity's possible attributes, finding again a God of limited power contending with an intractable creation. Also—more surprisingly, considering the horrors depicted in "Nature"—he is a benevolent God, Mill arguing that pleasure not pain seems to be the intended norm in this God's workings. Ultimately, Mill's God resembles not so much the Old Testament Jehovah as the Demiurge of Plato's *Timaeus,* a well-intentioned deity trying to mold into some kind of order the refractory materials of a universe he did not create.

Turning from such vexed theological matters, Part Three struggles with the evidence for immortality, and ends in a draw: no evidence one way or the other is forthcoming from experience. Still, a crucial change has taken place in Mill's persona. Though the hope of immortality remains no more than a hope, Mill is now among those who hope. A dramatic change from the conclusion to "Utility of Religion."

But what of revelation? Aren't Biblical doctrines concerning God's nature and doings attested by the miracles accompanying Judaeo-Christian events? In Part Four Mill wades into this hoary controversy, conducting an exhaustive investigation which has about it the quaint flavor of the eighteenth century—when disputes over miracles were all the rage. Indeed, Mill's discussion is peppered with the names of Butler, Campbell, and Hume—eighteenth-century disputants all. The conclusion seems eminently foregone: "Miracles have no claim whatever to the character of historical facts and are wholly invalid as evidence of any revelation."

After all the wintry skepticism of previous sections, Part Five melts in springlike hope. The question is raised: since so many supernatural doctrines can be neither proven nor disproven, ought one to go on hoping for the best? Mill answers with a resounding "Yes." Such imaginative hope does not pervert reason.

> Truth is the province of reason, . . . but when the reason is strongly cultivated, the imagination may safely follow its own end, and do its best to make life pleasant and lovely inside the castle, in reliance on the fortifications raised and maintained by Reason round the outward bounds.

A last harmonious blend of organic and architectural imagery, the passage represents Mill's final solution to the conflicts between religion and science, poetry and logic. Whenever reason cannot decide an issue, utility may. Survival after death cannot be proven one way or the other. But because it is both bracing and comforting to hope for immortality, such hope is permissible. With their legitimate areas of operation thus mapped out, reason and imagination need not infringe upon each other's territory.

It is necessary to note, however, how bounded reason's territory is in this essay. Beyond suggesting a benevolent deity of limited power who governs through natural laws (not miracles), reason draws pretty much of a blank, leaving imagination to wander at large dreaming its dreams. The island image from "Utility of Religion" would fit in "Theism" quite nicely: the small island is the province of reason, the boundless sea is imagination's.

The benefits from such dreams are incalculable. To Mill an imagination cleaving ever to the sunnier side of doubt (like Tennyson's Ancient Sage) invigorates one's emotions, and lifts the whole tone of one's existence. It exorcises the feeling of "not worth while." Letting the imagination paint its ideal portraits of humanity can recharge one's moral life. And seeing one's existence as a battle to aid the purposes of providence lends meaning and nobility to it—for though Mill has abandoned his Manichean bias, he has not surrendered his vision of a God struggling to bring meaning and order out of chaos. Humanity's glory is to lend a hand in this combat.

Such is the concluding drift of "Theism." The overall movement of the three essays can be charted in their references to Christ, such allusions serving as guideposts to the persona's journey from defiant "No" through skepticism of the supernatural to qualified "Yea." In "Nature" the allusions are largely negative. Christ is even quoted as endorsing nature's injustice: "To him that hath shall be given, but from him that hath not, shall be taken even that which he hath." In "Utility of Religion" the references vary from praise of Christ's ideals to critiques of their shortcomings. Actually, Marcus Aurelius's teachings are held to be nearly as lofty, while Christ's reliance upon eternal rewards and punishments—to say nothing of his belief in hell—is repugnant. "Theism," however, softens and elevates the picture of Christ. His moral revelations are an invaluable heritage even if they did not come from God—and they may have. And Mill's final tribute to Christ glows with sufficient warmth to justify John Morley's fears for his master's skeptical reputation. Though not about to confer godhead on Christ, Mill does argue that Christianity has pitched upon the right person to revere. In the end, his persona's hostility to Christ in "Nature" has been transformed, not into belief, but into wondering admiration.

So "Theism" closes not in faith, but in imaginative hope. Halfway between dogmatic belief and unqualified disbelief, Mill's stance recognizes both the difficulties of supernatural certitude, as well as humanity's tremendous impulse to worship and wonder. Fittingly enough, the essay's final glimpse of Mill shows him still on the intellectual high wire, delicately balancing religious hope against the cautious thinker's rational skepticism:

> But it appears to me that supernatural hopes, in the degree and kind in which what I have called rational scepticism does not refuse to sanction them, may still contribute not a little to give to this religion [of humanity] its due ascendancy over the human mind.

Completed during the winter of 1869–70, the first draft of "Theism" was laid aside to let its ideas ripen. Mill was never to revise it.

In 1871, the lease at Blackheath Park being up, he moved back to London, nearer to his circle of friends and followers. At sixty-five he was not up to par in health, and perhaps even his prodigious mental energies were at last beginning to flag. At least it seems an ominous sign that in 1869 he republished his father's *Analysis of the Phenomena of the Human Mind* instead of writing his own analysis. Certainly he needed to rethink his position on psychology. His life-long animosity toward innate ideas had the unfortunate side effect of discouraging him from penetrating very deeply into the human psyche. Most likely it had also blocked his work on ethology, the study of character formation. And now, in the light of newer psychological revelations, the old associationism looked more threadbare than ever. But rather than reevaluate it wholesale, he reissued his father's book embellished with footnotes that gamely tried to bring it up to date. Darwin's theory was another case in point. Clearly its social and ethical ramifications called for study, but Mill declined to grapple with them at length in "Theism." Perhaps he was tiring. In any event, when George Grote died in 1871 and Mill served as pallbearer, he left the elaborate Westminster Abbey obsequies muttering to Bain: "In no very long time, I shall be laid in the ground with a very different ceremonial from that."

At the moment, however, he was very much alive. Having become an almost legendary figure whose utterances held oracular power, he found his correspondence growing ever more massive. Only Helen's heroic services as secretary and occasional coauthor enabled him to cope with it at all. Meanwhile, work on *Chapters on Socialism* went forward. Essays were written, speeches were made. The Land Tenure Reform Association was formed. And all the while Mill's disposition grew sunnier. He even made peace with his family, generously coming to the aid of his luckless sister Mary and her children. But it was at Avignon that he truly blossomed. A thirty-foot covered walk and an extensive terrace had been added to the house so he could continue his constitutionals in bad weather. Like Bentham in exuberant old age, he christened them playfully his "vibratory" and his "semi-circumgyratory"—and reveled in them. He cherished the avenue of dense trees that led up to the house, and the tame nightingales that followed him from tree to tree as he walked. Unfortunately, little of this Benthamite geniality came through in G. F. Watts's celebrated portrait, painted in London during March 1873. Mill emerges from the dark canvas as the austere patriarch of reason, mulling over yet another syllogism.

And then suddenly he was dead. No sooner had Watts put the last daub to the canvas, than John and Helen had decamped for Avignon. Soon he was gustily botanizing. On Saturday, May 3, he scoured the Orange district in a fifteen-mile hike with a French admirer, Jean Henri Fabre. That night he caught a chill. By Monday he had developed a fever. A Dr. Chauffard was called in, and immediately wired Dr. Gurney at Nice. Arriving the following day, Gurney diagnosed the illness as erysipelas and solemnly told the patient there was little hope. Mill remained calm and resigned, wishing only that he might

John Stuart Mill in old age. Portrait by G. F. Watts, 1873.

not outlive his mental faculties or linger through a long wasting disease. His wish was granted. On Wednesday morning, May 7, he died in his sleep.

"Work while it is called Today; for the Night cometh, wherein no man can work." It was Mill's favorite motto—and, significantly, the words used by Carlyle to close his chapter on The Everlasting Yea.

Sometime before he died, Mill murmured half-deliriously to Helen: "You know that I have done my work." They were his last words, a final Yea to that gospel of work which aims at the greater human good.

And naturally biographers have wondered whom he was addressing. Was it Helen herself, that stepdaughter who had become more than a real daughter to him? Or was he addressing her beautiful, quick-minded mother who had been his Beatrice? Or was the dying philosopher returning in memory to Queen Square Place, justifying himself to his father and Jeremy Bentham as the worthy successor they had dreamed of? Or was he thinking of those Saints of Humanity— Socrates and Jesus, Turgot and Washington—whose approval he would like to feel he had won? Or was he addressing that hoped-for benevolent God whose struggles to perfect the world he had perhaps always dimly labored to aid?

The answer went with him to the grave on the following day. So suddenly had he died, that the only intimates on hand for the funeral were Helen, the two doctors, and Avignon's Protestant pastor and his wife. At the cemetery gate, however, a large gathering of townspeople waited silently in the mild May rain. Pastor Louis Rey made a short address and even ventured a brief prayer—for which he later ran into trouble from some of his scandalized flock. Then Mill was laid beside Harriet in the white marble mausoleum that he had planned so reverently fifteen years before. At last the mourners departed. Night came down over the small St. Véran cemetery outside the old walled city of Avignon. Far to the south the Pyrenees lifted their peaks to the night sky and the faint clear stars.

When news of the death reached England, the first wave of shock produced a round of expected tributes—and a few not unexpected attacks. Then came the memorials—the statue in the Embankment Gardens, the portrait in the National Gallery, even the bid—well-meaning, misguided, unsuccessful—for a Westminster Abbey burial.

But his memory required no such things. He had constructed his own most enduring monument from language and logic. "You know that I have done my work." And he had—in all the splendid essays and books that had poured from his pen during a lifetime devoted to lifting his fellow human beings ever nearer toward an ideal humaneness. Everything he had written was dedicated to destroying some privilege or oppression, some ignorance or abuse that arrested people's development and kept them shackled to the barbarisms of the past. So great was his devotion that he searched everywhere—into every discipline he could master, into every salient public issue—probing for sources of stagnation, and excising them root and branch. In the process he created a body of work stunning in its breadth and many-sidedness. Indeed, his contributions to any one of a half dozen areas of knowledge would have made the reputation of a lesser man. Seen as a whole, his work represents an almost incredible intellectual and moral achievement.

For he bequeathed to humanity not only his best thought, but his best self as well. Each of his works carries the impress of his own extraordinary character. The portrait's lineaments are somewhat idealized, it is true—but only to convey better the image of human regeneration toward which all the arguments point. For Mill, it was not enough to present Bentham and Coleridge as completing counterparts; he had to show the reader a portrait of the whole thinker capable of appreciating both halves of the truth. It was not enough to expound the principles of political economy; he had to show what the humane economist was like. It was not enough to argue for liberty; he had to embody in his narrator's voice a vision of heroic individualism. So that even when argument failed, artistry would carry the day. Plato's Socrates—perhaps the philosopher he earliest knew and loved—had taught him that.

Ultimately, then, Mill was a prophet-moralist, seeking to win people's hearts as well as their heads. Yes, truth was known by reason, but reason alone could not fire the will to strive toward greater self-perfection, toward the fuller happiness of humankind. Yes, rational argument could do much: it could clear the ground of nonsense, it could point the way, it could even set the thinker on his feet. But it could not generate the emotive power to move him onward. That power could be acquired only from "those we love and reverence," from those —living or dead—"whose lives and characters have been mirrors of all noble qualities," or from poets or artists who could "breathe" it into us through our imaginations.

And so in the end Mill became a poet as well. From his impressive resources of logic, he forged his arguments; but he shaped them imaginatively as well—with image and allusion, with metaphor and grammar, with all the nuances of language. So with argument and art for weaponry, he fought the good fight for reason itself when allied with deep emotion, for freedom to develop as each individual saw best, for equality before the law, for compassion, for the glory of adding to the sum of human happiness. And, finally, he translated the letter of

The Mill mausoleum at St. Véran. A photograph taken shortly after Mill's burial.

his argument into the spirit of a living voice that mirrored the very qualities he championed—fearless intelligence, strong feeling, tolerance, responsible individuality.

It is a superbly realized voice, whose accents of luminous logic and deep feeling even today draw many to its vision of human excellence.

FURTHER READING

The following list is intended as a guide to some of the available editions of Mill's works and to some of the important books and articles about him. It makes no pretense of being a full, much less a complete, bibliography of Mill. Those wishing to do more detailed research into Mill's life and work should consult section VI of this list.

The annotations appended to each entry are intended to inform the reader briefly of its contents and value, but they should not be taken as the definitive or final word on the listing.

A (p) after the entry means that the work is available in paperback edition. The abbreviation "rpt." means "reprinted."

I. SOME EDITIONS OF MILL'S WORKS

It would be impossible to list here all the currently available editions of Mill's writings. Instead, the reader will find below: (a) important hardcover editions of Mill's works, (b) some recent paperback editions of separate works, and (c) some valuable collections of Mill's writings. The reader should be aware that numerous other editions are readily available.

Alexander, Edward, ed. John Stuart Mill, *Literary Essays*. Indianapolis: Bobbs-Merrill, 1967. Mill on literature from 1827 through 1869. (p)

August, Eugene R., ed. Thomas Carlyle, *The Nigger Question*, and John Stuart Mill, *The Negro Question*. Northbrook, Ill.: AHM Publishing Corp., 1971. The two nineteenth-century giants square off against each other on racial matters. (p)

Carr, Wendell Robert, ed. John Stuart Mill, *The Subjection of Women*. Cambridge, Mass.: M.I.T. Press, 1970. Illuminating introductory essay. (p)

Cohen, Marshall, ed. *The Philosophy of John Stuart Mill: Ethical, Political, and Religious*. New York: Random House, 1961. Handy Modern Library edition, containing all of "Bentham," "Coleridge," "M. de Tocqueville on Democracy in America," *On Liberty, Utilitarianism*, "Nature," "Utility of Religion," plus selections.

Fletcher, Ronald, ed. *John Stuart Mill: A Logical Critique of Sociology*. New York: Scribners, 1971. Book VI of the *Logic* complete, plus other writings illustrating Mill's social thinking. (p)

Gorovitz, Samuel, ed. *Utilitarianism, with Critical Essays*. Indianapolis: Bobbs-Merrill, 1971. Mill's text and twenty-eight scholarly essays. (p)

Hayek, F. A., ed. John Stuart Mill, *The Spirit of the Age*. Chicago: University of Chicago Press, 1942. Important reissue of this neglected work.

Himmelfarb, Gertrude, ed. John Stuart Mill, *Essays on Politics and Culture*. 1962; rpt. Gloucester, Mass.: Peter Smith, 1973. Complete texts of eleven works including both essays on de Tocqueville, *Thoughts on Parliamentary Reform*, and "A Few Words on Non-Intervention."

Leavis, F. R., ed. John Stuart Mill, *On Bentham and Coleridge*, 1950; rpt. New York: Harper, 1962. Leavis's famous introduction, plus Mill's two classic essays. (p)

Lerner, Max, ed. *Essential Works of John Stuart Mill*. New York: Bantam, 1961. Excellent introductory essay by Lerner, complete texts of *Autobiography*, *On Liberty*, *Utilitarianism*, "Nature," and "The Utility of Religion." (p)

Magid, Henry M., ed. John Stuart Mill, *On the Logic of the Moral Sciences*. Indianapolis: Bobbs-Merrill, 1965. Book VI of the *Logic* complete. (p)

Mill, Anna Jean, ed. *John Mill's Boyhood Visit to France*. Toronto: University of Toronto Press, 1960. Journal and notebook kept by fourteen-year-old Mill during his 1820–21 visit with the Samuel Benthams in France.

Mill, James. *Analysis of the Phenomena of the Human Mind*. 1829; 2nd ed. 1869. With illustrative and critical notes by Alexander Bain, Andrew Findlater, and George Grote; ed. with additional notes by John Stuart Mill, 2 vols., 1878; rpt. New York: Augustus M. Kelley, 1967. James Mill's famous study, with his son's commentary.

Mill, John Stuart. *Auguste Comte and Positivism*. Ann Arbor: University of Michigan Press, 1961. (p)

Mill, John Stuart. *Dissertations and Discussions*, 4 vols. London: Longmans, Green, 1875. Mainly essays reprinted from the *Westminster* and *Edinburgh* reviews.

Nagel, Ernest, ed. *John Stuart Mill's Philosophy of Scientific Method*. New York: Hafner, 1950. Abridged version of *A System of Logic*, with related selections from *An Examination of Sir William Hamilton's Philosophy* and full text of "On the Definition of Political Economy, and on the Method of Investigation Proper to It." (p)

Nakhnikian, George, ed. John Stuart Mill, *Nature* and *Utility of Religion*. Indianapolis: Bobbs-Merrill, 1958. (p)

Robson, John M., gen. ed. *Collected Works of John Stuart Mill*. Toronto: University of Toronto Press, 1963–. The most authoritative and fullest edition of Mill's works ever published, ably annotated and introduced by a number of scholars under Professor Robson's direction. As of this writing, the following volumes have appeared:

> II, III: *Principles of Political Economy*, edited by J. M. Robson and V. W. Bladen (1965).
>
> IV, V: *Essays on Economics and Society*, edited by J. M. Robson and Lord Robbins (1967).
>
> VII, VIII: *System of Logic: Ratiocinative and Inductive*, edited by J. M. Robson and R. F. McRae (1974).
>
> X: *Essays on Ethics, Religion and Society*, edited by F. E. L. Priestley and D. P. Dryer (1969).
>
> XII, XIII: *Earlier Letters, 1812–1848*, edited by F. E. Mineka (1963).
>
> XIV, XV, XVI, XVII: *Later Letters, 1849–1873*, edited by F. E. Mineka and D. N. Lindley (1972).

The following volumes are in preparation:

> *The Autobiography and Literary Essays*
> *Essays on Current Affairs: Britain and the Empire, Speeches, and Journals*
> *Essays on Philosophy*
> *Essays on Politics and Society*
> *An Examination of Sir William Hamilton's Philosophy*

Robson, John M., ed. *John Stuart Mill: A Selection of His Works*. New York: St. Martin's Press, 1966. *On Liberty* and *Utilitarianism* complete, plus selections from other works. (p)

Rossi, Alice S., ed. John Stuart Mill and Harriet Taylor Mill, *Essays on Sex Equality*. Chicago: University of Chicago Press, 1970. Contains two early essays on marriage and divorce, "The Enfranchisement of Women," *The Subjection of Women*, as well as Rossi's introductory essay "Sentiment and Intellect." (p)

FURTHER READING

Schneewind, J. B., ed. *Mill's Essays on Literature and Society.* New York: Collier, 1965. Compact and useful collection; includes full texts of *The Spirit of the Age,* Mill's essays on poetry, "Bentham," "Coleridge," and more. (p)

Schneewind, J. B., ed. *Mill's Ethical Writings.* New York: Collier, 1965. Valuable and handy collection, including *Utilitarianism* and twelve related selections. (p)

Shields, Currin V., ed. John Stuart Mill, *Considerations on Representative Government.* Indianapolis: Bobbs-Merrill, 1958. The complete text. The introduction reaches some questionable conclusions about Mill's political thought. (p)

Smith, James M., and Sosa, Ernest, eds. *Mill's Utilitarianism: Text and Criticism.* Belmont, Calif.: Wadsworth, 1969. Mill's text and eleven other selections from Bentham, Mill, and the critics. (p)

Stillinger, Jack, ed. *Autobiography and Other Writings by John Stuart Mill.* Boston: Houghton Mifflin, 1969. Best available text of the *Autobiography,* plus *On Liberty,* "Bentham," "Coleridge," and more. (p) The *Autobiography* has also appeared as a separate volume. (p)

Stillinger, Jack, ed. *The Early Draft of John Stuart Mill's Autobiography.* Urbana, Ill.: University of Illinois Press, 1961. The 1850s text, containing intriguing variants from the final version.

Taylor, Richard, ed. John Stuart Mill, *Theism.* Indianapolis: Bobbs-Merrill, 1957. Mill's late essay on religion. (p)

Winch, Donald, ed. John Stuart Mill, *Principles of Political Economy, with Some of Their Applications to Social Philosophy,* Books IV and V. Baltimore: Penguin, 1970. The last two books of the *Principles* complete, plus two chapters on socialism and property bequest from Book II. (p)

Wishy, Bernard, ed. *Prefaces to Liberty.* Boston: Beacon Press, 1959. Generous selection of Mill's writings on liberty, many of them little known and difficult to find elsewhere. Also full text of *On Liberty.*

II. MAINLY BIOGRAPHICAL

Bain, Alexander. *John Stuart Mill: A Criticism, with Personal Recollections.* 1882; rpt. New York: Augustus Kelley, 1969. This invaluable biography by one of Mill's close friends also contains important observations on the works.

Borchard, Ruth. *John Stuart Mill the Man.* London: Watts, 1957. Brief, readable.

Hamburger, Joseph. *Intellectuals in Politics: John Stuart Mill and the Philosophical Radicals.* New Haven: Yale University Press, 1965. Mill amid the political turmoil of the 1830s. Valuable, though some of its conclusions are questioned. See, for example, the review by J. H. Burns in *The Mill News Letter* 1, no. 2 (Spring 1966), pp. 26–27.

Harris, Abram L. "John Stuart Mill: Servant of the East India Company." *Canadian Journal of Economics and Political Science* 30 (1964): 185–202. Mill's career at East India House.

Hayek, F. A. *John Stuart Mill and Harriet Taylor: Their Friendship and Subsequent Marriage.* 1951; rpt. New York: Augustus Kelley, n. d. The pertinent documents strung together with connecting narrative. Intriguing, enlightening.

Levi, A. W. "The 'Mental Crisis' of John Stuart Mill." *Psychoanalytic Review* 32 (1945): 86–101. Everything you always wanted to know about Mill's mental crisis but were afraid to ask. Fascinating, persuasive.

Mill, Anna J. "John Stuart Mill's Visit to Wordsworth, 1831." *Modern Language Review* 44 (July 1949): 341–50. Mill in the Lake District.

Packe, Michael St. John. *The Life of John Stuart Mill.* 1954; rpt. New York: Capricorn, 1970. The fullest and best biography of Mill, written with style and wit; a delight from start to finish. (p)

Semmel, Bernard. *The Governor Eyre Controversy*. London: MacGibbon & Kee, 1962. The Jamaican riots of 1865 and the English controversy, with some emphasis on Mill's role. Reprinted as *Jamaican Blood and Victorian Conscience* and as *Democracy Versus Empire*. (p)

Waller, John O. "John Stuart Mill and the American Civil War." *Bulletin of the New York Public Library* 66 (October 1962): 505–18. Mill's support for antislavery.

III. AN IMPORTANT PERIODICAL FOR MILL STUDENTS

The Mill News Letter. Currently edited by John M. Robson and Michael Laine (Department of English, Victoria College, University of Toronto, Toronto, Canada). Since Fall 1965, this twice-yearly newsletter has offered perceptive articles and reviews, as well as useful bibliographies and Milliana.

IV. COLLECTIONS OF CRITICAL ESSAYS

Some of the most significant articles on Mill have been gathered into the volumes listed below. The reader should also see the two editions of *Utilitarianism* listed in section I, one edited by Gorovitz, the other by Smith and Sosa.

Friedrich, Carl J., ed. *Nomos IV: Liberty*. New York: Prentice-Hall, 1962. Collection of outstanding essays on Mill's *Liberty*. David Spitz's "Freedom and Individuality" deserves special mention for blowing the whistle on various misreadings of Mill's book.

Radcliff, Peter, ed. *Limits of Liberty: Studies of Mill's On Liberty*. Belmont, Calif.: Wadsworth, 1966. Ten essays on Mill's classic. (p)

Schneewind, J. B., ed. *Mill: A Collection of Critical Essays*. Garden City, N.Y.: Doubleday-Anchor, 1968. All-star cast of contributors explores facets of Mill's many-sided mind. Essays range from general assessments of Mill to specialized studies. Seven of the nineteen contributions focus on aspects of *Utilitarianism*. Superlative collection. (p)

V. SOME BOOKS AND ARTICLES ON MILL

In the following list the reader will find: (a) important studies of large segments of Mill's thought, (b) studies that illuminate some significant aspect of Mill's work, and (c) studies that focus on artistry in Mill. In general, writers sympathetic to Mill are listed, although a number of his most important critics are cited.

Many excellent specialized studies have been omitted here for lack of space, including those found in the collections of critical essays listed in section IV, as well as those in the Gorovitz and in the Smith and Sosa editions of *Utilitarianism* listed in section I.

Albee, Ernest. *A History of English Utilitarianism*. 1902; rpt. New York: Collier, 1962. Devotes three chapters to Mill. (p)

Alexander, Edward. *Matthew Arnold and John Stuart Mill*. New York: Columbia University Press, 1965. They agreed about ends, if not always about means.

Anschutz, R. P. *The Philosophy of J. S. Mill*. London: Oxford University Press, 1953. Mill's manysidedness was at odds with his tendency to wedge disparate ideas into a utilitarian framework. For a different view, see Alan Ryan's book listed below.

August, Eugene R. "Mill as Sage: The Essay on Bentham." *Publications of the Modern Language Association* 89 (January 1974): 142–53. How Mill's artistry works to undercut Bentham in the classic essay.

August, Eugene R. "Mill's *Autobiography* as Philosophic *Commedia*." *Victorian Poetry* 11

(Summer 1973): 143–62. Mill's journey from Benthamite inferno, through the purgatorial mental crisis, into the realms of philosophic thought and action.

Axelrod, Rise B. "Argument and Strategy in Mill's *The Subjection of Women,*" *The Victorian Newsletter,* no. 46 (Fall 1974), pp. 10–14. Perceptive study of Mill's argument and art.

Barber, William J. "The Revisionism of John Stuart Mill." *A History of Economic Thought.* Baltimore: Penguin, 1967. Brief, thoughtful introduction to Mill's economics. (p)

Black, R. D. Collison. *Economic Thought and the Irish Question, 1817–1870.* Cambridge: Cambridge University Press, 1960. Discusses Mill *passim.*

Britton, Karl. *John Stuart Mill.* 1953; rpt. New York: Dover, 1969. Introduction to Mill's life and philosophy, with chapters on ethics, politics, and logic. (p)

Carr, Robert. "The Religious Thought of John Stuart Mill: A Study in Reluctant Scepticism." *Journal of the History of Ideas* 23 (1962): 475–95. One of the few studies that manages to bring light instead of heat to this topic.

Cowling, Maurice. *Mill and Liberalism.* Cambridge: Cambridge University Press, 1963. This assault on Mill as a totalitarian in disguise has drawn considerable fire from commentators. For openers, see articles by John C. Rees and C. L. Ten listed below.

Duncan, Graeme. *Marx and Mill: Two Views of Social Conflict and Harmony.* Cambridge: Cambridge University Press, 1973. Rather forbiddingly scholarly, but a needed study.

Feltes, N. N. " 'Bentham' and 'Coleridge': Mill's 'Completing Counterparts.' " *The Mill News Letter* 2, no. 2 (Spring 1967), pp. 2–7. The essays complement each other just as the thinkers do.

Grube, John. "*On Liberty* as a Work of Art." *The Mill News Letter* 5, no. 1 (Fall 1969), pp. 2–6. Overly ambitious title, but the article contains some splendid insights. Don't miss the intriguing footnote.

Hainds, J. R. "J. S. Mill's *Examiner* Articles on Art." *Journal of the History of Ideas* 11, no. 2 (April 1950): pp. 215–34. Revealing look at an often ignored aspect of Mill's artistic sensibility.

Harris, Abram L. "John Stuart Mill: Liberalism, Socialism, and Laissez Faire." *Economics and Social Reform.* New York: Harper, 1958. Lengthy, packed essay.

Heilbroner, Robert L. *The Worldly Philosophers,* 4th ed., rev. New York: Simon and Schuster, 1972. Brief, warm appraisal of Mill as economist and person. Delightful reading. (p)

Himes, Norman E. "John Stuart Mill's Attitude toward Neo-Malthusianism." *The Economic Journal* (*Economic History Series,* no. 4, Suppl.), January 1929, pp. 457–84. Explores Mill's views on birth control.

Himmelfarb, Gertrude. *On Liberty and Liberalism: The Case of John Stuart Mill.* New York: Knopf, 1974. Argues that *On Liberty* and *The Subjection of Women* were written largely because of Harriet's influence and that both are out of line with Mill's other more conservative works. For a critique of this view, see review by David Spitz in *The New York Times Book Review,* 28 July 1974, pp. 15–16.

Himmelfarb, Gertrude. "The Other John Stuart Mill." *Victorian Minds.* 1968; rpt. New York: Harper, 1970. The "other" Mill is the conservative Mill of the 1830s and the 1860s. The liberal Mill was beguiled by Harriet. For a reply to this view, see article by C. L. Ten listed below. (p)

Jones, Iva G. "Trollope, Carlyle, and Mill on the Negro: An Episode in the History of Ideas." *Journal of Negro History* 52 (1967): 185–99. Next to the racism of Trollope and Carlyle, Mill's egalitarianism looks better than ever.

Kubitz, Oskar Alfred. "Development of John Stuart Mill's *System of Logic.*" *Illinois Studies in the Social Sciences* 18, nos. 1–2 (March–June 1932), pp. 1–310. Though superseded in part by Robson's textual introduction to the *Logic* in the *Collected Works* edition, Kubitz's study still remains a valuable commentary on *Logic.*

Mackie, J. L. "Mill's Methods of Induction." *The Encyclopedia of Philosophy*. Edited by Paul Edwards, 5: 324–32. New York: Macmillan and the Free Press, 1967. Superior explanation, refinement, assessment, and defense of Mill's inductive methods.

Man, Glenn K. S. *The Imaginative Dimension in the Writings of John Stuart Mill*. University of Notre Dame, 1970. An unpublished Ph.D. dissertation that ought to be in print.

Matthews, Charles. "Argument through Metaphor in John Stuart Mill's *On Liberty*." *Language and Style* 4 (1972): 221–28. Convincing study of art in Mill's great book.

Mazlish, Bruce. *James and John Stuart Mill*. New York: Basic Books, 1975. Full-length "psychohistory" of the father and son.

Millett, Kate. *Sexual Politics*. 1969; rpt. New York: Avon, 1971. The entire book is fascinating, but "Mill versus Ruskin" (pp. 88–108) is a "must" for anyone interested in the relevance of Mill's thought on sexual equality. (p) This segment from *Sexual Politics* can also be found in Kate Millett, "The Debate over Women: Ruskin versus Mill." *Victorian Studies* 14 (September 1970): 63–82.

Mueller, Iris Wessel. *John Stuart Mill and French Thought*. Urbana, Ill.: University of Illinois Press, 1956. Thoroughgoing study of the French influences—the Saint-Simonians, Comte, de Tocqueville, Fourier, Louis Blanc.

Neff, Emery. *Carlyle and Mill: An Introduction to Victorian Thought*, 2nd ed., rev., 1926; rpt. New York: Octagon Books, 1964. Placing Carlyle and Mill against the historical and intellectual settings of Victorian times, this readable study wears its age extremely well.

Rees, J. C. *Mill and His Early Critics*. Edinburgh: R. R. Clark, Ltd., 1956. The response to *On Liberty*. Also argues convincingly against attributing *On Social Freedom* to Mill.

Rees, John C. "The Reaction to Cowling on Mill." *The Mill News Letter* 1, no. 2 (Spring 1966), pp. 2–11. Informative survey.

Rinehart, Keith. "John Stuart Mill's *Autobiography*: Its Art and Appeal." *University of Kansas City Review* 19 (1953): 265–73. Perceptive look at the *Autobiography* as an imaginative work.

Robson, John M. *The Improvement of Mankind: The Social and Political Thought of John Stuart Mill*. Toronto: University of Toronto Press, 1968. A leading Mill scholar traces the development and maturity of his social thinking, making a convincing case for considerable unity in Mill's diversity.

Robson, John M. "John Stuart Mill and Jeremy Bentham, with Some Observations on James Mill." *Essays in English Literature from the Renaissance to the Victorian Age Presented to A. S. P. Woodhouse*, edited by Millar MacLure and F. W. Watt, pp. 245–68. Toronto: University of Toronto Press, 1961. Informed survey of Mill's fluctuating responses to his philosophical godfather.

Ryan, Alan. *John Stuart Mill*. New York: Pantheon, 1970. Arguing that Mill expounded a philosophical system here labeled "inductivism," this scholarly study has illuminating things to say about most of the major works. (p)

Schneewind, J. B. "John Stuart Mill." *The Encyclopedia of Philosophy*. Edited by Paul Edwards, 5: 314–33. New York: Macmillan and the Free Press, 1967. An important scholar incisively surveys Mill's life and thought—his logic, epistemology and metaphysics, ethics, social and political philosophy, and religious views.

Schumpeter, Joseph A. *Economic Doctrine and Method: An Historical Sketch*. Translated by R. Aris. 1912; rpt. New York: Oxford University Press, 1967. Chapter III places Mill among the classical economists, with enlightening results. (p)

Schumpeter, Joseph A. *History of Economic Analysis*. Edited by Elizabeth Boody Schumpeter. New York: Oxford University Press, 1954. A classic in its field; generally sympathetic account of Mill as economist.

Schwartz, Pedro. *The New Political Economy of J. S. Mill*. Translated by B. Leblanc. Durham, N. C.: Duke University Press, 1972. New look at Mill's economic thought. Controversial in places.

FURTHER READING

Sharpless, F. Parvin. *The Literary Criticism of John Stuart Mill.* The Hague: Mouton, 1967.
Enlightening study of Mill's aesthetic theory and practice.
Steele, E. D. "J. S. Mill and the Irish Question: The Principles of Political Economy,
1848–1865." *Historical Journal* 13 (1970): 213–36; and "J. S. Mill and the Irish Question: Reform and the Integrity of the Empire, 1865–1870." *Historical Journal* 13
(1970): 419–50. Interesting factual details, but almost obsessively anti-Mill.
Stephen, James Fitzjames. *Liberty, Fraternity, Equality.* Edited by R. J. White. Cambridge: Cambridge University Press, 1967. Handsome edition of this famous attack
on Mill, which grew out of a series of articles published by Stephen in 1872.
Stephen, Leslie. *The English Utilitarians,* 3 vols. 1900; rpt. New York: Peter Smith, 1950.
The third volume is devoted entirely to Mill.
Stigler, George J. "The Nature and Role of Originality in Scientific Progress." *Essays
in the History of Economics.* Chicago: University of Chicago Press, 1965. Peppery
defense of Mill's originality in economic thought.
Stokes, Eric. *The English Utilitarians and India.* Oxford: Oxford University Press, 1959.
Valuable background, though surprisingly little about Mill in this study.
Ten, C. L. "Mill and Liberty." *Journal of the History of Ideas* 30 (January–March 1969):
47–68. Argues against Cowling and Himmelfarb, presents evidence to show that the
traditional picture of Mill as Liberal is valid.
Viner, Jacob. "Bentham and J. S. Mill: The Utilitarian Background." *The Long View and
the Short.* Glencoe, Ill.: The Free Press, 1958. Masterful look at Bentham and his
wayward disciple.
Williams, Raymond. "Mill on Bentham and Coleridge." *Culture and Society, 1780–1950.*
1958; rpt. New York: Harper, 1966. Penetrating study. (p)
Wolf, Howard R. "British Fathers and Sons, 1773–1913: From Filial Submissiveness to
Creativity." *Psychoanalytic Review* 52 (1965–66): 197–214. Like Gosse, Lawrence, and
Joyce, Mill became an artist in order to imitate the mother's creativity and to reject
the father's masculine rationality. Thought-provoking.

VI. BIBLIOGRAPHIES

Readers should also see section III; *The Mill News Letter* carries lists of recent publica-
tions on Mill.
Hascall, Dudley L., and Robson, John M. "Bibliography of Writings on Mill." *The Mill
News Letter* 1, no. 1 (Fall 1965) through 5, no. 2 (Spring 1970). Probably the nearest
thing to a comprehensive bibliography of Mill in print.
MacMinn, Ney; Hainds, J. R.; and McCrimmon, James McNab, eds. *Bibliography of the
Published Writings of John Stuart Mill.* 1945; rpt. New York: AMS Press, 1970. Mill's
list of the works he published during his lifetime. Indispensable.
Robson, John M. "John Stuart Mill." *Victorian Prose: A Guide to Research.* Edited by David
J. DeLaura. New York: The Modern Language Association of America, 1973. A
master Mill scholar surveys the primary and secondary sources. Enormously help-
ful.
Victorian Studies. The June issues of this scholarly journal contain annual bibliographies
of writings on the Victorian age. See entries under Mill.

INDEX

INDEX